MERLIN

MERLIN

NORMA LORRE GOODRICH

Franklin Watts 1987
New York Toronto

Library of Congress Cataloging-in-Publication Data

Goodrich, Norma Lorre.
Merlin.

Bibliography: p.
Includes index.
1. Merlin (Legendary character)—Legends—History
and criticism. 2. Arthurian romances—History and
criticism. I. Title.
PN686.M4G66 1987   809'.93351   87-15987
ISBN 0-531-15060-7

. . . .

To
Dr. Otis E. Fellows
Avalon Professor of Humanities
Columbia University in the City of New York

Dear Teacher. Dear Friend.

CONTENTS

ACKNOWLEDGMENTS

· · · · · · ·

My thanks to librarians at the Bacon, Denison, and Honnold Libraries of the Claremont Colleges, Butler at Columbia University, Cal State Los Angeles, Claremont Public, Cleveland Public, Harvard University, University of Illinois at Urbana, Kansas State University, San Francisco State, Los Angeles State, Stanford, Trinity College at Hartford, Conn., Upland Public, and Wisconsin State College. I also thank G. Langshaw, Scottish Development Department, Historic Buildings & Monuments, Edinburgh, Scotland, for answers to queries. Especial thanks to the Clan MacKay, U.S.A., and to the Isle of Man.

I thank colleagues who shared their work in progress: Dr. Michael J. Curley and Dr. Clifton Snider; Dr. Jeffry Young of California State University at Fullerton; Dr. Joan Milliman for her work on my behalf, her services, and her friendship; Dr. Ralph Ross for willing counsel.

The following have offered generous support: Mrs. Joan Starr, Mrs. Jil Stark, Mrs. Marjorie Logan, Madame Laurence Novell, Mrs. Marie Rooth, Mrs. Sharan Cherbak, Ms. Molly Ann Squire, Ms. Jana Seely by her sculptures of Merlin, Mr. John Daniels, Mr. Bruce Peterson, Mr. Arthur MacArthur, and Mr. William S. Stinson.

I also wish to thank Mr. Harold Schmidt, Mr. Kent Oswald, and Mr. Ed Breslin.

• • • • • • •

❧

• • • • • • •

"Pass in, pass in," the angels say.
"In to the upper doors,
  Nor count compartments of the floors,
But mount to paradise
By the stairway of surprise."

Ralph Waldo Emerson
Poems
(from *The Works of*
Ralph Waldo Emerson,
Vol. III, New York
and London, 1897,
pp. 130–34).

PREFACE

· · · · · · · ·

In 1978 I found what I had long been searching for: a detailed description of the Castle of the Holy Grail. With that information the site proved easy to locate on the map of Britain. This archaic site lay where ruins rise today, on Saint Patrick's Isle, adjacent to the Isle of Man, in the middle of the Irish Sea. The ancient Grail Castle of King Arthur once stood, then, at the very center of Great Britain.

Other ancient holy sites are also customarily said to lie either at the earth's center or at the center of the sea. They too received the bodies of wounded gods and beloved heroes. All claimed to be Paradise, or to duplicate it.

In 1979, still engaged in the search for King Arthur, my husband and I spent our summer vacation in Britain. We also went to study the Isle of Man. As ancient writers had said, its beauty was spectacular. After two days of general observation, we parked the car one morning on the top of the hill, at the entrance to the small city of Peel (Palisade). To commemorate the day, we took a photograph. Then, in great suspense, we descended quietly through the dark streets of Peel, and came out suddenly over a golden beach. Despite the blinding light, we saw, opposite us, beaten by huge waves, a quadrangular, rocky islet. There were masses of yellow, orange, and red ruins above emerald grasses and sea thrift. The brilliant, sapphire sea stirred all about the isle. Yes, there was still a curtain wall above a crown of black crags.

From time immemorial rumor had named this islet a wonder of the world. It was also a hidden wonder—remote, difficult to come across, the secret and royal residence of kings, King Arthur among them. Numerous other holy sites also constituted the retreats and treasure houses of kings. All were held to be paradisiacal, sweetly perfumed, adorned with tropical blossoms, hung with silver bells, lighted with golden chandeliers, swept with soft breezes, safe as churches: Paradise.

My book *King Arthur* was published in New York and Toronto in May 1986. On December 1 of that year I received a telephone call from the representative of the Manx government in Washington, D.C. He called to tell me (what Lila Kreutz, a reader of *King Arthur*, had already told me by postcard from Man) that archaeology confirmed to some degree what I had said about King Arthur and the Isle of Man. Excavation proved that Saint Patrick's Isle had been an important Christian center in the Dark Ages. Graves there dated from King Arthur's lifetime. The islet appeared to have been the residence of an important personage.

At 7:00 A.M. on December 7 Charles Guard called to tape a telephone interview with the Manx radio station. On December 8 Ian Faulds, editor of the *Peel City Guardian*, called to read me his December headline: SECRET ROYAL RETREAT AT PEEL. SENSATIONAL DISCOVERY. On December 14 my husband and I left Los Angeles for the Isle of Man, as guests of the Manx and British people. On the afternoon of Tuesday, December 16, Manx newspaper reporters and I set foot on Saint Patrick's Isle again. Three English television crews followed us there again on Wednesday, December 17.

As I responded to their questions, I kept thinking of Merlin and Arthur, and of *Merlin*, which I had just finished: "Despite you, the twentieth century will make you both historical," I told them. "And you thought time would end."

What a paradox that these two great men, Merlin and Arthur, both of whom were in their time so radically antihistorical, should now have to become mere mortals. Their archaic culture, which had raised and trained them in its religious faith, still presented them as above the irreversible events or "facts" of history. Unshaken it still maintains its worldview, as it argued

2

with King Henry II in the twelfth century. Henry insisted that King Arthur and his Queen Guinevere be dug up and declared dead once for all. He demanded that Arthur and Merlin submit to history. But voices from the archaic world still insisted: King Arthur did not die. Merlin said so. He was the king who will come again.

Thus, the defeated Celtic peoples remained victorious over death. No grave would be found for Arthur, they said. The reason being, he did not die. Their view was ahistorical. Arthur and Merlin became myths, grew larger and larger until they were almost absorbed into the cosmos.

And so, Celtic poets, who are today to be trusted and whose words can be believed, welcome Merlin and marvel at his solution in the face of utter, approaching, irreversible defeat.

While the Manx people by and large were astonished to learn of Christian settlements on Saint Patrick's Isle that dated from the Dark Ages, the Scots were not surprised to have discovered the like on the south coast of Scotland.

In March 1987, David L. Niven of Castletown, I.O.M., informed me by letter of the great interest generated at Whithorn, Scotland, on the Rhinns of Galloway where he was born and raised, by the ongoing archaeology commenced in the 1950s and 1960s there. As the reader of *Merlin* will soon see, such excavations in Scotland relate directly to Merlin's lifetime.

The peninsula of Whithorn, Scotland, faces the Isle of Man to the south of it, across an expanse of the Irish Sea about eighteen miles in width. Whithorn has long been recognized as the oldest Christian site in Scotland. Royal and other pilgrims down the ages have made at least one trip there during a lifetime. Christian graves dating from King Arthur's and Merlin's lifetime have already been found at Whithorn. According to my evidence in the *King Arthur* of 1986, the king himself was probably born in Galloway, Scotland, not many miles east of the Whithorn ruins as described, when they were not ruins, in the Arthurian literature.

New excavations were launched at Whithorn, then, in 1986,

3

announced in the *Galloway Gazette* and *Daily Telegraph* on May 24 of that year, sponsored by the Whithorn Trust and the Church of Scotland. Their archaeologist was Peter Hill.

The Royal Museum of Scotland hosted at Edinburgh in the summer of 1986 "a small display" of "important relics" from Whithorn. Curator Dr. David Caldwell then welcomed that opportunity to show these objects "discovered at the site" and that had been "buried for centuries."

One such object was a copper gilt and enameled crozier once belonging to a bishop.

INTRODUCTION

Strangely enough, despite centuries of writings, Merlin, the man, is an enigma. His name is known as that of a wiser, older man who counseled King Arthur. It is believed that, in fact as in legend, he arranged for Arthur to be born. He is purported to have reared Arthur expressly to defend Britain from foreign invasion. However, competing claims, nationalistic prejudices, superstition, and even ignorance have muddled his history.

Both Merlin and Arthur, who was probably his junior by twenty-five years, undertook a defense of Britain in the fifth century. Rome had been sacked in 410. At this time of dire calamity and wholesale massacre of civilians, Rome had been obliged to withdraw from its Roman province of Britain the four Roman legions stationed as an army of occupation for the past five hundred years.

Large numbers of Romano-Britons had decided to remain in Britain on their landed estates. The line of the "Roman" commanders-in-chief, —Maximus—Constantine—Ambrosius— Uther Pendragon—Arthur, stepped in to defend the formerly Roman forts along the two walls of defense: the Antonine to the north (Glasgow–Edinburgh line) and Hadrian's Wall to the south (Carlisle on the west to the North Sea on the east). [1] These east-

---

[1] King Arthur's military and civil administration must be thought of in terms of the Roman occupation of Britain as the distinguished Welsh Professor Emrys George Bowen (University College of Wales, Aberystwyth) said in his *The Settlements of the Celtic Saints in Wales* (University of Wales Press, Cardiff, 1956). Speaking of the Bishop or Arch-

west lines of defense separated what is now England from what is now Scotland, the northern line erecting a barrier between the lowlands and the highlands, where the northern Picts dwelled, a still largely unknown people. (The modern area between these two walls is still called Borders). These lands constituted Merlin's and Arthur's battlegrounds.

At this time the Scots from Ireland were still emigrating into what is now Wales, Cornwall, and the western Isles, and establishing their new kingdoms. But the Anglo-Saxons from across the Baltic and North seas had, by the time Arthur reached the command age of fifteen, already taken eastern Britain and were holding east of the line Southampton to Edinburgh. The situation was not only grave for the resident peoples, but desperate.

For Merlin to be so fondly remembered in Scotland today, far and near, high and low, he must have been a very exalted personage—indeed, even someone more exalted than King Arthur himself. Then who was Merlin? What was his profession? What was his title?

These are questions that have been argued back and forth by scholars for some time now: Were there not two Merlins? Or was there only one? The archives of Wales claim that, in fact, there were two Merlins and give the two genealogies. The

• • •

bishop Dubricius, who attended Arthur in military and religious affairs, Bowen says specifically (p. 44):

> We have noted that references to Dubricius indicate a leader more in the tradition of a Roman territorial bishop than a recluse of the Celtic type. Likewise, the writer of the early twelfth century 'Life' of St. Cadog thinks of him, too, in a strong Roman setting. He is made out to be a direct descendant of a long line of Roman emperors in unbroken succession from Augustus, and to love the work of Vergil and even to regret that he (as a Christian) will be unable to meet the distinguished pagan poet in the Hereafter.

Geoffrey of Monmouth thought of King Arthur and of his religious leader Dubricius in similar terms.

6

older one *is* King Arthur's Merlin. He was born probably about 450 and died in 536.

The theory of only one Merlin even now seems to stumble on the fact of dating, by extending his life span too long—by several decades. One Merlin could not have been the victorious contemporary of King Arthur, who died in 542, in the first half of the sixth century, and also a defeated contemporary of a British chieftain of the Old North called Gwenddolau, slain at the battle of Arthuret (Arfderydd), Scotland, in 573.

One must now commence a new search through the primary documents to discover who the mysterious Merlin was and how he was related to Arthur, what his profession was, and what his accomplishments were while he lived. Such an investigation will also answer questions about Morgan "le Fay," the Lady of the Lake, and about the biggest mystery: Who killed Merlin?

The first person in question was a warrior and supporter of King Arthur, and he was named Merlin. The second person in question, one who survived the battle of Arthuret—because of which he went insane—was named Myrddin. He lived on for many years after 573 as a wild man in the "Caledonian" forests of Scotland.

Both candidates for the prestige and rank of Merlin were authors, Merlin of orations and the world-famous *Prophecy*. The latter, Myrddin, wrote, probably, a body of obscure verse in Old British, which was a language similar to modern Welsh, and this verse is stored in Wales. It has unfortunately been much rewritten over the centuries.

The former, Merlin, was interred on the seashore of western Scotland in the year 536. The latter, Myrddin, was still alive between 573 and 600, for at some time in those years he conversed with and was blessed by Saint Kentigern (Mungo), the older patron saint of Scotland. Myrddin was probably interred in the border uplands of Scotland.

Merlin was called Merlinus in Latin, Merlin in French and in English, in which three languages his major exploits as a counselor to four British kings (Vortigern, Ambrosius, Uther, and Arthur) are told. His death, while King Arthur was still living, is also recounted in several texts. In none is he ever called Myrddin, which is a Welsh name. Neither his Latin name (Merlinus) nor his French and English name (Merlin), occurs in Welsh or in a Welsh dictionary.

King Arthur was always known as a Romano-Briton, Roman on his father's side and British on his mother's side, both families being warriors or commanders of the line. Merlin was at least twenty-five years older than Arthur and *probably* a near relative. Freeborn Romans and Celts customarily bore three names, and sometimes four. The Romans were given:

1. a *praenomen*, or first name,

2. a *cognomen*, family or last name,

3. a *nomen*, or middle name indicating his *gens* (clan), and sometimes, if a man was very distinguished,

4. an *agnomen*, which was a surname often bestowed as a title of honor, or fondly as a nickname.

In Britain any noble Celt such as Merlin would also have had three personal names, as we see now in Welsh, his *ennwau personau: cyfenw* (a surname), *enw bedydd* (a baptismal name), *llwyth* (a tribal name), or *tylwyth* (a family name, ancestral name), or *brychan* (his plaid, or tartan name). Without a clan name, both Briton and Roman would been scorned as a nobody (*sine gente*).

A premonition suggests that "Merlin" was an agnomen. It urges a search through those languages primarily connected to King Arthur's Merlin: English, Latin, French, and Scottish. The personal name "Merlin," one remembers at once, is also spelled "merlin" as a common noun. This suggests that "Merlin" was the man's familiar name, fondly bestowed, his affectionate nickname. More than any man alive, King Arthur's Merlin would have merited a title of honor, an affectionate tribute, for meri-

8

torious service well beyond the call of duty. He was, like Arthur, a father to his country.

Doubtless, Merlin and Myrddin have long since merged into one personage held in equal affectionate remembrance by one and all, one man in the public mind. But it seems imperative now, in the name of justice, to separate them into the Arthurian hero and battle leader, adviser to the four British kings, scholar and mysterious, great, but still unrevealed noble personage, and the pitiful, suffering poet Myrddin, who went mad, ate apples, wandered for decades, naked, cold, and starving through the forests. Myrddin was forgiven and blessed by Saint Kentigern about 600, and was even seen centuries later by Saint Waldhave while recuperating from a serious illness.

Even during his lifetime Merlin was largely ahistorical and unrevealed. He is even unrevealed in the manuscripts that recount his life story. He was always largely unknown to the greater public, except as "Merlin." When he was summoned by the kings or needed desperately to recruit other noble allies, he came silently, disguised as a poor shepherd, as a woodcutter, or as a peasant. Even the sovereigns failed to recognize him under his various disguises. He practiced this concealment habitually and for a long period of time. It would be useful to examine the written texts to see if this practice can be explained.

Who in Arthur's day would have been obliged to disguise himself as he passed through the battle lines into Arthur's command post? But more significantly, how was Merlin occupied when he was away, neither advising Arthur nor leading Arthur's battle line ahead of the king?

Merlin played many roles, it would seem, since he wore many costumes. Yet, contrary to King Arthur, Merlin's physical appearance is so meticulously detailed as to make him instantly recognizable in any street of Carlisle, Peel, Glasgow, or Edinburgh.

There is the story of Merlin's birth and the story of his childhood as a prodigy. He was a rare case in history. Having satisfied ourselves as to his name, it is possible to follow him as a child, as a youth, and as a prodigy. In Scotland he is still hailed as "Marvelous Merlin" because he worked such wonders for Arthur that he has come down as the very prototype of the shaman, or wizard, or magician. And yet these words do not sit well upon Merlin's august shoulders. He is too venerable even for them, too imposing.

Although it may be impossible to persuade the modern reader of this fact, Merlin's chief glory rests not in any magical performance but in his famous *Prophecy*. This great work of art, *which has changed history down through the centuries* in Europe, overshadows even his exploits as standard-bearer and foremost warrior of Celtic Britain, which is saying a good deal.

His principal attraction for poets and readers throughout the centuries has been his physical attraction to women. He must have been a beautiful man. Morgan "le Fay," who was the Queen of Ireland and the Out-Isles and a mother to at least one of the clans of present Scotland, was said to have been romantically involved with Merlin. She was also romantically involved with Lancelot and with Accolon, to name only two of her other lovers or luckless suitors. Merlin's greatest romantic attachment was to the Lady of the Lake. That Lady Niniane, or Vivian, for her names are double at least, has always been said to have seduced Merlin, which seems to have been every woman's wish in those days. As the gossip goes, after having seduced him, the Lady persuaded him to teach her his most difficult magic tricks. Such stories supply us with the larger part of Merlin's legend. Its end is sad enough to please all lovers and to shock others, for the Lady then killed Merlin. What were her reasons for murder?

Even murder could not silence Merlin. It continued his legend with a new breath of wind. He was then afforded a voice from beyond the grave where the cruel beauty had shut him in his cold, stone sarcophagus. As he lay so treacherously entombed, Merlin cried out messages for posterity. He did not die at once but lingered on as long as he had breath and words to transmit. One must have another look at these stories, judge their merits, fathom their secrets, discover how Merlin died and where, and reach some satisfactory truth behind the legend.

Yet Merlin's claim to immortality during the Middle Ages rested upon his Christianity and upon his authorship of the *Prophecy*. That text was eagerly seized by the leading churchmen of northern France in the twelfth century since it came from the pen of Geoffrey of Monmouth. Geoffrey first translated it from Old British into Latin, which was then the universal language of all churchmen. Fragments of this prophecy or of others still circulate in Scotland. However, and here is the bitterest controversy among scholars and theologians today: they do not accept as truth the words of Geoffrey of Monmouth. They also reject Merlin's authorship. Too many scholars still believe that Geoffrey of Monmouth forged the Merlin *Prophecy*, that Geoffrey wrote it, and that the *Prophecy* refers to twelfth-century politics at the court of King Henry II. Thus, the famous Merlin *Prophecy*, for centuries the wonder of world literature, has fallen into modern disrepute. Even so, it is retranslated in this book so that new readers may form their own opinion and judge for themselves. (The retranslation is placed in the middle of the book since it once formed the center of Merlin's life.) Merlin's major work, then, was a *Prophecy* in the manner of the ancient prophets of Israel and Judah whom in life and dress Merlin imitated. We know of King Arthur's dedication to the Virgin, and that he and Merlin re-Christianized the Grail Castle on its western isle adjacent to the Isle of Man.

The *Prophecy* may still be what the Middle Ages considered it in those later days of faith, as imaginative literature from a great mind that had allowed memory to wander among openended symbols back to the frenzy of combat: naked warriors covered in blood; black whips flailing naked flesh like the sting of vipers; animals tearing, clawing, rending, raging in uncontrolled savagery. The battle frenzy of the archaic Celtic warrior explodes before us like a cornered, bristling boar charging from the thicket. Over the battlefields of this war for one's home territory soars like some ancient dragon Merlin's flaming red banner, a dragon sometimes called gargoyle, called sphinx, an image of death and fire that the Saxon hero must fight and extinguish.

When Merlin himself was not more than one year old, his future symbols were already revered among the Franks in Gaul. The Frankish King Meroveus, who is said to have killed Attila the Hun, dreamed he had been fathered by just such a dragon, a dragon-king, or some coiled serpent-king. Another Merovingian sovereign dreamed of a horrible three-headed monster and was informed that his dream summarized history: the way France was ravaged by three successive conquerors—a lion (the Celts), an eagle (the Romans), and a venomous toad (the Franks). Here is Merlin's animal symbolism of the *Prophecy* already made. Another Frankish noble who became a saint also dreamed that the eagle (Rome) was destroyed by a lion (the Celts) and then by a serpent (the Welsh); this was not a dream but a nightmare. Similarly, Britain was lashed by the Saxon chieftain Hengist, a German worm, said the Celts, that swam underwater like wolves or like Beowulf. They were wolves of the ocean, says Merlin.

Then Merlin's *Prophecy* takes off to float freely onto another association: the Lion of Scotland, the Pictish Boar from the Highlands, the Red Dragon of Wales. Altogether his archaic symbols shift so often that they become incomprehensible to us. They are so ancient in the history of man, so much older than our books, that they are really relics of a truly forgotten prehistoric past.

Merlin's use of symbols in lieu of history, conveys to us some lost past of the human race where we merely glimpse in the mind's eye the olden Germanic kings and also their preferred insignia: beasts that represented each heathen monarch. The British Celts, who had been converted to Christianity directly from Jerusalem, it is still believed, gasped in horror.

But among the ancient Celts of Gaul, who did not even remember them, birds and animals once symbolized rivers, forests, and even mountains. The animal drawings of the Picts still impress us with their vivid beauty. In Merlin the three limbs of the tree seem in one flash to symbolize the three tribes of the British Celts. Such seemingly accidental associations in the Merlin *Prophecy* convey spontaneously and better than a thousand words Merlin's hopes and fears for his time. His masterful use of animal symbolism, especially when compared to the Pictish glyphs, puts his modern readers not before Merlin, but beside him, looking out with his eyes at wild hogs, at white giants of iniquity in the mountains of Wales, at bear cubs born to a lioness, at the oracular heron, harbinger of the storm, who flew like a druid, or like the soul of Hercules, who was also Merlin's Arthur, up into an oak tree.

In one passage of the *Prophecy* Merlin almost falls into a coherent narrative. In that passage he tells how the heron gave birth to a king of Scotland. Her firstborn offspring was a fox who devoured its dam, wore an ass's head, bit a boar, became a wolf, devoured the boar, became a boar, and slew the wolf. Afterward he was kinged, that is, he metamorphosed himself into a royal, rampant lion. Every now and then, despite himself, Merlin corroborates our knowledge, such as that those ancient sub-kings wore gold torques instead of crowns. He always stimulates recollections of the modern history books, with his symbols that persist in reminding his reader of Maximus, Constantine, Ambrosius, Uther Pendragon, and Arthur. Even the ubiquitous, evil King Vortigern seems almost to float to the surface. These evocations remain only that, however, as they slip from our grasp and float off into freer air. We are left with Merlin's view.

Thus, in Merlin's *Prophecy*, the lion, the wolf, and the fox have not yet been confined to their set roles, as in the medieval fable (or beast-epic). This later medieval form was political and attacked the monarchy. The ancient Merlin has no comic relief and no homely, barnyard domesticity. Merlin is like a biblical prophet. He never veers away from his given task, which is to present war in its unrelieved horror. His is a fierce, crude portrayal of ancient warfare at its worst. Nor does he confuse his terrible images of a bloody history with the consecrated symbols of his Christianity.

The *Prophecy*, which long ago slipped from the pens of Merlin and Geoffrey, escaped alone into the world where like all great literature it still lives a life of its own, as public property. Thus, we shall all be free to decide finally if it seems truly to be an eyewitness account of the Dark Ages. If so, it is doubly precious, for such firsthand accounts are very rare indeed. The Celts were not trained in history, which is a modern discipline.

1

THE
NAMES
OF
MERLIN

. . . .

Who can escape then, who can know,
What things the ancients have laid on us?
A secret thing that one of us does,
Can be remembered and done again
By flesh that is not yet borne of our pain.
This darkened earth, the hollow in hills,
Invisible water that sings and fills
The deeps of air with silences—
Alert and watchful in unstirred trees—
Remember too: and they tell the most,
Without intercession of fetch or ghost
To those in whom the memory brings
The past and magic of all lost things.

"Merlin's Grave,"
Scenes and Plays.
Gordon Bottomley.

• • • • • • •

Standing upon a higher step and facing him, or equal with the young king but just behind his right shoulder, the tremendous figure of his mentor Merlin overshadowed King Arthur for most of the younger man's life. When over the fifteen intervening centuries poets and chroniclers have referred to Merlin, they have most frequently used this key word: "tremendous." Straining to characterize such an imposing presence, they have returned again and again to assure us Merlin was, to put it plainly, "tremendous"; he had once made Britain tremble. The political power Merlin wielded from the fifth into the early sixth centuries of the Christian era shook those islands down to bedrock.

So far as is known, the first writers to portray scenes from Merlin's life or to supply the briefest bits of his biography wrote in Latin and in British (Old Welsh).[1] Geoffrey of Monmouth again introduced Merlin to the Latin Middle Ages in 1134 with the briefest of identifications: "Merlinus qui et Ambrosius dicebatur": (his name is Merlin) and he was also called Ambrose. Or, Geoffrey continued, he was named "Ambrosius Merlinus," but either way he was a major prophet and difficult to name.

Geoffrey stopped writing his *History of the Kings of Britain* long enough to give his eager readers an interlude, Merlin's longest prophecy. Europe was enchanted, for the fame of King Arthur's Merlin had never faded from people's minds.

• • •

[1] *Merlin*, edited by W. E. Mead, EETS (Early English Text Society), Original Series 10, 21, 36, 112 (London), p. XLIVff.

17

For their part, the Welsh have always believed in their poet, or that Merlin's original name may have been Myrddin, a Welsh name that, they say, Geoffrey may have rendered into Latin, correctly and phonetically. Less well-read scholars still insist that Geoffrey dreamed up Merlin, or invented from his "wild" (Welsh) imagination both the name "Merlin" and the prophet himself. Thus, we have as rivals Merlin and Myrddin.

There probably are two separate Merlins, the first being King Arthur's Merlin, born about 450 and died in 536. This is the prophet called "Merlinus" by Geoffrey of Monmouth in his *History of the Kings of Britain* and in his *Prophecy* of Merlin. This is also the Merlin of the many other medieval narratives in Old French, Latin, English, Icelandic, and Italian. He is the Merlin not only associated with King Arthur but responsible, in fact, for King Arthur. This Merlin is such a famous figure in the history of the Dark Ages that we shall also look for him in all the more ancient archives we can find. He was a man of many names, of many parts. He was buried in Scotland, in a very prominent place or national site. His story belongs to what are now two separate Celtic realms: Scotland and Wales.

The successor to this first Merlin was a minor poet named Myrddin in Welsh, or Old British. He is the subject of a brilliant, recent book of admirable scholarship: *The Quest for Merlin* by Nikolai Tolstoy (New York, 1985). He was the Wild Man of the Woods, the Merlin Sylvester, the poet Myrddin who went insane at the Battle of Arderydd in 573, by which time King Arthur's Merlin and King Arthur himself had long been dead. Tolstoy calls this successor, this Myrddin "heir of the Druidic tradition," a descendant of shamanistic cults in Siberia, and a pagan Druid. Thus was he represented by many artists: Thomas Jones, Gustave Doré, and the unknown illustrator of Thomas Heywood's *Life of Merlin*. But, despite his illustrator's confusion, Thomas Heywood was writing about the first, or King Arthur's Merlin, the prophet who was as eminent a man and personage as lived in the entire Dark Ages. Here is another case of an illustrious man whose identity was assumed by an innocent poet and madman some fifty years after the death of the great personage.

Vicious charges against both Merlin and his first historian Geoffrey of (or from) Monmouth (in Wales) commence from the very first ascriptions of his *Prophecy* to Merlin. However, they form a part of the violent anti-Celtic prejudice among men of letters, which over the centuries has accused the Welsh, the Scots, and the Irish of being "wild," "wily," "treacherous," and worse.[2] There have been many examples of great men and great writers who have been debunked. One finds commonly applied to Merlin such stock epithets, plus the belittling of Merlin's powers with the term "mere conjuror." His dearest pupil, for Merlin was called "summus doctor," whose name was either Niniane or Vivian, but who was in her lifetime honored by the title the "Lady of the Lake," has generally also been dismissed as "wily Vivian," just as King Arthur's learned and royal half sister, Queen Morgan, has been scorned as "Fay," or Fate, or crazy. Warning of this jealousy on the parts of less talented men should make it easier to dilute or even to smile at such allegations.

By output, because of their total of twenty-nine major manuscript treatments, the French-language authors of the Middle Ages, who discarded Myrddin, control the Merlin question. They wrote the most varied, the longest, the most resourceful, vivid, overbearing, and entertaining accounts of Merlin's life and achievements. Since they also drew up a once theologically acceptable and perfectly rational account of his "birth," it is possible to follow Merlin from conception to death, and thanks to his written and spoken words, even to well beyond the magnificently sculpted sarcophagus that was to hold his body. The French authors were fascinated with the prophet Merlin *primarily*

• • •

[2] Edward D. Snyder. *The Celtic Revival in English Literature 1760–1800* (Cambridge, Mass., 1923). The phrase "American Celtomaniac" appeared in A. H. Krappe's article in *Romania* LX (1934): 83. (See Bibliography.)

because he had been a child prodigy, and only later because he was a superb warrior. He seemed to echo the old Frankish savagery, their animal symbolism, and their admiration for men of war. He predated their own battling orators, like the Archbishop Turpin, who under Charlemagne's leadership slaughtered so many Saracens in the passes of the Pyrenees.

The French-language examinations of Merlin and the studied elaborations upon this theme so charmed readers on the continent that other authors selected from this now large body of material those aspects of Merlin's life story that most interested them.

In fact, Margaret J. C. Reid in 1938 observed that Merlin is "ageless and selfless, he cannot die." He later became not only Prospero, the protector, said Reid, but further than that, the touchstone by which his critics more often than not show their own attitudes rather than any that might conceivably have been Merlin's in that time long ago. Thus, each Merlin variant offers up not so much Merlin as each author for judgment.

In *The Idylls of the King* ("Vivian"), Tennyson had allowed the Lady of the Lake to concur:

> . . . *so is it with this rhyme:*
> *It lives dispersedly in many lands,*
> *And every minstrel sings it differently; . . .*

In its final development and scholarly extension, the Merlin material later found successful authors in Dutch, English, German, Icelandic, Italian, Portuguese, Provençal, and Spanish. Several major alterations result from this four-handed method of operation: (1) there occurs more than one Merlin, (2) there is more than one perfectly logical geographical setting, (3) Merlin displays at least two different characters, careers, and personalities, and (4) the whole is dominated, one might say overwhelmed, by the French clergy and by Roman orthodoxy, both of which strongly opposed the British Church.

20

In Merlin's case it is important to avoid their major error, which was to assume that Druid priests and the Druid religion had survived the Roman occupation of western Europe. The evidence fails to support such romantic notions. It is true that the word "magus" (pagan magician) survives in Merlin's day and even widely for another few decades, or into Saint Columba's prime, as into our days; but any pagan magicians or "wise men" were seen only rarely, wandering naked and insane like poor Myrddin in some deep forest or far away in the Highlands of Scotland. Merlin once punished two or three such "wise men" but no taint of such delirium, much less of the Pelagian heresy, tainted the great Merlin himself. Nor was he examined by Papal Legates sent from Rome or from France during his lifetime, but the same cannot be said with absolute certainty about Saint Patrick. Even the officiant sub-King Bademagus at the Grail Castle, or his heirs, probably found it expedient to modernize his name to Baldwin, and a subsequent orthodox Baldwin became an Archbishop of Canterbury.

Several generations of ancient authors have written a great deal about Merlin, how covered with coarse, black hair the newborn child was as he lay in his mother's arms; how as a stern warrior he demanded recruits for King Arthur; how he decorated the walls of Carlisle with the heads of slain enemies; how Perceval or Queen Morgan was his last pupil; how he castigated Gawain's brothers for incompetence, gross negligence, and cowardice; how he stood finally, a tall, white-headed old man, our Father Time with the rolled scroll of some ancient, lost Annals of Britain in his right hand. The last view anyone had of Merlin, according to an otherwise unknown author called Richard of Ireland, was as he lay down in his stone tomb, attended at the end by the most brilliant and gifted of all his students, Niniane/Vivian. She was about to murder Merlin.

Whether or not the Lady of the Lake murdered Merlin, and how and why, is still a mystery. In any event, Merlin's story did not end there. By that time, he had already rejoined those few

21

people unanimously hailed as the greatest writers of the world. Like them, Merlin also possessed one of those tremendous voices from beyond the grave that still sends shivers down the spine.

Before commencing to know Merlin by studying the Latin, Welsh, French, and English texts and other narratives, one should first turn to the word "merlin" as recorded in dictionaries. One must first try to understand how language has preserved his name.

The Welsh name, Myrddin, even though it seems not to occur before 930, is supposed to indicate the place of a Merlin's birth in the Latin town of Maridunum, which became Caer/marthen (Citadel of Marthan) in South Wales. If *Merlinus* is an approximation of the British *Marthen*, then it should have no other meaning in Latin. Tradition has said that the town of Carmarthen took its name from Merlin, and not the other way around. Avoiding the controversy by striking off in an untried direction, one finds, surprisingly, that "Merlin" does have meanings of its own. Geoffrey of Monmouth's Latin name for Merlin, or *Merlinus* (tonic accent on the second syllable), derives from classical Latin:

merul + inus > merula = blackbird,

meruleus = colored like a blackbird,

merula solivaga = a wandering bird, solitary, not gregarious.

The Romans tell us "unde et avis merula nomen accipit, quod solivaga est" (whence the blackbird receives its name, because it is solitary).

By medieval times[3] the Latin word had been simplified into "merlina" and "merlinus" the blackbird, or the falcon (pigeon hawk). Therefore it seems reasonable that *Merlinus*, or Merlin, was the great leader's nickname or agnomen, and furthermore

• • •

[3] R. E. Latham. *Medieval Latin Word-List from British and Irish Sources* (London, 1965).

22

that it did not stem either from the Welsh Caer/marthen, nor from the corresponding Welsh word for blackbird (which is *mwyalch*).

"Black" and "solitary bird" both suit the French lives of Merlin, according to the French dictionary (*Littré*, 1863), where the word *merlin* occurs commonly as:

1. *merlin*—a noble personage, traditionally Celtic, possessing a high magical power, knowing sciences.

2. *merlin*—archaeological term for an ancient weapon, a hammer or club from the ancient world, made of bronze and/or iron. Butchers today use such a weapon, and so do woodcutters in splitting wood.

3. Hercules's club is called a *merlin* in French, and it was gnarled and spiked. Such clubs were used in combat between priests in the time of Saint Augustine (fourth century).

4. Cain used a *merlin* to kill Abel.

With its vastly expanded vocabulary, the English dictionary adds considerably to the notion of what the name *Merlinus* meant and what it tells about Merlin himself. Unlike the French dictionary, the English dictionaries, such as *Webster's Third International*, do not affirm that the common noun *merlin* comes from the man Merlin himself. *Webster's* lists:

1. *merlin* (from M.E. *meriloun*, O.F. *esmerillon*, etc)—the small European falcon (*Falco aesalon*), which is a diurnal, flesh-eating bird of prey with long wings, very swift in the air. This bird often signals, in symbolic language, a messenger from afar.

2. *merlin*—a single-bit ax, which has an edged head affixed to a handle. It was used by ancient Celts as a weapon in war. Such an ax is also a symbol of ancient, Celtic royalty; just as in Imperial Rome it was carried as an emblem of high authority.

3. *merlin*—a blackbird, a common thrush *(Turdus merula)*, a passerine bird of perching habits, a warbler, a whitethroat. In America it is the robin, or robin in the wood.

4. *merlin*—an ocean fish such as a whiting or silver hake related to the cod; a sea carp.

5. merlin's-grass *is so named after Merlin,* "the fifth-century wizard" from Wales. This grass is quillwort *(Isotes lacustris)*, also called joe-pye weed, and butterfly weed. The plant grows about three feet in height, has greenish-purplish stems, and flower heads of perfumed white, pink, and lavender flowers. The plant secretes latex.

Merlin's-grass belongs to the famly *Asclepias*, named for the Greek healer Asklepios, the hero-physician and god of healing. Sick people thronged to his round shrines.

The dried root of this plant was used as a diaphoretic and expectorant in the treatment of lung diseases. It is also called pleurisy root.[4]

Because the Lowlands of Scotland were the ancient home of the Welsh before their migration into what is now Wales, evidence is also found in the *Scottish National Dictionary* and in the *Dictionary of the Older Scottish Tongue:*

1. *merlin, merling*—used erroneously for the blackbird, as in these examples from Hoggs's *Jacobite Relics:*

A. *Hae ye heard at eve the merlin,*   c. 1827
    Within the greenwood grove?

B. *Whan the weary sun gaes down*   c. 1869
    Gladden'd by the merlin's tune.

• • •

[4] In backcountry Vermont in the 1920s and 1930s, doctors used the hairy leaves of this weed in poultices for the throat inflamed with scarlet fever and diphtheria.

C. *I' in tree and the bush*   c. 1870
    Sing the bullfinch and thrush,
    The goldfinch and merling.

2. *merling*—a mermaid[5]

    The ship's in the howe o' a roarin' wave   c. 1866
    An' thy luve's i' the merlin's cell . . .
    But the merlin he noo maun wed.

3. *merling*—

    He was brought south by a merling,[6]   c. 1821
    Got a hundred and fifty pounds sterling,
    Which will make him bestow the auld carlin;
    He winna be guidit by me.

The original Latin name for the prophet Merlin (Merlinus) contained a treasury of meanings after all, including one mythological suggestion, an allusive hint that sets the mind wandering back to an early Greek poet whose lament "Woe is me!" rings so reminiscent of the British prophet's cry of agony: "The Celtic peoples will lose Britain to the invaders!"

This Greek musician and poet was Linus (linus), whose name occurs as the Latin accented syllable.[7] Linus was said to have invented melody and rhythm, to have suffered an untimely death in a wasteland, and to have lamented the death of Adonis. But perhaps in Merlin's case, this name derived from the early Pope Linus (d. A.D. 76). If Merlinus derived from the proper name Linus, then the prefix "Mel" or "Mer" can be chosen from an assortment of possibilities:

· · ·

[5] In other words, a maiden from an island? The Lady of the Lake?

[6] The older meaning for *merling*, as perhaps here, is a whiting.

[7] In Scotland today "Merlin" sounds to an American ear like our pronunciation of the woman's name "Marilyn."

Mel = black-haired, used commonly as a prefix in Greek personal names,

Mer < *merus* = true, genuine in Latin,

mel < *melos* = song in Greek,

mel < *mellina* = sweetness in Latin.

It would be too much to expect to be able to trace the names to the Gaelic *linne* (pool) or Welsh (llyn = pool) although Merlin did haunt the healing pool in what the Bretons and French still insist was and is the Forest of Broceliande.

It seems appropriate that Merlin, who was solitary and not allowed to marry, should be associated with a bird, blackbird and pigeon hawk, since both the dragon and the birds were always protective symbols for the Celtic peoples. Merlin seems to have designed the dragon banner for Kings Uther and Arthur. Like the boar and bull ensigns, dragons also appear in jewelry, in manuscript illustrations, in carved stones and wood, and over doorways.

A vague conception of Merlin's biography now begins to form from mere words adorned with their extended webs of significance, with their archaic symbolism that conveys hours and hours of associations. From the dictionaries it is clear how deeply and persistently Merlin has descended into the common consciousness of speakers throughout Great Britain and France, from French Brittany to Provence. Thus, persons taught in those languages, also as in Spanish, German, Italian, Icelandic, and Portuguese, join the Anglo-Saxons, whom the Celts have conquered with their own special culture, history, and myths.

Many people have seen Merlin as that great father figure of absolute authority: stern, swarthy, black-haired, judgmental, teaching, reprimanding cooly. Every New Year's Eve he is pictured as Father Time when one looks, as Merlin did, Janus-like, forward into January and backward into the dying year. Merlin himself must have been remembered popularly, as the dictionary attests, as the solitary, wandering blackbird hidden in the forest thicket, whistling, assembling his twilight flock, and remembered in battle as that stone that dove with folded wings from the clouds upon the foe.

With everything in full dissolution in the ancient world, and with the fall of Rome to Alaric in 410, warriors like King Arthur could not for one second take their eyes off the point of the sword. But the prophet Merlin—like Daniel even in captivity, or Isaiah, or Jeremiah—applied himself to portents, to warnings of imminent evils, knowing from the Bible, and perhaps also from Cicero's essay on divination that from its beginning the world was so constituted as to signal special messages by symbols clear to anyone who could read their warnings before catastrophe struck.

And what greater compliment than to be remembered by the dictionary as Asklepios at his healing waters and near his medicinal grass. But how sadly to have been labeled as a mere trickster, a sleight-of-hand magician when he had devoted his years to science. Such a study was at that time forbidden learning, only reestablished by the Church in Geoffrey of Monmouth's twelfth century, which may explain why Geoffrey proudly proclaimed to all who listened that he had found the lost prophecy of a great unknown scholar.

The ax more than the crystal ball announces Merlin's royal signature. Not only did Merlin wield his ax in battle against illicit sorcerers and foes, and carry it in ceremonies so that all could contemplate this visible symbol of his power of life and death, but as the Green Giant he also used the ax to convey a reprimand, for it left a permanent red mark upon Gawain when he promised more than he could fulfill. Decollation was also practiced, as shown in the hard story of the future Welsh Saint Winefred, who was fortunate in finding another saint nearby who could attach her head to her shoulders again so that she also had only the thin white or red scar to bear.

To this day guidebooks claim that people still see the gallant warrior Gawain near Spanish Head on the Isle of Man, with

MIGRATIONS AND CONQUESTS from c. A.D. 150

NORTHMEN

NORTHMEN

NORTHMEN

NORTHMEN

ANGLES

SAXONS

ATLANTIC OCEAN

FRANKS

VANDALS

FRANKS

BURGUNDIANS

FRANKS

LOMBARDS

EAST GOTHS

Ravenna

WEST GOTHS

Rome

MEDITERRANEAN SEA

the red scar from his wound on the neck still clearly visible. The Green Giant (Knight) and his ax seem otherwise forgotten along that fierce seashore. The heroic sagas of Ireland clearly recall several occasions when the horrifying sound of the beheading ax cut the air, making a hiss as loud as the whistling of treetops thrashing about in the cyclone.

Finally, it would help to turn again in our dictionaries to allusions to the Isle of Man and to this Irish Sea. They are all appropriate but less immediately understandable. Whatever tale there once was of Merlin and the fish has not survived. But he has his own special isle in the sea, called Merlin's Isle. More wonderful, he also had his own special maiden whom he discovered and adored for her beauty and her intelligence, his beloved Lady of the Lake, that "Lake" also being the Irish Sea, with in its center the Isle of Man.

French authors believe that Merlin's mother was a religious, that it was she who gave him his other name Ambrosius. He was probably named either for the great fourth-century Saint Ambrose of Milan or for the British King Ambrosius of the previous generation. Those who have thought that the name Ambrosius was a place-name from the hill or promontory of Ambrosius in North Wales fail to grant that it could as well be that the place took Merlin's second name from some dramatic presence of Merlin at that spot.

Another version is that Merlin's name was rooted in the Latin comparative *Melius* or *Melior* (better) because he declared himself the son of the world's best mother, *Optima*. No other name in Latin has been as widely recorded for Merlin's mother; and mother and son had in French no husband/father, but only a father confessor named Blaise.

If no sure conclusion can as yet be drawn concerning the names of Merlin, Ambrosius appears possible, and the name *Merlinus* describes him rather than names him and his illustrious family. An easy target for blame regarding his name is the great poet Taliesin. In the generation after Merlin, he formally forbade all teachers in the Celtic realm (the present Scotland and Wales, at the least) to explain personal names on the grounds that they contained the keys to the sacred stories, or Celtic classics, that formed a basis of the ancient curriculum. The Celts believed that the name of a person and his soul are one and the same. To know and to speak a person's name is to gain dominance over that person. The question "Who am I?" became not only a common Welsh riddle but also a standard teaching device.

Both James Frazer in *The Golden Bough* and Sigmund Freud in *Totem and Taboo* have written at considerable length concerning the widespread taboo of names, which allows a nickname such as "Merlin" to answer such a riddle by explaining who and what he was rather than what his name and ancestry were. Even if the Welsh *Brut*—which is a translation of Geoffrey of Monmouth's *History of the Kings of Britain* into the Welsh language—is correct and Merlin's name in Welsh was "Annvab y llaiann," Son-of-the-Mother, that again fails to satisfy because it merely means that the youngster was enrolled in school for the long and rigorous education of those days.

The multiplicity of these names of Merlin, with their heavy symbolic counterparts, indicates only that he represents what the contemporary anthropologist Anne Ross identifies and describes in *Pagan Celtic Britain* as a tradition deeply ingrained in *religious* thinking. A surmise that Merlin was a prophet in the Judaic tradition gains some seconding here. In speaking of the perils of the soul and of the terror of names, Frazer notes that names of the dead were generally tabooed, but that names of kings were always tabooed. The weight of such injunctions inside Britain was such that subjects were put to death in Merlin's day, say the Celtic scholars, if they so much as pronounced the birth-name of a personage, that is, Lancelot (Galahad). At the sacred shrine of Eleusis in classical Greece, nobody was permitted even to name one of the priests' names, much less to write it. These names were actually buried in the depths of the sea. The purpose of this Greek taboo was the same: to protect people, royal personages, and sovereigns. As a general rule, adds Frazer, the mightier the person, the grander his name.

The tellers and now the writers of Irish fairy tales gave one of their most impressive personages a clearly descriptive name that recurs in most collections of these tales from ancient times. This character is the Grúagach, or Laughing Grúagach, laughter that precedes the burst of prophecy being typical or even essential to the prophet wherever he feels that spell coming upon him. (All the Merlin authors have noted this laughter, as it swept over Merlin, and detailed endlessly each particular onset, and what it was that Merlin prophesied.) This account parallels the Latin annals concerning Merlin's functions in his society. In these tales Ireland remembers Merlin, and it would be strange were they to have forgotten him.

The Isle of Man has probably not forgotten him either, for the word in Manx is *gruagagh*, which now means a brown-haired' gnome, or a brownie. Anthropologists realize that popular memory rarely repeats historical memory.

These old Gaelic tales, as collected by Jeremiah Curtin, for example, are so charming in their weirdness and mystery, their memorizers so intent upon recounting the awful spell of this "teacher of high pedigree," that listeners down through the ages certainly remained enraptured by mystery. The name of this exalted professor hits his physical appearance right on the nail; he is the black, "hairy guy" (from *grúag* = hair). He "takes" little "boys," even a fisherman's son, for a period of *twelve* years, during which discipline they are his *"birds,"* or his *"doves."* In first grade they are "doves"; in second grade, horses; third grade, hounds; and then they are put in the *cave of concealment* for graduation (?).

When the fisherman's son got into fourth grade, he was such a slippery *eel* that he managed to wriggle out of the cave and flop into the river; but the Grúagach chased him. In grade five the rascal turned himself into a *salmon* ("the salmon of knowledge" is a well-known symbol), but he was chased by the Grúagach and the others. Grade six found the stubborn lad metamorphosed into a *whale*, but bigger ocean whales got him back. In grade seven he turned himself into a *swallow*, but the falcon (Merlin's hawk) brought him down. By grade eight he had been fairly well-yoked academically, for he turned himself into a *golden ring*, which fell into the lap of the Princess of Erin. After that he became really hard to handle when he was a *spark* (the fire of the intellect), until the *tongs* caught him. Even as a *grain of wheat* in grade nine he could not escape the *roosters* (emblem of the Gauls or Franks). In grade eleven he bit off the heads of Father Grúagach and his eleven other "sons" so that by grade twelve he had turned himself into a *prince*, married the Princess of Erin whom earlier he seems to have seduced, and became king of Ireland.

The story suits Perceval admirably, his twelve or so uncles even more, who sponsored him as their pupil as he strove to marry the Isle of Man's Irish princess and install himself in Gaelic territory as king of the Grail Castle. The Isle of Man, or Avalon, was known in Arthur's day as the "foreign land" because Gaelic (Q-Celtic) was spoken there and not Welsh (P-Celtic). The tale also corroborates a French *Merlin* (and the *Didot-Perceval*) that Perceval was one of that great man's last pupils, that he was obdurate, hardheaded, not easily teachable, and that Merlin died before Perceval, and the Merlin was interred in a cave in Scotland.

The fairy tale is psychologically so true that we sympathize with Merlin's and the Grúagach's efforts to bring back into line a recalcitrant student who had been allowed to run wild. Merlin's student Perceval "had problems" as all students phrase it. Perceval "felt" that he had succeeded because he "tried" to master the lesson, or because his father had died when he was an infant. His mother had so "overcompensated" for that loss that she had turned her son into a lout. Doubtless, Perceval preferred running through the forest with the deer to attending school. Merlin or the Grúagach was stumped when either had to teach a lad like Perceval.

The Irish recall another traditional tale about the Grúagach and his "sons," but this one is somewhat more grim. A certain fairy prince will wed the king of Erin's daughter if he can pass these tests: discover why the Grúagach no longer laughs, guard five golden coins successfully, and watch the bull without horns. He will succeed if he can then decapitate five horrid giants and kill the old wizard hare. Hardest of all, he will inherit a realm if he can bring back to life the Grúagach's twelve sons. So it was this student alone who perceived that his old taskmaster had on his back *a strip of black hair*, such as a black sheepskin, perhaps. There it was: thick, black wool. The Grúagach laughed once more when his twelve sons were restored to life. The prince

32

married the Irish beauty named Sovereignty of Ireland, which is a proper fairy-tale ending.

The more one looks back over this apparently guileless tale, the grimmer it seems and the longer it turns restlessly in the mind. The tasks of the prince look overwhelming. His situation looms more and more grave. The twelve sons, or heroes, are already dead. The Grúagach has failed to prophecy, for his prophetic outbursts must all be preceded by wild laughter. When leadership, heroism, and prophecy have all failed to save the Britons, what shall avail? Magic? Perceval?

But we are fairly sure of recognizing one person here, and that is the Grúagach. He wears a hair shirt next to his skin and, like his mother he does not marry, and like his mother he is a religious. Merlin, then, seems to be the Grúagach, or Hairy One, of Irish folk tales, someone so unforgettable and so impressive that for ages he has remained symbolically in the public mind. Another legend might also have him as the Grúagach Gaire, the Laughing Hairy One, personal names being frequently alliterative. He is probably also the towering, glossy Green "Knight," or dead-green, ghastly warrior from the isolated Land of the Dead, from that green Ireland that then lay isolated in the farthest west of the known world. Like other majestic personages, he carried his own head in his hands until, like the saints, he proudly put it back on again, without harm, and like an avenging angel then swiped Gawain on the neck without entirely laying him down into death. The Arthurian hero Lancelot wept bitter tears when he heard his teacher's voice, Merlin's voice, saying, "You will *never* achieve the Grail." Even the feat of bringing to Merlin at the Grail Castle the head of John the Baptist could not earn another Arthurian hero, Gawain, a place among the most sacred of men there.

This brief preview of Merlin's names should awaken a sense, an intuition, which will point the way as we commence a more disciplined, scholarly examination of the French texts that recount "The Birth of Merlin."

33

The functions of Merlin have always been common knowledge and the property of the world. Famous as he is today, he was as famous in the year A.D. 500 and A.D. 1500. He instantly gained immortality among mortals.

His title about A.D. 500 was probably the Roman title of "Draconarius," bearer of the dragon standard, or ancient rainmaker (the dragon symbolizes rain), or the Roman imperial official so dignified. He carried it into war beside, and after the first onslaught, before the teenaged boy Arthur, not yet fully grown, said Merlin. In this duty he resembled the Roman *Aquilifer*, or Eagle-bearer to the Legion, for like that brave officer there was only one Merlin to an army and one red dragon pennant streaming over his head into the wind.

Since that red dragon on a green field is still the flag of Wales, one should take very seriously those scholars of British, which is the Old Welsh tongue, who have searched with such longing to find Merlin's name and to keep him among the modern Welsh people. They especially long for him in Wales, into which land they were moving in Merlin's day, from the Edinburgh area and the Lowlands of Scotland. The *Cambridge* 80 manuscript, detailing Merlin's military feats, will call him "Only-Son-of-the-Nun," which in Welsh would sound like "Merlin:" "un mab llian."

The Welsh poem "Englynion y Bedew" also calls him "An ap llian," observed the Welsh scholar D. W. Nash. This or "merch llian" (child of the nun) amounts to calling Merlin fatherless, a child of a woman only; or, consulting the Gaelic *Etymological Dictionary* of Alexander Macbain (Inverness, 1896) we find that the name "Merlin" might be derived from "mac" (son, magician) + "linn" < "plenus" (century, age, offspring): Merlin = Magician of the Century. To someone in the Dark Ages such an appellation designated an "initiate" or "accolyte." It referred to a male child born into a priestly family, where inheritance of education, office, and dignity came by right to the child from the distaff side of his family. The father had sired a royal child in a hierarchy where distinguished mothers bore distinguished sons. Modern psychologists have for some time been telling

34

teachers faced with a highly creative youngster to look at the mother. Her influence on the small child has been the telling influence on a charmed childhood. When they call it the Jocasta complex, they are not talking of "slowly wise" Percevals, of course, but of a superior class of creative youngsters who will become learned men and women.

There was a time in the history of religions, says Frazer in his chapter on "Incarnate Human Gods," when both gods and men were considered as living persons of equal rank. In later years there stretched between them an ever-widening gulf that divided them into separate species: god-man and man-god, the one with supernatural faculties impossibly beyond those of the other. Frazer gives us instances that led him to so theorize. The Sicilian philosopher Empedocles declared himself a god because he could make the wind blow or subside, because like black Merlin he could make rain fall during periods of summer drought, because he could make the sun shine, banish illness and old age, and raise the dead from their western isle.

Matthew Arnold's admirable poem "Empedocles on Etna" (v. 280ff.) has the lone philosopher apostrophize the stars: "Have *you*, too, survived yourselves?" You too once lived, in a younger world, "among august companions" . . .

> *In an older world, peopled by Gods,*
> *In a mightier order . . .*

but now you kindle your flames

> *For a younger, ignoble world,*

and wheel each night across the heavens

> *Above a race you know not.*

When he had finished speaking, Empedocles hurled himself down into the crater of the volcano Etna, choosing to perish while he still had command of his faculties.

Even as it is glimpsed unclearly in modern times, Merlin's life seems to have united him with his most beloved ward Arthur just as in classical Greece and Rome king (Arthur) and priest (Merlin) shared a single supreme power. In ancient Sparta two such kings, one representing political power and the other, religious authority, together performed the state ceremonials; those rites that seem truly ancestral and hereditary should then be performed by Merlin and Arthur. Expecting this, one cannot believe that Merlin was absent at King Arthur's coronation, and yet this is the case in Geoffrey of Monmouth's first and primary account. This is yet one more mystery unsolved since the year 1134.

Important men in the Dark Ages often performed a double function. The French art historian Emile Mâle notes how the early Frankish saints were also defenders of the state: *defensores civitatis*. In southern Scotland the bishopric of the premier British Saint Ninian, who lived before Merlin, exercised both civil and ecclesiastical power. Because he was a prince of the Irish blood royal, Saint Columba, who lived after Merlin, administered Iona not only spiritually and politically, but also militarily as a soldier of Christ, a *miles Christi*. The seventh-century Anglo-Saxon Saint Cuthbert had his banner carried into battle.

Merlin also has become immortal, or as close to that prestige as man has reached. He was the keeper of royal genealogies. He was a military and personal adviser to four kings: Vortigern, Aurelius Ambrosius, Uther Pendragon, and Arthur. As prophet he demonstrated his foreknowledge of persons, deaths, punishments, rescues, and the fate of Britain. From his own superior intellect he bested kings, astrologers, magicians, and his own students. For the Arthurian kings he drew up campaign plans, strategies, and battle plans. He released slaves, organized the officers corps, enrolled and searched for suitable recruits, brought rain, calmed tempests at sea, raised winds and dust storms, and confounded armies. He provided advice about food, and food itself. He even provided a male infant when the throne lay vacant and prepared the nomination and inauguration of Arthur. He also ordered the deaths of two evil kings. He constructed in Britain national services and national monuments, decorated them, and presided at their consecration. He also founded the revered institution and fellowship of the Round Table.

A chief reason for Merlin's immortality must be, however, his *Prophecy*, which was first issued in manuscript copies in 1134 by Geoffrey of Monmouth. Almost all modern scholars of Arthurian history and literature have followed the common belief that this *Prophecy* was written by Geoffrey and that it referred only to current events of 1134. For now, we shall have to leave that question open also. However, when turning to the first written records that tell "The Birth of Merlin," one should bear in mind that in Merlin's day prophecy was at best a dangerous occupation.

As early as A.D. 11 the Emperor Augustus by imperial edict frowned upon all prophecy in the Roman Empire and banned all practitioners from the city of Rome. The Code of Diocletian (c. A.D. 300) decreed the death penalty for prophets and astrologers in the Roman Empire. Constantius repeated this death sentence; it was again reinstituted in 373, and again in 409, only three years after contact was cut between Rome and its province of Britain. Even though Britain was suddenly free, and free by the time of Merlin's birth, prophecy was still a dangerous, risky profession. This accounts for the many names for Merlin, which was definitely not his real name.

We know that Merlin lived in this Roman world in its era of collapse. Yet it was probably only in Rome itself that Merlin's equals could be found during his lifetime: the British theologian Pelagius, gone to Rome to ask his embarassing questions (What will the Christian Church do about the poor? What about the common man and women?); Saint Augustine, who died at Hippo in Africa after the barbarians had vandalized his city (430); the great writer and noble Roman theologian Boethius, put to death by the barbarian Emperor Theodoric.

Prenotions of Merlin have led us to the one place where his

memory was stored permanently: the dictionaries. There one can find several common words denoting those emblems that bring Merlin to life again:

whiting	pigeon hawk
battle-ax	hammer
black hair	club
blackbird	font (fountain? well?)
hair shirt	robin in the wood
medicinal plants	herbs
enchanter	wizard
healer (like Asklepios)	master teacher ("summus doctor")
red dragon banner	Father Time
prophet	son-of-the-mother (like Saint Augustine)

Dictionaries reinforce the claim that Merlinus can be distinguished and can be disentangled from Myrddin, if respect for Geoffrey of Monmouth as historian can be sustained. Such respect was suggested as early as 1929 by Geoffrey's American editors, Jones and Griscom, at Columbia University.

After thirty years as author of the standard and only scholarly book on Merlin, Paul Zumthor (*Merlin le prophète*, Lausanne, 1943; Geneva, 1973) in his second preface concluded that Geoffrey of Monmouth, in fact, invented less than has previously been thought, that his vision of Merlinesque history had by 1973 *finally managed to stifle all other accounts.* Although in conversations and lectures Zumthor's primary interest remained the tracing of Merlin's *Prophecy* throughout the later Middle Ages, he knew of the progress made in Wales. Welsh scholars meanwhile were methodically tracing Merlin backward, into the Dark Ages.

The most highly respected Welsh scholar of Merlin to date, A. O. H. Jarman, in *Legend of Merlin* (Cardiff, 1960, 1970), had already established three principal areas of inquiry in the Dark Ages: Ireland and what are now Wales and Scotland.

2

❧

THE
BIRTH
OF
MERLIN

· · · · · · ·

LUCINA.

In honor of this childe, the Fates shall bring
All their assisting powers of Knowledge, Arts
Learning, and Wisdom, all the hidden parts
Of all-admiring Prophecy, to fore-see
The events of times to come. His Art shall stand
A wall of brass to guard the Brittain Land.

The Birth of Merlin, III, iv.
William Rowley.

. . . .

The orthodox, original, and only explicit version of Merlin's birth comes from a French clergyman named Robert de Boron, supposedly native to eastern France, who wrote between 1188 and 1212. His Merlin work came some fifty years after the Latin prophecy of Merlin burst upon the century, recovered, or composed, by Geoffrey of Monmouth in England. Merlin's birth followed Robert's *Story of the Grail,* also entitled *Joseph of Arimathea.*[1]

Robert commenced his Arthurian legends all the way back to the crucifixion of Christ. Saint Joseph was said to have taken the body of Christ down from the Cross. The saint subsequently migrated to Britain, carrying the Holy Grail with him. He died in Britain and was interred there. Robert introduces his Grail text as follows (my literal translation from the Old French original):

> *I do not dare to relate or reconstruct,*　　　　　v. 929
> *Nor should I be able to do so,*
> *Not even if I desired to do it,*
> *If I did not have the Great Book*
> *Where all the stories are written, (that are)*
> *Made and quoted by all the great scholars,*
> *Therein are written the great secrets.*

. . .

[1] French manuscript (B. N., ms. fr. 20047) edited by William A. Nitze (Paris, 1971), *Joseph d' Arimathie (Le Roman de l'estoire dou Graal).* (Robert de Boron is the author.)

41

Merlin's birth story of 502 verses follows this Grail or *Joseph* section of Robert's narrative. The rest of his original *Merlin* is lost, but recoverable fortunately from later prose adaptations in Old French.

Robert de Boron's introductory verses by way of substantiation are still unclear, for by "the Great Book" he could have meant any number of great books, including the Bible. Joseph of Arimathea himself has been known to theologians and was once widely accepted among the Christian saints. Furthermore, had Robert de Boron not later established himself as a first-rate narrator in his unique Merlin-birth story, he would, if judged by the larger part of his production, be long forgotten.

Robert begins his first or Grail section (vv. 1–716) on Joseph of Arimathea with a reference to the Gospel of Nicodemus as it recounts Christ's descent to hell; his "Romance of the Prophecies of Merlin," as he terms his second section, begins similarly with a second reference to Christ's bursting open the Gates of Hell:

> *Mout fu li Ennemi courciez*   v. 1
>
> (Much was the Enemy outraged)
>
> *quant enfer fu ainsi brisiez.*
>
> (when hell was thus sundered).

A council of demons, Robert continues, was once urgently invoked to deal with Christ's descent into hell. The issue set before the learned fiends was this: how to be revenged upon Christ for His having broken down the Gates of Hell, and having released Adam and Eve. "If we managed," their chairman said, "to endow a man with our knowledge and our spite, then we could gain immense satisfaction from this man. Since he would know all that was said and done, near and far, in past centuries and in the present, he would have no trouble wielding over mankind a sovereign authority."

The demons then selected a family of five for their plot, Robert continues, because these parents had three unmarried daughters upon whom they could work their foul scheme. The father and mother were past their youth, and, best of all, from the devils' point of view, the father had just been obliged to declare bankruptcy. This business failure, which commenced the ruin of a once fine and highly respected family, tokened their final and total ruination. Their two younger girls presented so little difficulty that the demons were easily able to debauch and deflower them.

Their plight is passed over quickly. However, in the early Christian Church as established in France, the crime of extramarital sex or adultery, was classed along with murder as a capital crime that was, in the eyes of the Church, an unforgivable sin. Medieval illustrators delighted in making hideous, pornographic pictures of the demon in bed with his victims in the act of rape. Their ultimate punishment is assumed.

As she sorrowfully watched her sisters fall into utter, irreclaimable humiliation and damnation, the oldest daughter forced herself to understand so as to resist further attacks by the demons, plus all offers whatsoever of seduction, all promises from them, all pleasantries, and all pleas. She consulted her confessor at once and memorized his counsels, which she practiced assiduously until the one fatal evening that, upon preparing herself for bed, she forgot her special prayers. During the night, while she slept, she was raped by a demon. Thus was Merlin conceived, upon a lovely elder daughter and a virgin. All this happened in France, agreed subsequent readers and storytellers, or in *South Wales*, for the suspicion has always lingered that Robert de Boron should not have located Merlin's birth inside France.

This business of fiends, this association with demons or devils at one stroke of Robert's pen condemns Merlin's antecedents and the infant Merlin himself as outside the pale of Christianity. In fact, Robert's was a device usually employed by such orthodox writers to downgrade a famous person and to imply that he was excommunicate, heretic, and identifiable thereafter as pagan. Robert de Boron so easily associates Merlin with black magic that even without any further condemnation he besmirches his reputation for several ages to come. Henceforth, Merlin and his actions sink under Robert's scornful terms: "wizard," "conjuror," "pagan," and "devil." Merlin was subsequently condemned by the Church, and no wonder.

It was in fact pre-Christian, uneducated Romans of more ancient Rome who practiced black magic, which plebeians then considered good medicine for all ailments. There existed demons, they thought, who brought sickness upon them. The Romans purchased bronze mirrors engraved with hideous demons and hung them in their poor homes as a prophylactic measure to drive away illness and to protect them from epidemics. Of course, since science and the study of science were subsequently outlawed and formally prohibited in the earliest centuries by the organizers of the Christian Church, then Merlin as a healer fell all over again, becoming doubly a magician, practicing magic. Ancient superstitions died hard even in old Rome.

Robert's story of Merlin's antecedents follows classical rather than Celtic literature. *Daemon* was originally a Greek word latinized by Apuleius, the famous author of *The Golden Ass* (c. A.D. 155). Robert de Boron also took a cue from his immediate predecessor in England, for Geoffrey of Monmouth in his *History of the Kings of Britain* had theorized in 1136 that

> As Apuleius wrote in his treatise concerning Socrates, live spirits actually dwell between the earth and the moon, and we call them *incubi* (the plural of *incubus*), or demons. Their nature is partly human and partly angelic, but they can at will take on a mortal appearance and have sexual relations with human women. Perhaps such an *incubus* or *demon* got her pregnant with Merlin.

These more careful, less superstitious words by Geoffrey precede his world-famous prophecies of Merlin.

Both Robert de Boron and Geoffrey of Monmouth, who were male religious of the twelfth century, lived and were supposed to follow the precepts of Saint Augustine (354–430), the renowned Bishop of Hippo in Africa, Doctor of the Church, and one of the four Latin fathers. Among his voluminous writings, Saint Augustine had resolved forever, he thought, the question of an *incubus* or a demon, by declaring both "infernal spirits."

The ancient Celtic sun god named Hu was also condemned by early Christian theologians, who relegated him to the category of "demon" gods. This sun god Hu was often represented pictorially as a "rouge dragon," the same symbol of power that centuries later flamed and rippled along Merlin's red war flag.

Words such as demon, *incubus*, and (female) dragon probably join another word that causes some consternation on the part of modern readers every time they come upon it strangely situated in an Arthurian text. This is the word "chariot," often applied to tarnishing the reputation of Queen Morgan. By "chariot" the ancients were referring to oracular temples or to places of pagan worship, where the "old hag" (Demeter or Ceres) and her daughter Proserpina were once worshiped.

The ancient Greeks would have looked more kindly upon *daemons*, for Plato says in his *Symposium* that everything *daemonic* is to be considered intermediate between God and mortal man since God has no direct contact with man. But sometimes the loudest voices win theological arguments, and the French clergymen of the Dark Ages carried two big sticks: (1) their closer association with Rome, for France has always claimed that as a country she takes precedence even over Italy and sits at the right hand of the pope, and (2) excommunication. Twice during Merlin's fifth century, Papal Legates, the most powerful churchmen of France, were dispatched to Britain to investigate goings-on there and to report back to Rome if any measures were required at the moment. And we know with what an awed reticence and trembling voice Saint Patrick stammered out his deathbed *Confessions*.

Robert de Boron takes no kindly view of Merlin's mother, and he enjoys telling this shocking story of demons and rape.

Upon awakening, the elder daughter knew instantly that she was pregnant. The poor girl keeps her head, however, and calls two friends and a servant to escort her as she consults her confessor. Unfortunately, "sergeants" immediately arrest her for criminal sexuality punishable by death. She is shut up in a stone tower so that she can be isolated or quarantined from contaminating the public. Inside this tower she is sequestered and then walled up with two matrons, who will remain at her side to assist her until the child is delivered and nursed during a first period of unspecified length. One does not know whether the mother was allowed days, weeks, or months, only that soon her baby was to be "taken from her."

God meanwhile had granted the baby to know her, says Robert, and to know the future as well. Merlin is to have this gift as a counterbalance to the demon's gift, *which was knowledge of the present and of the past!*

The two matrons shrieked when they saw the baby Merlin born, for he emerged as a swarthy male child completely covered with thick, black hair. It was a sight such as they had never before seen! The mother again kept her head. She prayed at once to the midwives that her baby might be let down in a basket in that very instant to be baptized at once and named for his maternal grandfather Merlin (or Mellin).

The infant Merlin is from birth a prodigy and precocious beyond belief. At eighteen months he consoled his condemned and weeping mother, "You will not be burned because of me." Even the matrons heard him speaking clearly. Terrified, they abandoned both mother and child. The mother's death sentence, for her offense is aggravated, is to be carried out in forty days. She was also condemned by the judge for not naming the baby's father. Then the baby Merlin speaks again. He argues with the magistrate in terms that make us suspect he has already been studying Plato: "I know whose son I am," he cried. "These enemies," he goes on to explain, "are called 'Incubes' (our *incubi*), who are evil spirits and who have sexual relations with women in their beds at night. But God granted safety to my virtuous mother," the baby cried, "by granting me knowledge of the future."

The child Merlin then delivered a personal attack on the judge, attempting to disqualify him by daring him to condemn his own mother, guilty of adultery, before he decided to condemn Merlin's mother. "I see that the man who was your real father will commit suicide today," he added, "now that I have unmasked him." And so it happened that the baby Merlin caused the judge to disqualify himself.

The trial ended happily for Merlin's mother, with her release in the custody of her confessor Blaise. She became a nun. Merlin is, therefore, truly "the only son of a nun." Robert de Boron's story has proved valuable after all.[2]

At this point the clergymen who are the *Merlin* continuators pick up the story, after verse 502. As Paul Zumthor wrote in 1943, if one clearly understands that the baby Merlin was born in prison, then his case was considered unique in the history of the world. Merlin the man was saved by the redemption of his mother so that he was able to turn his devilish powers to good, that is, from engineering the coming of Arthur to calling up the last Grail King, Perceval. Therefore, according to theological

• • •

[2] Paulin Paris (1800–1881), who was the dean of Arthurian studies in France and a first translator into modern French of Arthurian material in Old French, pointed out in his pioneer edition of this *Merlin* text by Robert de Boron that the confessor Blaise is therefore named as the first guarantor of the story's authenticity. Generations have done their utmost to locate Blaise, to no avail, unfortunately. So far, Robert de Boron has dropped the name in vain. One must observe, also with a smile in the direction of a favorite French scholar, that those who strove so valiantly to locate Blaise were the very ones who believed the whole story of Merlin's birth in the first place. Paris

47

argument, Merlin was ordained prophet by the grace of God. He was saved because he was baptized, thus becoming a loving symbol of the power of Christ.

Merlin tasted victory in his first exploit, which was his battle against the magistrate for the life of his mother. His second exploit will pit him against an evil British king named Vortigern, to save his own skin and blood, for at that early age Merlin in his turn is to be put to death sacrificially. The triple themes of guilt, punishment, and death, which commence nine months before the birth of Merlin, follow him all his life and echo his words that come to us from beyond the grave.

Robert de Boron's initial verses have left everyone with three critical problems: that of Merlin's mother, that of his father for whom thus far we have the name Ambrosius, and that of the confessor Blaise. Contemporary medievalists such as A. R. L. Bell, California State University at Long Beach, explain that the absence of a father presents less difficulty since the uncle-nephew relationship, or the custom whereby the young hero was fostered by an uncle, was preferred over what has become the institution of fatherhood, which Robert Graves also said is modern. The mother presents us with a more urgent need to know because ancient Britons regulated their lives by the system of tanistry, meaning that the right of succession inherited from the mother remained in the family rather than residing in the individual.

Mothers figure prominently in some lives of illustrious contemporaries. The example of Saint Augustine was probably also

* * *

first suggested that it was not entirely Celtic but that it came, at least in part, from the Near East.

Not just Robert, but through the twelfth century everybody who tackled Merlin's story floundered when they set about finding guarantors: the confessor Blaise, the Welsh bard Taliesin, Saint Gildas, Saint Waldhave, Saint Kentigern, to name the choicest candidates for the honor.

present in the thought of Merlin's chroniclers. Augustine's mother, Monnica, followed her son from Africa to Rome, where he fell spellbound before Saint Ambrose, underwent his great change, and was baptized at Easter in his mother's presence. She died in his arms, wrote F. W. Vroom, and his grief was openly expressed: "Let me die that I die not, that I may see Thy face. . . . I am cramped in the house of my soul. . . ."

While the oracular priestesses (Merlin's mother became a nun) at Delphi in ancient Greece inherited their posts from mother to daughter, there is also some evidence for prophets such as Merlin having inherited this function from their mother. In his fascinating book, *The Secret of the East* (Boston, 1883), Felix Oswald wrote:

> A year after the death of the prophetess Sospitra, says the pagan historian, Eunapius, her son was one day standing before the temple of Serapis, when the prophetic spirit of his mother fell upon him. "Woe be our children!" he exclaimed, when he awakened from his trance. "I see a cloud approaching: a great darkness will fall upon the human race."

Like Merlin, in his long prophecy, as recorded by Geoffrey of Monmouth, Sospitra's son was a prophet of doom. When we come upon a virgin's son, added Oswald, we call him that; he was *parthenogenitus*, like the Indian god Krishna. Very early in Oswald's book appears the first western scholar who was also an Orientalist; but there were others who by 1883–86 had read Gaston Paris and were only warming up to inform the Celtic world where their "Birth of Merlin" had originated. Before allowing the celebrated Orientalist Moses Gaster to scoff at Robert de Boron's text, which Gaster in 1905 laughingly termed the "Gospel of the Infancy," one should look once more around Britain for ancient mothers like Merlin's.

Interestingly enough, two such may be found in Merlin's age and vicinity. Two Arthurian celebrities, both holy men of the Celtic Church, had similar relationships with their mothers. Saint David is the patron saint of Wales. Saint Kentigern (Mungo) is a patron saint of Scotland and is entombed in the Catholic Cathedral in his own Bishopric of Glasgow. Saint David, said Geoffrey of Monmouth, attended the coronation of his relative, King Arthur, and David's mother was a nun of Dyfed (South Wales) named Nonnita. Her churches stand today where she founded them, in Wales, Cornwall, and Brittany. Saint Kentigern's mother (Kentigern means "Beloved Lord"), as the Arthurian text called *Yvain, ou Le Chevalier au lion* tells in such thrilling form, was another sovereignty herself, or the daughter of a king of Lothian, Scotland. The Celtic scholar, W. F. Skene, explained in *Celtic Scotland* that this mother's name was Denw or Tenyw,[3] and that she became Saint Tenoc; but unfortunately her name was later confused with the more familiar biblical man's name Enoch. It was apparently easy to forget the distinguished women of Merlin's day.

Arthurian scholars have not as yet arrived at any consensus in the first question of Merlin's mother. John Veitch, writing in Glasgow in 1903, felt that Merlin's mother must have been a Vestal Virgin held over in some round temple, possibly from Roman imperial days. In 1929, Edmond Faral in Paris accused Geoffrey of Monmouth of having invented both Arthur and Merlin, if not Great Britain itself, out of his pipe dreams. In her 1938 book, Margaret J. C. Reid concluded that Merlin had existed but that the authentic *Birth of Merlin* had long since been lost, leaving us with Robert de Boron. Paulin Paris had already castigated Robert as a mere "arranger" of events to suit himself. Marie-Louise Sjoestedt pointed to the many names given gods and personages in this Celtic world; fifty-nine names for Mars, she noted, reinforces a hunch that the prophet in question was

• • •

[3] (She is named variously: Thenew, Themin, Thameta, Thaney, and Taneu, which probably indicates her popularity as noble mother and saint.)

perhaps only familiarly called "Merlin" in his leisure or off-hours, and then to conceal his real name and hide his high position.

The second problem of Blaise, who according to Robert de Boron was Merlin's "Master" (teacher), as well as his mother's confessor and his own, becomes more and more intriguing. Two of the most creative of Arthurian scholars, Jessie L. Weston and the Breton-French Hersart de la Villemarqué, agreed that one should search for a real man called "Blaise." Alternate suggestions have come from various scholars who have tried to identify him as any one of a number of puzzling names that recur in medieval texts, either as the name of a king or as the name of a great and original author of Arthurian chronicles: Bleheris, Breri, "Bledhericus fabulator," Blederic, and so forth.[4] An excellent review of this search for Merlin's Master was drawn up by the Breton scholar Ferdinand Lot in *Romania* (1925).

Villemarqué's pioneering book situating Merlin in Brittany, France, and giving him the Breton name "Myrdhinn," from the Old Breton "Marthin," has fallen by the wayside as too poetic and fanciful to be relied upon; but it contains some very interesting insights, especially for 1863 when important Arthurian scholarship could hardly be said to have commenced. Only the historian Sharon Turner (1840) and the poet Tennyson (*The Idylls of the King*, 1859–1885) had preceded him. Villemarqué noticed how, in the probably spurious poem *Vita Merlini*, Merlin's companion in the forests is called *Lupus* (wolf), which in Breton is a proper name spelled *Blaidd* but pronounced *Blaiz*, or like the French *Blaise* (pronounced *blez*). Now, continued Villemarqué, *Lupus* is the Latin name of the Bishop of Troyes in France, who was twice sent to Britain in the fifth century. He was held to be the greatest prelate of his age. He would have been a fit master for

• • •

[4] These names occur, for instance, in Wauchier de Denain, the Thomas *Tristan*, the Gerald of Wales *Description*, in Geoffrey of Monmouth, and in the poem *Vita Merlini* (Life of Merlin) attributed since the 1920s to Geoffrey.

Merlin who, thought Villemarqué, came from Brittany, France, in any case, and not from Britain.

This novel theory merited another good look, particularly since many French Arthurian manuscripts were written at Troyes, France, but it proved again incorrect because of the dates. Saint Lupus traveled to Britain for the second and last time in 445–446, which probably antedated the birth of Merlin. Even if it is impossible to mark the year of Merlin's birth exactly, Merlin surely lived well into the sixth century, and Saint Lupus died in 478. He could therefore not have been Merlin's companion, scribe, and confessor at any time up to and including his death.

Jessie L. Weston suggests the working hypothesis that Blaise *was* a real person. However, the searching of one hundred years has failed to discover a personage of this name. Therefore, if the real Merlin is found one day, his lifelong companion will, hopefully, be beside him. The real name of this companion was probably not Blaise, but concealed, and intentionally so.

Concerning Blaise, a final word from Glenys Goetinck in his *Peredur* (the Welsh name for Perceval) of 1975 makes very good sense. The man's name was Welsh, says Goetinck, and was spelled "Bleddri" (pp. 33–34). He was not Merlin's companion, but only an unimportant singer of Welsh material, neither a court poet nor a chief poet. Had he been either court or chief poet, the Welsh would have known about it and honored him accordingly. So when the man called Merlin is found, he will undoubtedly be somebody the Welsh do know about, and beside him will probably be his equally well-known secretary and companion.

In 1905, Celtic scholars received what seemed to them at the time a terrible affront, which was resented and contested by Jessie L. Weston. In *Folklore*, the Orientalist Moses Gaster published an article entitled with good intent "The Legend of Merlin." This title alone would suffice to alarm serious students eager to prove Merlin not legendary but historical and a real person. Merlin was, advised Gaster, "an uncanny prophet and magician," and his "Gospel of the Infancy" derived not from any history or any archives of Great Britain but, by way of well-known middle eastern intermediaries, from the far older cycle of King Solomon and the demon Asmodeus. In the Hebrew original of this birth tale, said Gaster, the mother is variously called daughter of the prophet Jeremia(h) or even daughter of King David. She also represents another appearance of the Roman oracle Sibylla, said Gaster, which is no less than a reappearance of the Queen of Sheba. Her son was originally Sira, or Sirach, at the court of King Nebuchadnezzar. Intermediate versions in Germany and Russia adopt still another notion, however: that Merlin was another son of the Greek centaur Chiron, who was his demonic or semi-human father.

Gaster concluded that Geoffrey of Monmouth was a "later genius" because knowing this Old Testament and legendary material, he left it for such a poor writer as the French Robert de Boron to dress up the birth-of-Merlin. Thus, said Gaster, the birth-of-Merlin material does not belong to Merlin the prophet and is quite separate from any evidence one might be able to accept as historically accurate.

An earlier brilliant riposte from England in 1662 should have more than served to relegate Robert de Boron's version of Merlin's conception to oblivion, for that year in London the witty intellectual William Rowley (c. 1585–1642) presented his "vigorous and entertaining play," *The Birth of Merlin; or, The Childe Hath Found his Father*. The play was advertised as a collaborative effort between William Rowley and William Shakespeare. However, it was printed in Germany and labeled what it is, a pseudo-Shakespearean play.

The cast of characters included the usual minor personages in Merlin's lifetime: Aurelius, Uther Pendragon, Vortigern, and Cador of Cornwall, but it stopped short of offering any indignity to King Arthur. The Devil now is the *incubus*, and so he is Merlin's father, who conceived the child one dark night *in the woods*, leaving the largely pregnant Joan Go-too't to grope about in the trees after him, alone with her brother, a local clown like those craftsmen whom Shakespeare had presented more genially in *A Midsummer Night's Dream.*

Rowley has used the usual appurtenances of Merlin's situations: the forest, storms, meteors, the Saxons defeated, Merlin predicting his own death, the prodigy confounding vested authority, Merlin's forest cave, his compulsive laughter before each prophecy, and his (?) popular prophetic utterances to or concerning lowly persons. Here again Merlin protects his dear mother by driving away the Devil, who wants to make love to her again, and by promising to build Stonehenge (built c. 1750 B.C.) for her tomb (c. A.D. 500). The fifth act ends properly:

> All future times shall still record this story,
> Of Merlin's learned worth and Arthur's glory.

Historically, Rowley adopts an early theory that Merlin, and Arthur too, were not British but Bretons:

Devil: And Merlin's name in Brittany shall live,
   Whilst men inhabit here or Fates can give
   Power to amazing wonder; envy shall weep,
   And mischief sit and shake her ebbone wings,
   Whilst all the world of Merlin's magick sings. [*sic*]

The Devil himself, says Merlin in the play, "Keeps a Hothouse i'th' Low-Countries." Pointing to the Devil, Merlin says: "The Childe has found his Father, this is he." The idiotic Clown quips, "I think his Ancestors came from Hellbree in Wales. . . ."

The ribald passages must be very comical on the stage, like this one in Act III, iv:

Clown: (*to his sister Joan*): Let me see, is your great belly gone?
Joan: Yes, and this is the happy fruit.
Clown: What, this Hartichoke? A childe born with a beard on
   his face?

Merlin: Yes, and strong legs to go, and teeth to eat.
Clown: You can nurse up your self, then?

A third dramatist, a contemporary of Shakespeare and Rowley, had chosen to compose a treatise about Merlin that for its beauty and depth of thought stands head and shoulders above any other work to date on this subject. Rather than dwell upon the awkwardness in pregnancy and low birth of Merlin's mother, Thomas Heywood (c. 1574–1641) in 1641[5] offered the fairest solution to several Merlin questions.

He disdained the Three Fates and also Juno or Diana Lucina, goddess of childbirth in Rome, and the good fairy in folklore. He had already established Merlin in full dignity before Rowley turned him into a farce. A specialist in Greek mythology, Heywood would have recognized it in the Merlin situation had he really come across evidence of it. Author of dramatic masterpieces in which the characters resemble real people in real situations, Heywood was able to avoid pornography and propose a rational view of a nice woman having a baby. He called his book on Merlin: *The Life of Merlin, Sirnamed Ambrosius. His Prophesies, and Predictions Interpreted; and their Truth made good by our English Annalls.*

Heywood begins his Book II, Chapter I, (p. 1) by explaining the sanctity of prophets, predictors, and seers; but prophets, being highest, are restricted to *divine Mysteries.* There have been prophetical poets: Orpheus, Linus, Homer, Hesiod, and Vergil; but the prophets are loftier. They were Moses, Samuel, David, Isaiah, Jeremiah, Daniel, and John the Baptist. Heywood explained, therefore, what company Merlin will be keeping, where he will be found, and whom he will resemble.

He treats Merlin's birth casually, believing that the mother alone seems "certain," but the "father doubtfull." Heywood then

• • •

[5] A beautiful first edition (1641) of Thomas Heywood's work is in the Francis Bacon Library in Claremont, California.

offers what seems the only kind and understanding evaluation there is in all the Merlin literature to date: the young mother probably could not subject the father, who was her sweetheart, to "imminent danger" by exposing him. Therefore, she never did name him.

He wrote that Plato's mother had congregation with the "imaginary shadow of *Apollo*, and brought into the World him who proved to bee the Prince of Philosophers" (p. 2). However, he continued, both Apuleius and Plato believed in *Incubi* between "Moone and the earth" (p. 3), living creatures envious of man because, for the sin of pride, they had been precipitated there and were "so libidinous and luxurious" that they did assume human shape and "commixe themselves with women and generate children." The Romans called them *Fauni*, as Saint Augustine mentioned (p. 3), Heywood added for the sake of completeness.

Was Merlin a pagan or a Christian? "For the first, it is not to be doubted but hee was a *Christian* as being of the *British* Nation: This Kingdome having for the space of two hundred and odde yeares before his birth, received the Gospell under King Lucius . . . and Pope *Eleutherius* . . ." (p. 4).

One should not doubt Merlin on this score when even the pagan priestesses, or Sibyls at Rome, predicted the coming of Christ. It was the *Sibylla Cumana* on the Bay of Naples who so predicted, which we should honor because such a renowned Doctor of the Church, Saint Augustine himself, quoted her words—and, it might be added, because Michelangelo himself painted her on the ceiling of the Sistine Chapel in the Vatican at Rome.

Heywood did concede in a spirit of fair play that some people might still harbor certain doubts about Merlin, and justifiably so, for on and off he has been loosely termed no better than a soothsayer or a wizard. Anyone who doubts him should read the following, said Heywood, which he then quoted from the Universal Doctor Alanus de Insulis, rector of the Paris Academy about 1200, who wrote a splendid "Justification" of Merlin:

In all his prophecies I find nothing dissonant, incongruous, or absurd: nor anything foreigne, or averse from truth: and those who shall live in ages to come, shall finde those his predictions as constantly to happen in their dayes (according to the limit of time) as wee have hitherto found them certain and infallible ever to the age in which we now live. And for these signes and tokens which before the consummation of the World shall appeare, he divineth and foretelleth of them in the Sun and Moon, and the other five Planets; *Iuno, Mars, Mercury, Venus, Saturne,* and other stars, how they shall confound and alter their courses which they had in the Creation, according to that in the holy Evangelist Saint Luke, cap. 21. v. 25. Then there shall be signes in the Sun, and the Moon, and in the stars: and upon the earth trouble amongst the Nations with perplexity, the Sea and the waters shall roare, and mens hearts shall faile them for feare, and for looking after those things which shall come in the World, for the powers of Heaven shall be shaken, etc. But of the new heaven, and the new earth, and the resurrection of the dead to new life, how truly he spoke according to the Propheticall, Evangelicall, and Apostolical Traditions; it is manifest that hee no way deviated or erred from the orthodoxall Christian Faith, and so much Doctor *Alanus* concerning the truth of his prophecies, with whom I conclude this first chapter.[6]

Proceeding with his story, Heywood writes that Merlin was found by the messengers of the evil King Vortigern not at Carmarthen (Caer-Merlin) in South Wales, but at "Kaier-Merlin, id est, Marlborrow" in southern England, not far from Stonehenge.

• • •

[6] Only two *Commentaries* on the *Prophecy* of Merlin were made in the Middle Ages, and Heywood quotes here from the seven books of Latin *Commentary* written by this most learned of doctors, between 1174–1179. See Paul Zumthor in the Bibliography.

His mother, Heywood adds, was "daughter to King Demetius and lived a Votaresse in that Citie, in a Nunnery belonging to the Church of Saint Peter. . . . ." The grandfather's name "Demetius" locates the family in Carmarthen and South Wales, however, which during the Roman occupation of Britain were inhabited by a tribe called *Demetae.* Heywood, too, lends his voice to a support of a Welsh home for Merlin. He also substantiates calculations as to Merlin's birth date, having read in his sources that the prophet was born during the reign of King Vortigern, crowned in 448. The chronology in the Appendix suggests that Merlin was born about 450, and that King Arthur, who was the fourth king Merlin served, was born twenty-five years after him, about 475.

Before turning to the next part of Merlin's story, the terrible contest of Merlin versus King Vortigern, with Merlin's mother an anguished witness, one should look briefly at the five long manuscript accounts that offer the primary evidence of the adult Merlin. While they do follow Robert de Boron, they have between them accumulated additional traditions about Merlin's birth. For instance, he was probably nine months old, one says, when he predicted that his mother would not be burned. After her rescue from the court, Merlin commissioned Blaise to write the story of his life, and to do so at the Grail Castle where, when he was able to break free from his duties, Merlin would go to bring Blaise up to date. We hear again that Merlin was black-haired as a newborn, with "hide as rough as a swine," adds an English translator. Both Merlin and Gawain are connected to this same Grail island, which is the Isle of Man. Old verses tell us:

> He lett him see a castle faire,
> Such a one he neuer saw yore,
> Noe wher in noe country.
> The Turke said to Sir Gawaine,
> "Yonder dwells the King of Man,
> A heathen soldan is hee."

The well-known *Cambridge* 80 manuscript disagrees: Merlin was eighteen months old when he predicted that his mother would not be executed. The mother's confessor is named "Blasy, a worthy clerk." Most interesting correction of all, "Blasy" is to await Merlin's visits and write his biography in a tower in Northumberland (v. 2288), which is said to be "a wild country."

Merlin does not escape the complications of his birth, however, without severe censure from one last anonymous author, who wrote in eastern France and who dealt with the story long after Merlin as a character had disappeared into his tomb. This author of an alternate *Prose Lancelot* (which was recently edited by Elspeth Kennedy) summarizes the birth story laconically, in this vein:

> Voires fu que Merlins fu anjandrez an fame par deiable at de deiables meesmes car par ce fu il apelez li anfes sanz pere.

> (It was true that Merlin was engendered on a woman by the devil and from devils themselves, for by this was he called The Fatherless Child.)

Where was he engendered?

> —en la maresche de la terre d'Escoce et d'Irlande.

> (—on the march of the territory of Scotland and of Ireland.)

This day's "march" between Scotland and Ireland would seem to indicate that his conception took place at the Rhinns of Galloway, between Carlisle and the modern (and Arthurian) embarkation port for Ireland, that is, Stranraer on Loch Ryan.[7]

· · ·

[7] We have finally come back, then, as we did so often in searching for King Arthur, (see Norma L. Goodrich, *King Arthur*, New York and Toronto, 1986) to the nexus of that kingdom: the Rhinns of Galloway.

Explaining the birth of Merlin, the author of the alternate *Prose Lancelot* reviews, also cursorily, the Cupid and Psyche story from *The Golden Ass* of Apuleius: a wealthy damsel told her parents she would never have a man in her bed whom she had to look at with open eyes. Her will wanted a man, not her eyes. The Devil conceived on her a lad to be named "Mellins," (who was) not to be baptized. At age twelve he was taken to "Uter Pendragon," and went off to haunt the deep ancient forest.

> Il fu de la nature son pere decevanz et desleiaus, et sut quanque cuers porroit savoir de tote parverse science.

> (He was of the nature of his father, treacherous and disloyal, and knew as much as any heart could know about all perverse science.)

Here we see that our Merlin was far from being generally respected, not to mention beloved. This anonymous French author had no use for science, devils, extramarital sex, unbaptized infants, or youths who haunted forests. He did know his Greek literature, and he put Merlin up in Scotland and Ireland where the action was and where he would probably have had to be in order to advise the last three kings: Ambrosius, Uther, and Arthur.

3

THE
PRODIGY

· · · · · · ·

· · · · · · ·

VERSES BY TALIESIN

I will address my prayer to God that he would deliver our community.
O thou Proprietor of heaven and earth, to whom great wisdom is attributed.
  A holy sanctuary there is on the surface of the ocean;
  And at the time when the sea rises with expanded energy,
  May its chief be joyful in the splendid festival.
  Frequently does the surge assail the Bards over their vessels of mead;
  And on the day when the billows are excited, may this enclosure skim
    away
  Through the billows home beyond the green spot,* from the region of the
    Picts:
  And then, O God, may I be for the sake of my prayer,
  Though I preserve my institute, in covenant with thee.

(Stanza 1 translated by Rev. Edward Davies,
appendix, p. 507).

· · ·

* "Green spot" may translate Glas-gow, which would have been in the
land of the Picts, Scotland's oldest peoples. (Scholars consider Rev.
Davies a poor translator, but I admire him as a poet.)

・ ・ ・ ・ ・ ・ ・

Merlin is next heard of in Wales during the reign of Vortigern, a ruler generally understood as having been "evil" for several reasons: murder, incest, treachery, tyranny, and treason on an unbelievable scale. He may have seized power about the year 425.[1] Merlin and his mother are said to have been brought before Vortigern when Merlin was barely seven years old, by which time Vortigern was in deep trouble.

Saint Gildas writes with authority as eyewitness to the events that Vortigern's evil decisions brought about. Britain had been left unoccupied by the Roman legions. In Latin Gildas wrote:

> Then all his counselors, and the proud tyrant himself (Vortigern) went stone blind, for the method they concocted to safeguard our land only destroyed it. They were the ones who invited into Britain those blood-thirsty Saxons! Don't even mention their names to me! God and man loathe them all! Like letting wolves into your sheep pens, and they were supposed to beat back (into the Highlands) the peoples of the North (the Picts)!

Once the Roman legions withdrew in order to defend Rome itself from the Goths, Huns and other "barbarians" (bearded)

・ ・ ・

[1] The earliest narrative sources are Welsh, by Gildas and Nennius, both texts re-edited recently in London under the direction of the late John Morris. Our edition of Gildas here is by Michael Winterbottom.

warriors, the Anglo-Saxons poured into the vacuum that was Great Britain. "Like a litter of cubs!" cried Gildas. In their long, sleek battleships that could slide onto the sandy beaches, even well up the little rivers and into the marshes of Britain's low east coast; "it" came by threes at first and then like "satellite dogs" (Winterbottom, p. 26), in packs and litters and greedy hordes! If after five hundred years the Romans themselves, with all their up-to-date paraphernalia and Hadrian's Wall to patrol and barracks to live in, still could not keep the Picts from pouring out of Scotland and raiding the Roman province to the south, how then could Vortigern be expected to stop them? So the Anglo-Saxons, who had arrived first as Vortigern's paid mercenaries, proceeded to settle in what now bears their name: England. Soon, writes Gildas, they began "to lick their chops along the west coast too."

After agreeing with contemporary scholars that the Welsh Gildas was no modern historian—for he failed unscientifically to list names, events, places, dates, times, hours, numbers, and leaders other than Vortigern here—one may still be allowed to treasure his account for what it is: human, personal, honest, and heartbroken: Even the weather held, he moaned, so that the winds blew them straight (over the North Sea) upon us! And the augurs (left over from Roman days) tracked the migratory birds as they flew across our skies and told us the invaders would be not much less endurable than the Romans, for this new heathen crew would inhabit Britain for three hundred years. And the impious Vortigern married their pagan princess and fell madly in love with her. She was probably a tall, gorgeous blonde but, some added spitefully, a heathen.

The natives fled for their lives, testified Gildas, to the high country, into the deepest forests, up on the highest mountains along the west coast. There hundreds died of hunger and exposure before they could find food and build shelters for themselves. Those who gave up and came down into the Saxon-occupied valleys were massacred. They could not understand Anglo-Saxon. Others made it safely across the sea (probably

64

from the northern shores of the Forth and Clyde rivers down into the forested border country adjacent to Hadrian's Wall).

Saint Gildas, who told furiously what he could of this tragic moment in time, lived from c. 500 to c. 572, according to the well-known Arthurian scholar, P. K. Johnstone.[2] Gildas was himself a Pict, and so were the names of his family. He was therefore a Celt from the British Highlands, who later became a revered pan-Celtic saint. He belonged to the royal family of Caw Prydyn, and his sister's name was Peithien (Pict-born), a "Celtic name to the nth degree." Gildas was called "Badonicus" because he was born in Scotland, according to some scholars, in the year of the first resounding Celtic victory of Mount Badon. Before the native peoples could manage to bring about any victory over the invaders, Merlin had to come into the picture.

The story of Vortigern's deep troubles, his escape from a massacre, his flight into the highest mountains, and his hurried attempt to build a sanctuary for himself, writes Charlotte Guest, "led to the discovery of the enchanter Merlin, which opens the great drama of Arthurian Romance."[3] This story, she adds, is found in the "Nennius" papers, of the Nennius "who wrote in the eighth century, and . . . whose works, some copies as old as the tenth, are still extant." Nennius told, at least, "the substance of the tale."

According to the Nennius compilation collected c. 829 and called *Historia Brittonum*, history of the Britons, Vortigern attempted to build for his own protection and that of his followers and army "a citadel in Snowdon," Wales, writes a contemporary Welsh historian, Wendy Davies.[4] Such early citadels were strongly

• • •

[2] See "The Dual Personality of Saint Gildas." *Antiquity* 22 (1948): 38–40.

[3] See Charlotte Guest's notes to the *Mabinogion*, p. 305 passim.

[4] There are five references to Vortigern in Davies's *Wales in the Early Middle Ages*.

defended, she adds, but Vortigern (whose Welsh name is Gwrtheyrn) "failed in his attempt . . . despite the carpenters and stonemasons he had brought in from abroad for that purpose." Gerald of Wales tells us (c. 1188) about the terrain:

> Then we continued our travels (going east) along the coast of North Wales, having on one side the ocean (our left) and on our other hand a steep cliff, until we came to the Conway River estuary, or to fresh water. Not far from the heights where the Conway rises the high mountains of Snowdon begin.[5]

They stand as a towering mass protecting this huge, high promontory of northern Wales, fronted to the west by the Menai Strait and the massive, low-lying island of Anglesey. Up the stony ramparts where the Conway River rises stand the ruins of the Fortress of Ambrosius, where Ambrosius Merlinus is said to have sat on a rock and delivered to King Vortigern his world-famous *Prophecy*. The view Gerald describes is one of the most awesome anywhere, especially when darkness falls.

Vortigern's story as it is told in the Nennius papers (*British Museum/Harley* manuscript 3859) is confirmed by a French life of Saint Germanus written soon after all this happened, for the pope sent Saint Germanus of Auxerre to reprimand Vortigern, and the prelate first traveled to Britain with Saint Lupus from Troyes, France, in the year 429. Vortigern had by that time married the daughter of the Saxon chieftain Hengist (Hengistus) and subsequently had also married his own daughter. Saint Germanus cursed her and him formally. He also forbade Vortigern to believe in the Welsh, Irish, or Pelagian heresy.

Vortigern had told Hengist to summon more reinforcements from the Saxon coast, led this time by two more Saxon chief-

• • •

[5] *The Journey through Wales*, Chapter 8. See the translation and introduction (London, 1978) by Lewis Thorpe.

tains, Octha and Ebissa, who arrived promptly in forty "ciules."
They called their boats "keels" in their own language, Saint Gil-
das had already informed us. These mariners sailed all around
the Picts' coastlines, said Nennius, or "circa Pictos." They "vas-
taverunt Orcades insulas," laid waste the Orkney Islands, and
occupied several regions "ultra mare Frenessicum,[6] usque ad con-
finium Pictorum," beyond the Firth of Forth, all the way to the
northern confines of Pictish territory, at least as far north as the
city of Inverness. Inverness was then a Pictish citadel, or far
northern sanctuary.

> Hengist meanwhile continues to attract into Britain the
> keels of his compatriots in ever greater and greater flo-
> tillas each day more and more of them, to the point that
> the (eastern) islands where they had first come ashore
> now lay deserted, and growing in power they were now
> settled for good inside the city of the *Cantii* . . .

which Edmond Faral in 1929 said was the modern Canterbury.
From Inverness to Canterbury seems too long a jump even for
such swelling numbers, but Nennius is poor on chronology, and
poorer on geography. With a wave of the hand he might non-
chalantly calculate a hundred years for this expansion in his cus-
tomary manner: Christ to the birth of Patrick, 405 years; the
death of Patrick to the death of Brigit, sixty years; from the
birth of Columba to the death of Brigit, four years.

After Saint Gildas has torn his beard and the Nennius Ar-
chives have been amassed, containing the biography of Saint
Germanus and the *Annals of Wales*, and after the Anglo-Saxons
have written *Beowulf*, their *Chronicles*, and after their historian, the
Venerable Bede, has written his *History* of the English Church,

* * *

[6] The noted French Arthurian scholar and editor of this manuscript,
Edmond Faral, first noted in 1929 that "mare frenessicum," "fresi-
cum," or "frisicum" might turn out to be the Firth of Forth (vol. I,
p. 107ff.).

one comes in 1136 to a brilliant first historian of the Celtic peoples, Geoffrey of or from Monmouth, Wales. Because his *History of the Kings of Britain* has made him the best historian of the Middle Ages, and the most popular, he has also been the most reviled by academics until 1929, in the United States. In that year two American university scholars and editors, both of whom were historians skilled in Latin and Welsh, began his vindication.

In his *History of the Kings of Britain (H.R.B)*, Geoffrey has at hand all the sources mentioned up to now, and, in addition, a "little, small book" of history a churchman at Oxford had lent him. Charlotte Guest had written that the original documents, or ancient Welsh texts that she translated as the *Mabinogion* (or "tales," as she called them), were contained in "little, small" books, something like 3" × 6". Many scholars had doubted Geoffrey's assertion that he worked from a book of that size.

In the words of a great man and first-rate historian, Geoffrey of Monmouth, this whole Merlin story now comes alive and glows with pathos and color. Geoffrey backtracks in order to be tilting at full speed when he introduces Merlin and his mother at Vortigern's construction site, high up the vast, windy promontory, perhaps deep in the Snowdonia peaks (English translation, Book VI) of North Wales.

Geoffrey comes in with Nennius as his backup at a monastery of Ambrius,[7] near the Salisbury Crags, in the present city of Edinburgh, which lies on the south shore of the Firth of Forth. There Hengist and his reinforcements have arrived, inside a harbor wide enough and deep enough to hold a fleet of modern warships. Hengist invites Vortigern and the British chieftains to a banquet where they can cement a new alliance and divide real estate inside Britain. At a signal from Hengist, the Saxon warriors draw knives from their boots and massacre 460 British chieftains. Only two Britons survive, and Vortigern,

• • •

[7] See Norma L. Goodrich, *King Arthur* (New York, 1986) p. 53ff.

for one, escapes, Geoffrey believes, probably going across Britain at its narrowest point to Glasgow, and their fortress at Dumbarton, thence by ships down the Firth of Clyde until they could steer for the promontory of Great Orme's Head, and then upriver into the Snowdon Range. They left the bodies of the massacred men with the three hundred monks and the Abbot Ambrius, or his successor, at Kaercaradoc, now Salisbury, a suburb of Edinburgh. Vortigern, said Geoffrey, fled into the far parts of Wales, "in partibus Kambrie."[8]

Just as brutally Theodoric the Ostrogoth had massacred Odoacer and his officers at a banquet in his royal capital of Ravenna in 493 and seized "Rome." In literature a similar horrible deed, frequent in the Dark Ages, is done by the hand of the Lady Kriemhilde, this according to the Austrian epic, the *Niebelungenlied*. There, Theodoric is called Dietrich. Only the reasons differ from those of Hengist.

In his extremity Vortigern consulted his senators called *magi*, who advised him to construct one last extremely solid tower in which he could shut himself if the Saxons managed to ravage all Britain. He decided to build it on Mount "erith" ("erir"), or Snowdon, but his builders struck a snag. The tower collapsed each night so that by morning the work had to be done all over again. Vortigern was advised by his conjurors at this time that he should seek a fatherless youth: "iuvenem sine patre quereret."

The youth considered fatherless was "merlinus qui Ambrosius dicebatur," the Merlin also called Ambrose (p. 382), Geoffrey continues. Vortigern's messengers had found him in the town later called Carmarthen in South Wales, and he was the grandson of a Demetian king, presumably a member of one of the three royal houses of Wales: Cunedda, Brychan, and Caw. Merlin's mother was a nun in the Church of Saint Peter. It was she

· · ·

[8] Edition of Acton Griscom and Robert Ellis Jones, Columbia University (New York, 1929), p. 379. This is the diplomatic text of the *H.R.B.*, Latin and Welsh texts on each page.

who explained her son's parentage to King Vortigern, and his chief *magus* accepted her account as tallying with Apuleius, said Geoffrey, who had even as a Welshman probably forgotten that Merlin and his mother were accepted as members of a priestly tribe of the Welsh.

The boy Merlin did not wait to be spoken to, but asked Vortigern: "Why have my mother and I been brought here?" The boy's arrogance may be suspected to stem from this membership in a priestly caste, people accustomed to derive themselves from nine generations of a priestly family at the annual May Congress of the Welsh tribes.

"My *magi* have told me to sprinkle the blood of a fatherless child with the materials in my tower's foundations, and it will stand."

"They have lied to you," replied Merlin. "Let them come before me." After the king had summoned them before Merlin, the youth spoke to them. "You do not know why this tower does not stand, for which reason you called for my blood to be mixed with your mortar. You said that then it would stand. But you did not attempt to discover why it does not stand. What prevents it?" Vortigern's wisemen remained silent, fearing the solution of him called Merlinus Ambrosius, apparently already cowed by the boy. Merlin arrogantly called for workmen to excavate the area beneath the collapsed tower. They found a "stagnum sub ea (terra) quod turrim stare non permittet" (a pool under that earth which did not allow the tower to stand).

"Precipe ait stagnum hauiri per rivulos," Merlin said (Order that the pool be drained by ditches). And he advised that it be drained. "Underneath the water," he said to Vortigern, "you will find two concave stones within which two dragons are asleep." The king believed his words and that he had spoken truth about the pool of standing water, and he ordered it drained. He admired Merlin above all others.

[On this point the Welsh manuscript translated on each page of the diplomatic text differs.] Nobody could drain

the pool, and so Merlin diverted the water "by five run-
ning streams. *Annvab y llaiann* (the nun's son) he was
called before this, but myrddin after this, because he
was found in Kaer Vyrddin."

Thus, Gwrtheyrn understood that the lad possessed
great knowledge, so he asked him, "What is to happen
to me?"

" 'To be killed and burned,' " said Merddin.
'For today the sons of' " . . .]

Today the sons of Constantine are embarking to cross the sea,
we learn, and tomorrow they will land in Lloegr (then eastern
"Wales," now England).

As Charlotte Guest very aptly remarked, this scene between
Vortigern and Merlin opens the Arthurian story proper, for the
three sons of Constantine are Arthur's two uncles and his father;
these family members had been ousted and persecuted by the
false Vortigern. One uncle has already been ordained priest.
The Welsh manuscript has also embellished Geoffrey's story by
telling us that there were rushes growing on the pool and by
having the dragons enclosed within a stone chest. Upon awak-
ening they would rise and fight a long and terrible war.

Geoffrey's last line requires some comment since it is trans-
lated variously:

Admirabantur etiam cuncti qui astabant tantam in eo
sapientiam, existimantes numen esse in illo.[9]

1. Translation by Sebastian Evans, revised by Charles W. Dunn
(New York, 1958):

All they that stood by were no less astonished at such
wisdom being found in him, deeming that he was pos-
sessed of some spirit of God (p. 136).

.   .   .

[9] Acton Griscom (see Note 8 preceding this), pp. 382–93.

2. Translation of Lewis Thorpe (Penguin Books, England, 1966–1984):

> All those present were equally amazed at his knowledge, and they realized that there was something supernatural about him (p. 169).

The variant here hangs upon the Latin words *numen* and *ille*.

3. Literal translation:

> All who stood by were also marveling at so much learning in him (*eo*), thinking there was (that he was) *numen* . . .
> (a) divine-will, power of the gods,
> (b) godhead, divinity, deity, divine majesty,
> (c) (that he was) under the protection of the gods,
> (d) a god, a deity;
>
> *in illo:*
> (a) him, the great, the well-known, the famous man, the ancient man, the distinguished, the exceptional, the remarkable.

Geoffrey's text very definitely associates Merlin with Christianity by using the religious word *numen*, and furthermore emphasizes that here, in Vortigern's presence, the youth Merlin has undergone in the public eye a metamorphosis from *eo* (any old "him") to *illo* (a prodigy). The more timid, or intimidated, Welsh translation, probably knowing Merlin only as a mere sorcerer or common magician, avoided the whole issue by omitting the sentence except for "sapientiam," thus allowing him "great knowledge," but no divinity.

Elsewhere, such as in the justly celebrated *Huth-Merlin* manuscript [10] in Old French prose (so named because it was ac-

•   •   •

[10] *Merlin. Roman en prose du XIIIe siècle* (d'après le manuscrit appartenant à M. Alfred H. Huth), 2 vols., edited by Gaston Paris and Jacob

tually lent to Gaston Paris by an Englishman named Alfred H. Huth), the author uses another source that differs from those read by Geoffrey of Monmouth. Both Paulin and Gaston Paris, who was his son, observed long ago that there certainly existed a great amount of Merlin material, in various written and oral forms, which has not yet been recovered. For example, the *Huth-Merlin* author wrote that Merlin in person, and not just any fatherless child, was anticipated with dread by Vortigern's counselors. They had read the stars from which they had learned he would cause their deaths. In fact, Merlin sentenced them all by predicting their deaths, of the conjurers and of their master king, too.

The red dragon, which is usually said to symbolize the Celts, is here said to represent the past. The white dragon announces the Arthurian kings, of the lineage of Constantine: therefore, the red dragon is the doomed Vortigern, who will be burned at the port of Winchester (that is, Edinburgh) as soon as the brothers arrive at this harbor. They are already at sea and will arrive three months hence, which is a reasonable time if they are to bring an army from Brittany, France, as is often claimed. Thus, one can see that this account is one of many that places Vortigern in Scotland, where the advance body of Anglo-Saxons were by all reports arriving.

By its geography and miles of marshes in all directions, the Forth estuary would fit the story of an underground lake, pool, or pond. It would suit the battle array: Celt versus Saxon, red versus white dragon. It would support the story that Picts were crossing that sea called the Firth of Forth. It is a harbor, par excellence. And that area, just south of Stirling Castle, where King Arthur's Camelot will be erected, was a battlefield century after century. Arthur's "Knot" (castle) can still be seen on the wetlands below the Stirling cliff, as anyone who has visited the

. . .

Ulrich, S.A.T.F. (1886). Introduction by Gaston Paris (Paris, 1887), pp. I–LXXX.

site knows. Vortigern, specifies *Huth-Merlin*, was burned in his tower, as Merlin predicted, *on a riverbank*.

The English version called *Of Arthour and of Merlin*[11] says the "child" Merlin saw Vortigern's castle on the "Salisbury" plain (below the cliff of Edinburgh Castle Rock, or below the Salisbury Crags in Edinburgh), where the royal Holyrood Castle stands today. The structure was made of "wode and lime morter and stow" (v. 515), and Merlin's heart's blood was wanted, he knew. The underlying water, the old "North Loch," was "both swift and stepe" (v. 1450).

Whether Vortigern's citadel was located in North Wales, on the west coast of Scotland where archaeologists have sought it at Dumbarton Castle Rock, or whether it was located either at Stirling Castle or adjacent to Edinburgh Castle Rock is not yet clear. But there is more than a possibility that Merlin had gone to the Firth of Forth to await the arrival of royal brothers, Arthur's uncles and father.

Books on the Dark Ages often speak of "Wales" and "Scotland" as if they were the modern kingdoms known from the early Middle Ages, but instead these terms designate familiar geographical land masses, irrespective of later kingdoms and varying frontiers with "England," the kingdom. Merlin thus far has appeared in ports of what is now Wales, both northern and southern, and on the eastern shores of what is also "Wales" (Scotland), near the Firth of Forth. There he seems now to await the arrival of three or, at least, two sons of Constantine.

However disappointing the birth and prodigy stories may be, some parts of a lost "childhood of Merlin," claims to royalty, including Merlin's, should probably be taken seriously. As the British Commander Cunedda moved his people from the Edinburgh area into what became the two kingdoms of North and South Wales, his genealogists accompanied him. Because of this,

•   •   •

[11] EETS, 2 vols. (London, etc., 1973, 1979), Edited by Macrae-Gibson, also a diplomatic text (six manuscripts collated).

74

contemporary Welsh scholars like Rachel Bromwich can in her edition of the Welsh *Triads* derive the future King Arthur from two Welsh royal families. Thus, the clans of Wales and Scotland today, and their descendants throughout the world, proudly trace their lineages back to the Dark Ages.

Not only was Merlin descended from royalty, but his mother was a nun, which doubles the chances of a discovery of his true name. As Son-of-the-Nun he was not only priestly, but high born, and would have been highly educated. Therefore, it is safe to believe that he was a prodigy. He probably did meet King Vortigern, whose existence has been proved by archaeologists and, of course, is authenticated from France by Saint Germanus and his biographer. So far, only one Vortigern has been found, the name referring to this one king alone, just as the first person named Arthur is King Arthur, who appears to be a grandson of this same Constantine. His heirs are about to continue their rules in the north: Maximus, Constantine, Ambrosius, Uther, and Arthur.

The greatest remaining problem to discovering who Merlin was is a question of the geography. History has kept the reader running from southern to northern Wales, and up into whatever the ancient writers could have meant by "Northumberland," thence northward to the Firth of Forth (north shore Stirling Castle Rock, south shore Edinburgh Castle Rock).[12]

The later medieval manuscripts offer expanded geographical information, which will prove helpful, but some also fall into

• • •

[12] The references to the geography of Britain will inform at more length about all these places, excepting the site of Vortigern's citadel where he was burned to death, as Merlin had prophesied. In the *History* by Geoffrey of Monmouth, Merlin makes his great *Prophecy* to King Vortigern, or in his presence, and then reappears only at that point to counsel the sons of Constantine, for whom, it seems, he interrupted his education.

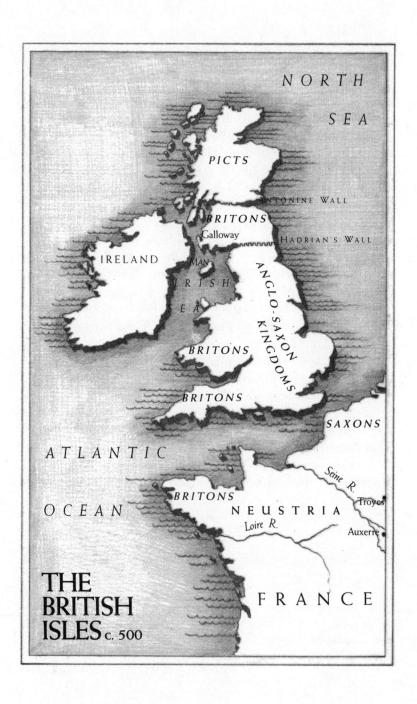

NORTH

SEA

PICTS

Antonine Wall

BRITONS

Galloway   Hadrian's Wall

IRELAND   MAN

ANGLO-SAXON KINGDOMS

IRISH

SEA

BRITONS

BRITONS

SAXONS

ATLANTIC

Seine R.

Troyes

BRITONS   NEUSTRIA

OCEAN   Loire R.   Auxerre

THE
BRITISH
ISLES c. 500

FRANCE

traps that the older sources, Gildas, Nennius, and Geoffrey of Monmouth, either avoided altogether or ignored in passing.

In an English text (*Cambridge* 80 manuscript), Merlin is not laughing when he predicts that his companion and confessor "Blasy's" book on Merlin shall be forever beloved, nor when he predicts that Merlin will attain his highest achievement during the reign of the fourth king, the one named Arthur (v. 2309), but along his road toward Vortigern's citadel Merlin is elsewhere held to burst out laughing each time he divines the future of persons met along the way. Vortigern's messengers have realized by this time that Merlin is "the wisest of mortals." Already Merlin has foreseen the white dragon, King Pendragon, prevail, and he already knows that Vortigern's *magi* are merely that, astrologers who will shortly be compelled to give up their unsanctioned practices. Merlin has previously characterized King Vortigern (Fortiger) as the slain red dragon. The Constantinian princes, he knows, are already rowing toward the evil king.

The late Latin verses called *Vita Merlini* in which has been inserted a statement to the effect that Geoffrey of Monmouth composed it—an opinion most scholars hold—slithers into ridicule, succumbing to sensational stories about Merlin's loud laughter. Now, the exalted personage called "Merlin" by persons who would not for the world have betrayed his real name or real mission in Britain's darkest hour does not strike the serious reader as possessing a hysterical temperament. This verse *Vita*, however, which maliciously debunks the great Merlin, sounds most unlike Geoffrey of Monmouth. There Merlin acts and laughs like a lunatic. The author then predicts the funny twists that ill Fortune ("sors importuna," v. 40, or chance, "O dubios hominum casus, v. 43)[13] blindly allows to govern this predestined

. . .

[13] The poet's words besmirch Merlin, making him at two strokes a pagan, worshiping the Roman goddess Fortuna ("bona aut mala Fortuna"), *sortes (sors)* lots cast by players or by a pagan oracle, and *casus (cadentia)* the fall of the dice in a crap game.

life of such great men as Merlin, which Geoffrey would neither have thought nor said.

The flippant versifier of the *Vita Merlini* has Merlin prophecy callously that a poor man will die three times: by falling, by drowning, and by getting hanged by his horse's reins. Incredibly he has Merlin mock a poor workman who has the leather soles of his shoes patched, although he will be dead before he reaches home. He also has Merlin scoff at a crippled beggar by the church door, crying for pennies, when he is all the while sitting on a treasure he has amassed.

Such stories are as unlike Merlin as his supposed oaths by Orpheus and Venus, or his vulgar remarks, after he sees a queen on the ground, about a cow urinating. Never would the warrior Merlin, who urged Kings Aurelius, Uther, and Arthur to die for Britain, have cried as this poet has him do:

O death, which strikes and drives the miserable life   v. 43ff.
   from the bodies of the warriors!
Daring youth, your daring has snatched away your sweet years of youth!
   Blood has flowed everywhere!

When in this poem the Britons attacked the Scots, Merlin supposedly threw dust on himself and rolled on the ground. He then (unbelievably) lamented for three days and refused food! Not likely. Not Merlin, whose life-style was undoubtedly abstemious enough on ordinary days, and doubly so on days spent rushing out into combat, bearing his dragon banner ahead of the heroes. Not Merlin, who told Uther to go to war on a litter if he was too ill to walk or ride! Merlin spent men as we spend coins. Nor would any person of priestly and royal birth ridicule a poor man because he wanted his shoes repaired, much less because he was soon to die, even if as a healer Merlin had read death on his face.

Therefore one welcomes again the support of two Orientalists, Moses Gaster in *Folklore* (1905) and Alexander Haggerty

Krappe (*Romania*, Paris, 1933), who proved the hypotheses of Paulin and Gaston Paris. This "Gospel of the Infancy," mused Moses Gaster, comes from the older cycle of King Solomon and the demon Asmodeus, where the mother is variously daughter to the prophet Jeremiah or to King David. Her son is Sira (Sirach), who at age seven at the court of Nebuchadnezzar discomfits his rivals. He also laughs at the man with the holes in his shoes. Intermediate versions of this story, particularly those in Germany and Russia, would represent Merlin as the centaur Sagittarius.

Gaster relates another intermediate version (Rumanian manuscript 71):

> The Archangel Gabriel was dispatched to take away the soul of a widow, but when he found her suckling twins, he left her soul alone.
>
> God punished Gabriel for disobedience, by sending him for a stone at the bottom of the sea. But when the Archangel cut it in half, he found two "worms" (dragons) inside.
>
> "*If I feed worms,*" said the Lord, "*do you think I would let twins starve?*"[14] God punished the erring angel for thirty years, and took the woman's soul.
>
> At the end of thirty years the Archangel laughed three times:
>
> (a) at a dying Abbot buying new shoes.
> (b) at a beggar sitting on a treasure, and

．　．　．

[14] To indicate how widespread this story is, may I add here that I heard it told verbatim, as here, in the early 1920s in Vermont. The narrator related it as original and true of his great grandfather, who had resided in Monkton, Vermont. The Lord replaced the word "worms" by "cows."

(c) at a governor and a bishop riding in pomp and cir-
cumstance, not knowing they were twins of the
widow.[15]

Moses Gaster furthermore traced the story of the underwater
dragons to a popular handbook of the Middle Ages (*Elucidar-
ium*) that made clear to students the cosmography of the world,
as follows:

1. the earth rests upon water,

2. the water rests upon a huge rock,

3. the rock rests upon two whales,

4. every time a whale moves, there is an earthquake.

He also traced it to apocryphal additions, or to a dream of Mor-
decai, in the book of Esther:

> Beloved, there was a great noise and tumult and the voice
> of terrible uproar upon the whole land and terror and
> fear seized all the inhabitants of the earth: and behold,
> there appeared two mighty dragons and they came one
> against the other to fight and all the nations of the earth
> trembled at the noise of their fury. And there was a
> small nation between these two dragons, and all the na-
> tions of the earth rose up against it to swallow it up.
> And there were clouds and darkness and obscurity upon
> the face of the earth . . . and the dragons fought one
> another with cruel fury and frenzy, and no one sepa-
> rated them. And Mordecai beheld and lo! a fountain of
> living water sprang and flowed between the two fighting

• • •

[15] In Scotland, Merlin, or another Merlin named Myrddin, was later
said to have had a twin brother named Lailoken. Freud calls this
process of inventing relatives "duplication."

dragons and stopped their fight. And the small fountain swelled into a mighty river and overflowed like a mighty sea and swept everything off the face of the earth. And the sun rose up and the rays lighted the whole earth.

Mordecai interprets his dream, continues Gaster, just as Merlin interprets his red and white dragons. Geoffrey knew all this legendary, religious material, said Gaster, and was surely a "later genius."

Krappe continued Gaster's scholarship by showing how the Hebrew originals migrated into Persia and India and then returned into Nennius, Geoffrey, and the *Mabinogion*. The Oriental structure is the same:

1. A king in difficulty,

2. His ministers stumped,

3. Child-prophet, or fatherless child is heard of,

4. Messengers seek him,

5. They take him from his comrades at play,

6. The child's power is validated immediately,

7. King and wizard desire to sacrifice the child,

8. They fail and/or are to be put to death,

9. Child reveals a crime,

10. Child becomes prime minister,

11. Child's connection with a serpent or serpents—or he is the son of the Great Serpent,

12. Child is fatherless, or the wizard(s) has killed his father.

Krappe's principal complaint is that the Celtic versions, contrary to those from the Orient, remain mysterious, unexplained, illogical. The Indian accounts, where actions follow consequentially, are therefore anterior to the Celtic, he claims, which conclusion perhaps fails to take account of the purposely unfinished nature of Celtic art. Such incomplete solutions appeal to active readers in whom they solicit collaboration. Moses Gaster came to the tantalizing conclusion that the birth and childhood of Merlin were separate from the man Merlin and his life. However, they have at least allowed a preview.

4

"MARVELOUS MERLIN"

. . . .

" 'Knowest thou aught of Arthur's birth?'
Then spake the hoary chamberlain and said,
'Sir King, there be but two old men that know:
And each is twice as old as I; and one
Is Merlin, the wise man that ever served
King Uther thro' his magic art; and one
Is Merlin's master (so they call him) Bleys,
Who taught him magic; but the scholar ran
Before the master, and so far, that Bleys
Laid magic by, and sat him down, and wrote
All things and whatsoever Merlin did
In one great annal-book, where after-years
Will learn the secret of our Arthur's birth.' "

"The Coming of Arthur"
The Idylls of the King.
Alfred, Lord Tennyson,
Poet Laureate.

・ ・ ・ ・ ・ ・ ・

When he had finished his long Prophecy of the far future, Merlin was applauded even by Vortigern, both for his words and for his great wisdom. At first, all were struck dumb in the sudden silence after Merlin closed with the words:

> *Confligent uenti diro sufflamine.*
> *& sonitum inter sidera conficient.*[1]

> (Shall clash together the winds in a dire blast.
> & that thunder shall bounce between the stars.)

At Vortigern's request Merlin went on to tell him what the near future would bring upon them all, a future that Merlin's cosmic vision and his interrogation of the heavens had revealed to him. Vortigern should fly, Merlin added, from the vengeance of Uther Pendragon and his older brother Prince Aurelius Ambrosius. They would be avenged for Vortigern's murders of their father, for his invitations to the Saxons, "that accursed people," adds Merlin, who ultimately will catch Vortigern in their crossfire. All will die: Vortigern by fire, Aurelius and Uther by poison, Hengist in battle. By next day's dawning the princes landed. It was too late for Vortigern to escape.

・ ・ ・

[1] See the diplomatic text, edited by Griscom and Jones, last line of the Latin prophecy, bottom of page 387.

Geoffrey of Monmouth's telling of these calamities is truly unparalleled in its forcefulness and the beauty of its Latin prose (Chapter 8 in the English translation: *The History of the Kings of Britain*).

Geoffrey's account presents Prince Aurelius, the noble Roman, who becomes king of the Celts, vanquishes Vortigern, and faces the oncoming Saxons until he dies. He brings Merlin forward as his viceroy, as it were, and viceroy also to the younger Uther Pendragon. Aurelius sought Merlin at a special spa or "Fountain," or Font, or healing well, where he was accustomed to reside, and had him brought to the Edinburgh area to construct a church in honor of the British chieftans massacred under Vortigern. Then Merlin joined the combat as leader and banner bearer.

Meanwhile, and this point is critical, Aurelius found that two archbishoprics had fallen vacant: "York" and "Caerleon." To York he appointed the holy Samson, and to Caerleon the holy Dubric. Both archbishops, notes Geoffrey, had been singled out by God as his choicest, chosen servants. Theologians since Geoffrey's day have spent much time disputing these lines concerning archbishoprics and appointees, and have chastised Geoffrey (and Gerald of Wales also) for championing Caerleon in Wales as having once been an archbishopric worthy of becoming so again. York remains to this day the seat of an archbishop, but Canterbury has long since replaced any legitimate or illegitimate claim that Caerleon has forwarded from Wales.

Many scholars in Wales and elsewhere have thought seriously that the Archbishop Samson, whom Geoffrey claims sat at York, was in reality "Sir" Lancelot's son Galahad, he who figured so prominently in the last of the Arthurian recordings. If so, another sort of problem arises: If Caerleon was never a prominent center for the pan-Celtic tribes currently warring in the Edinburgh area, then where was this archbishopric granted by Aurelius after his initial victories there?

King Arthur (Part I, Chapter 4) proved that by "Caerleon" Geoffrey meant to say "Carlisle" in northern Britain, a much more massive Roman fortress, anchoring the western end of

Hadrian's Wall. King Arthur was crowned there and the obvious conclusions arrived at were that Geoffrey of Monmouth either mistook "Caerleon" for "Carlisle" or that he wanted to see an archbishopric established at Caerleon. His literary contemporary, the Welsh prince named Gerald of Wales traveled to Rome three times in the twelfth century to argue in favor of Caerleon's claim to this very great honor.

Because of this patriotic and piously cherished desire on the part of Welshmen in the twelfth century, Geoffrey perhaps hastily presented his Merlin *Prophecy* to the public, taking it out of context from the middle of the book he was writing, his *History of the Kings of Britain*: Such a prophecy from a native prophet born of a Welsh nun in a priestly tribe, supposedly at the Welsh city of Carmarthen, should not fail to further Welsh claims in Rome.

Probably for this same urgent reason, Geoffrey spent an extra effort on his "Coronation" of King Arthur, the section in his *History* that follows the poisonings of Aurelius and Uther, and the birth of Arthur. At the "Coronation" scene, Geoffrey again brings to prominence the first and foremost ecclesiastics of ancient Celtic Britain: Saint Dubric, (Dubricius) who placed the crown on the young Arthur's head, and Saint David, patron saint of Wales, who also attended the new, young king. So, very probably, this was no mistake on the part of Geoffrey but an easy alteration by the pen: "Caerleon" for "Carlisle." Love of Wales seems to have overcome Geoffrey, or else he made an honest error. But either way, the evidence points to Carlisle as the coronation site of King Arthur, and Hadrian's Wall northward as the general area of his twelve battles.

It seems no error that Saint Dubricius crowned Arthur, and that he was the Archbishop Dubric, as Geoffrey identifies him. A biography of Saint Dubricius was being written in Wales, as Geoffrey wrote his *History*. Geoffrey might have had a hand in the second text as he wrote his own version of another and the same well-known Welsh saint. Geoffrey may have put his Archbishop Samson in York because he knew York was an archbishopric, second in importance to Canterbury. However, the Arthurian texts also frequently make such an error in geography, saying "York" when they mean "Stirling" in Scotland, claiming "York" as the birthplace of Perceval, for instance, when manuscript evidence in (*Perlesvaus*) names that hero's birthplace as "Camelot," that is, the present city and fort of Stirling.

Whenever he presents ecclesiastical claims for Wales, Geoffrey curiously drops Merlin from his text in order to name the proven historical ecclesiastics of Arthur's day, as here, and in order of importance: Dubric (Dubricius), David, and Samson. Geoffrey must receive one's sympathy, for he is twice bound to Wales, presumably as a native son first of all, and second, as a Cistercian monk, teacher, and scholar. A well-known fact is repeated by theologians and historians of the Celtic Church: the Cistercian Order remained during the Middle Ages close to Wales and to the Welsh people. For their part, the Welsh people reciprocated, admiring the simplicity of the Cistercian liturgy, ritual, and life-style, but not particularly admiring or identifying with Glastonbury's Benedictines, a much larger, wealthier order.

Geoffrey understandably drops "Marvelous" Merlin whenever he turns to purely ecclesiastical matters, as when he describes the coronation ceremony for King Arthur and Queen Guinevere. This disturbs a reader who cannot quite recover from this sleight of hand, especially when Merlin had already figured so prominently as a builder of churches in honor of the massacred British chieftains. Even in Geoffrey's rather terse and compact prose, we perceive that Merlin constitutes an elusive and a disappearing personage, one who turns up when summoned, only to drop out of sight inexplicably. Faced with this peculiarity, one gladly welcomes the Old French manuscripts, and their English translations.

Leaving Geoffrey of Monmouth momentarily and opening the pages of the English *Merlin*,[2] one discovers that Merlin has

•   •   •

2   *Cambridge* 80 manuscript. EETS, Extra Series, 3 vols. (London, 1904–1913), edited by Henry Lovelich (Louelich the Skinner), 27, 85 2 vv. Glossaries in Part II by Ernst A. Kock. This is a metrical version

been disappearing or disguising himself unaccountably ever since he first solved Vortigern's problem of the sinking tower. When messengers next sought him, they were stunned to come upon him disguised as a shepherd and hiding behind a huge, fearsome beard (v. 3035 ff.). When Aurelius (the first to be called Pendragon) sends for Merlin, he is again found disguised as a cowherd or herdsman. Merlin comes to announce that Hengist (Augwis) is dead, but on this occasion, too, he is disguised as a commoner or as a "seemly man." Disguised as an old man, he had actually witnessed the slaying of Hengist, the enemy chieftain, having managed to creep after dark into Uther's tent. Merlin had "taken governance" of Uther and his older brother.

Meanwhile, further prophecies of Merlin continue to be alarming: the Saxons will attack in eleven days, toward the end of June, with superior forces, near Salisbury (the Salisbury Crags outside Edinburgh). Aurelius will die there. But Merlin's massive red dragon will blaze across the sky. Here is our battle plan, says Merlin: Prince Uther will take half the Celtic forces and lie for three days in ambush between the invaders and the sea so as to cut them off from their ships and their retreat. Merlin for his part will instantly retire far into Northumberland. Prince Aurelius will attack with the other half of the Celtic army as soon as he sees the dragon burn above them as it crosses the sky. Then Uther's men will rush from their hiding places and attack the Saxons from the rear. Aurelius will gladly give up his life and his all that fatal day, for the Constantinian princes must prevail. Merlin will have the tomb for the hero Aurelius built on Calton (or the Royal Caledonian) Hill in Edinburgh and will advise King Uther to call himself Pendragon now, as his brother had done before him.

The very credible *Huth-Merlin*, or Old French version, tells us the same story but makes even clearer the military point of

* * *

made in English around 1450 of an Old French text. The *Cambridge* 80 manuscript is the unique and only text.

view. Merlin advised the princes that the Saxons would be arriving with a double force and would coast along the riverbank (south shore of the Firth of Forth). He showed the brothers how to call their men together and make a solid line of defense along the river, guarding back upstream to Salisbury but invisible from the water. As soon as the Saxons breach the line and come ashore, the men are to regroup, close the line, turn and cut them off from their ships and from their drinking water. The princes are to wait for two days and then attack on the third day when the Saxons are very thirsty.

Some Arthurian manuscripts, without evidence, transfer this Salisbury to the city of the same name near Stonehenge in southern England, and recalling Merlin's strategem, say Arthur lost his last battle on the chalk plains nearby because of thirst. In actual fact, King Arthur lost his last battle in this drastic war on Hadrian's Wall, say O. G. S. Crawford and P. K. Johnstone, where he killed and was killed by Vortigern's granddaughter Anna's husband Modred.

Huth-Merlin continues: the Saxons arrived on the coast the first week in July. For two days Uther harassed them so as to keep them hemmed in between his forces on the one side and the river and the Saxon ships drawn up behind the enemy on the other side. On the third day a red dragon breathing flames appeared in the sky and flew straight forward with a great-whooshing sound, directly over the Saxon warriors. It was not Merlin. Merlin had presumably gone back to Northumberland. Then the two princes caught the Saxons between them. Pendragon fell and died. Every one of the Saxons died, was wounded, or drowned—to the very last man.

"One of you [Ambrosius or Uther] must die here," were Merlin's words. "But I want you to know that over his grave I shall erect such a beautiful and splendid memorial to commemorate his name as long as Christianity itself shall survive."

The marble monuments on Calton Hill, Edinburgh, can be seen today from all over the city. Although they are not the ones Merlin built, they rise there in our century white and splendid anyway. Old engravings show fallen cut stones that have tumbled down the grass of the hilly slopes. Merlin had persuaded King Uther to send a fleet of ships to Ireland to commandeer the cut stones; for it seems to have been the cutting of the stones that required the longer time, and not their assembling into a church such as the one built there for Dark-Age Celtic Christianity.

After having established Uther safely in his kingdom, Merlin journeyed to "Carduel," near the modern Carlisle on the western end of Hadrian's Wall, so as to found there an institution that would attract to Uther's standard the most noble, most valiant chieftains throughout that dangerous Border area. He created the Round Table for twelve members, in memory of the Last Supper, with a thirteenth Seat of Dread for Judas Iscariot. The Order of the Round Table was to convene at Pentecost, with a full complement of fifty associate members, if the author of *Huth-Merlin* can be trusted here. The empty thirteenth seat would finally be safely filled or sanctified by one who is not yet even born, decreed Merlin, but he would be another magnificent Scot (that is Perceval), who would *pass many tests* "triumphantly" there where the Grail itself would eventually be deposited for safekeeping (that is, on Man, which is the Isle of Avalon).

As soon as he had arranged all this, completed the building, and established the desired aristocrats into an Order that all others would tirelessly strive to enter and in which they could advance even higher in the public esteem, Merlin retired to his Master's establishment somewhere in Northumberland. He is absent, in the company of Blaise, for a period of two years. Apparently, Merlin needed to spend two more years studying; it might also seem that in a dangerous time, with scores of hostile craft riding the North Sea, someone like Merlin also needed desperately to organize and supervise the eastern coast guards.

It is difficult to roam about this coast of the Border area, from Berwick-on-Tweed to North Berwick, without thinking of Merlin there in that ancient "Northumberland." One can picture him at the medieval ruins of Fast Castle, near some Wolf's Crag, looking out over the flat, white sea, a lonely seascape where the gulls wheel and the peewits scream as they soar out from the broken rock cliffs. The precipices there face north so completely that their faces are hidden in deep shadow all day long. There are hidden ledges for the coastal watchmen who climb narrow ridges of rock to reach their lookouts eighty or a hundred feet above the sea. If one looks directly down these red sandstone cliff faces, one seems to see Merlin perched on the rock, or on some large pulpit, some platform, as wide as a room overhanging the sea caves at the water level. One can imagine or remember from motion pictures what the fury of the northeasters must be upon that row of beetled cliffs as they sweep over such a shallow sea.

To the north stands Berwick and the solitary conical peak of Berwick Law, for centuries a rallying-post, or *maidan* castle for all of East Lothian, Edinburgh eastward to the seacoast. The bale fires or beacons that began down south near or on the promontory of Saint Abb's Head were quickly lighted and within minutes caught fire all the way up the coast to Dowlaw Hill, with three or four of them blazing out from Berwick Law and Tranent, wrote Walter Scott in *The Antiquary*. As a young boy Scott had spent summers recuperating and visiting along that coast.

When Merlin reappears, it is to handle a very delicate human problem, but one that is also dynastic: what to do about a male heir for King Uther. While the romancers freshened up their mythology to tell this tale scabrously as the Greek seduction of Alcmene by Jupiter disguised as her husband Amphitryon, people today may perhaps prefer it to be told differently: Merlin advised or superintended the Constantinian dynasty, as a modern archbishop in Britain might have done.

The Duchess Ygerne had recently lost her husband, explains the clearheaded author of *Huth-Merlin*. She haughtily sued for damages and demanded justified, handsome, and instant compensation. She had been married previously and had five or so grown but still unwedded daughters. Thus, her problems were multiplied by daughters needing real estate as dowries. Merlin seems to have heard the case, as a modern ecclesiastical court might do.

In this suit one can almost hear Merlin's restatement of this difficult situation. The plaintiff was a very important British personage, twice widowed at least, perhaps already thrice widowed, with at least four compliant daughters and one other maiden extraordinary for any day or time. The highborn personage in question was still a young, well-connected daughter of a chieftain, obviously very attractive to men, and evidently fertile. Then there is the hero King Uther, a survivor of fierce combat. His older brother Ambrosius, who was respected and honored far and near, had sacrificed himself without hesitation for the good of the cause. The odds were that Uther had not long to live and was probably scarred and in poor health from wounds and stress.

The solution comes to mind easily: Uther should wed Ygerne. As for the other matter of the five daughters, why should they not wed kings from the Border country, bind their husbands as best they could to the Constantinian dynasty, and set to work at once to breed a race of heroes, mother's sons who would be bound by blood to the Celtic cause?

Thus, the Duchess Ygerne was married to King Uther. One of her daughters—whose name a great many annalists never did agree upon—was married to King Loth, to whom she bore five illustrious sons: Gawain, Agravain, Guerrehes, Gaheriet, and Modred. Another "bastard daughter," perhaps of the duchess's first or second husband, married King Neutres of Sorhaut. Another daughter, perhaps named Morgain, was eventually married to an archenemy, King Urien (Urian) of Murray and the Western Isles, to whom she bore the great hero Yvain (Owain). Her husband later sired another illegitimate son of the same name. She seems to have been the same as the youngest, who was the daughter named Morgue. Her Merlin first dispatched forthwith to a "convent" so that she could study with her equals, if equals could be found. She was eager to master all seven liberal arts, plus astronomy, it is reported, plus the other physical and natural sciences.

The last daughter when grown is known as Queen Morgan, but her legend calls her "Morgan le Fay." She was certainly, like Arthur, set apart from her contemporaries, unique because of her descendants, her beauty, her brilliance, her wealth, and her great learning. Her real name was not "Morgan," for that is a man's name even in modern Welsh. Actually, "Morgan" was King Arthur's physician's name, say the Welsh tales.

The *Cambridge* 80 manuscript (called *Merlin*) states that Arthur had five sisters (half sisters): the first married Loth, the second married "Newtris," the third married Urien(s), and the fourth was a widow. This fourth sister would be, then, the celebrated "Widow Lady of Camelot," mother of Perceval. The fifth sister was reportedly sent to school in "London." She was more likely sent to the Edinburgh area, the Latin for Lothian (Lodonesia) having been again misread for "London."

Sir Thomas Malory gives us Morgawse as the name of King Loth's wife, Morgan le Fay as the wife of King Urien(s), and the English *Thornton* manuscript adds that the Widow Lady of Camelot was named Acheflour and that she was Perceval's mother. Geoffrey of Monmouth and his Anglo-Saxon translator Layamon call King Loth's wife Anna, but the German *Parzival* called her Sangive, who was Gawain's mother.

The double questions of the Duchess Ygerne's husbands and her daughters' names remain troublesome despite great interest in them. The French *Prose Lancelot*, which is in English *Of Arthour and Merlin* (Vol. 2), seems to think that Ygerne first married Harinan, then Hoel, then Tintagel, and finally Uther Pendragon. Her daughter named Blasine married a Nanters, and their son was Galathin. A daughter named Belisent married King Loth and bore Gawain and his brothers. A third daughter named Hermesent(e) married King Urien of Gorre (Isle of Man) and bore Yvain.

However, all narrators agree that Ygerne also bore a son

named Arthur to Uther Pendragon, that Merlin personally accepted the newborn baby as his "reward," and that he immediately sent him out for secret fostering (or hid him) for some fifteen years. The baby was carried immediately after birth to a secret, unknown place, where he absolutely could not be found and killed by any Saxon or any jealous rival. He was the future king and hope of the Celtic peoples, which probably by then also included Brittany.

The *Cambridge* 80 manuscript explains that they have him named Arthur (or Arthewr—v. 6503), and that he was handed out of his mother's chamber to an ugly old man recognized as Merlin. Merlin personally handed the newborn infant to a foster father named Ankor (or Antron). Only if Merlin were the baby Arthur's sole living, adult male relative, and a high ecclesiastic, would such a handing over of the precious royal infant become understandable.

By now we have probably seen enough examples of Merlin's disguises to be somewhat disconcerted by them, not knowing what to think or how to interpret this mania for concealing himself so often whenever he has to deal with other royal persons. The comical poet of the *Vita Merlini* (Life of Merlin) who openly calls himself "jocose," deals with this matter by means of the grossest slapstick. According to his riotous and farcical debunking of Merlin, he has Merlin given a wife, for which there is no evidence. Merlin's wife wishes to remarry, for her spouse is inveterately detained, allegedly in the woods of Northumberland. She has Merlin's consent, or her first husband's consent. Merlin in person plans to attend the ceremony, and he comes riding into the citadel courtyard mounted on a stag. When he glimpses the bridegroom, who is about to oust him from his marital couch, Merlin wrenches the antlers off his stag's head, hurls them at the bridegroom, and strikes him dead. Then he quickly gallops away. This concocted story could have been told straight: Merlin refused to perform a marriage rite. In any case, the stag symbolizes the highest holy man among the Celts.

This last disguise, Merlin mounted on a stag, can be taken comically since it is so like the Whitsuntide Mummers' plays where the Wild Man of the Woods, a medieval descendant of the pagan Italian priest of Nemi in Diana's Sacred Italian Grove, is chased by the younger king, or younger "stag," who will supplant him. Such mythical incidents, Merlin on the stag, says Malinowski,[3] must now be understood for what they once meant, that is, in terms of the priesthood having control of the universe, refuting death, maintaining a permanence unthreatened by contenders, and supplying a guarantee of security. The myth functions best when it deals with a terrified populace shaken by "profound historical changes" that have ripped apart the old ways and shattered a society. Only such a sacred tale is truly a myth, the anthropologist says.

The performance of Merlin is of concern, indirectly at least, to the work of anthropologists. In Bronislaw Malinowski's "Myths of Magic" (Chapter IV), for example, the magic attributed to Merlin over fifteen hundred years occasioned, the author writes, by situations when (1) danger is acute, (2) hope must overcome fear, (3) chance and accident are terribly dreaded, (4) society needs an organizer, (5) people long for some token of success, some powerful man, a Winston Churchill to inspire them with belief in their own powers, (6) some guarantee is needed against despair and anxiety, and (7) success appears possible by means of practical activity.

Merlin's disguises tie him not only to the myths of kingship but also to the historical and desperate plight of the Celtic peoples. They also suggest an interpretation of him recalled as an actor, wearing a costume, or as officiating or performing onstage, like some high priest during the four Celtic festivals: spring,

• • •

[3] See James George Frazer's *The Golden Bough*, pp. 88, 117, 287, and 344ff., and the work of his follower, the Melanesian anthropologist Bronislaw Malinowski.

summer, autumn, and winter. That thought may not be too impossible; nothing is known about the theater in Celtic Britain. And yet, Merlin is remembered as high priest, as an actor, a revered character, or a figurant even centuries after his death.

However, the question still tantalizes: Why all these roles and these disguises? One can understand that as the original British robin of the woods, as the herdsman who spoke the wordless language of the beasts, as the worshipful shepherd guarding his sheep, Merlin also took on their names: he became the Irish mystical guardian, or *bachlach*, pronounced "Bertilak" in *Gawain and the Green Knight*.

One should remember that Merlin must have lived a life of extreme danger, under threats of assassination. He was a public figure so well known to high persons and to the low that, like a modern celebrity, he could not move freely without being recognized. Since one cannot be sure who in actuality he was, it is unclear whether Merlin's position among the mightiest personages, duchesses and kings, required such absolute secrecy. Why did he alter his disguise from the door of the Lady Ygerne's bedchamber, to the antechamber, and again to an outer hall? Merlin trusted nobody, it would seem, with state secrets. What he said to people was often by way of command, as to King Uther lying ill with gout: if you cannot walk to battle or ride before your warriors, then be carried on a litter. But go today, now, and die bravely, if your time has come. I absolve you.

A new manuscript telling how Merlin raised Arthur after that, or what tests he made that wild boy undergo, will probably not be discovered. For once, in Arthur's case, the pejorative epithet applied in scorn to the Celts suits the case aptly. Only the adjective "marvelous" suits Merlin's case when he devised the test of the sword from the stone for Arthur. As the later poet-prophets of Scotland called him, Merlin was simply "marvelous." Arthur was "wild," but Merlin escorted him at age fifteen before the assembled chieftains of the Borders at Carlisle and let Arthur show publicly what he could do: only he could draw the sword from the anvil Merlin had devised or where Merlin had ingeniously put it. That was a marvel, indeed, not understood perhaps but never forgotten.

Even so, the chieftains refused to accept this fifteen-year-old Arthur. In fact, they scorned him as a nameless nobody from nowhere, a reaction that draws attention once more to Geoffrey's trump card and greatest triumph: King Arthur's final coronation some years after Arthur had drawn the perhaps fiery sword from the anvil of "hard stone" that was possibly "marbil gray."[4]

King Arthur's sisters and their royal spouses were present at this coronation. All proceeded according to their rank into the churches. The usual dignitaries and officers of the court were present, as was Archbishop Dubric, who placed the crown on the head of the victorious warrior, which Arthur by that time had become. Arthur's sisters, who were queens and mothers of his warriors, attended Queen Guinevere, and also proceeded in solemn state.

One dignitary is absent from Geoffrey's account, and his conspicious absence disturbs one considerably. In Britain every coronation includes the candidate's ascertainment of right to the throne. But in Arthur's coronation ceremony, which is otherwise spendidly enacted with all the pomp and panoply of British and ancient Scottish royalty and with all due honor, there is neither High Sennachie nor King Herald—nobody, in fact, to recite King Arthur's pedigree, which alone established his right to reign over the tribes, clan chieftains, and lesser aristocracy of the north. Such an ascertainment is duly and rigorously performed in Scot-

· · ·

[4] *Cambridge* 80 manuscript, v. 6999:

> . . . *an beholden where that a foure-quartered ston that there lay* . . .
> *bit of what maner ston that hit was,*
> *there knew no man In that plas.*
> *Somme there seiden hit was marbil gray.*

land today for all the clan chiefs, who today are members of Parliament.

It is therefore a relief to find in the Old French accounts that particular ascertainment ceremony. That is, it is both a relief and not. It is all the more wonder how Geoffrey came to miss it. When one ponders this omission, the more it grows in importance. Such an omission is unlike Geoffrey of Monmouth, one of the world's most meticulous scholars. He was a man with an acute sense of what is proper, and, moreover, a man endowed with a literary talent surpassed only by a handful of the greatest writers of history who have ever lived. Why did Geoffrey ignore the ascertainment ritual? He could not have failed to see it in his source, when the contemporary French-language writers found it, recognized it, and recorded it. The primary conclusion imposes itself. What happened to Merlin? Where was he? Where was the kingmaker?

Another author tells us that "syxe kynges" came to the coronation, where they rudely refused the gifts that were offered to them (*Cambridge* 80 manuscript, v. 7785ff.), disowned Arthur, and threatened to take his life. Then, and only then, did they haughtily summon not Dubric, but Merlin, to appear before them, made Merlin swear upon oath to tell them the truth about Arthur, and listened to the two witnesses Merlin summoned to this council. But was it not Merlin who should have convoked the courtiers to appear before the royal personages? asked the author of *Huth-Merlin*. The personages included Queen Ygerne, Morgain, Ulfin, and Auctor (Antor). Before such an assembly, Merlin himself then must have proved Arthur's legitimacy and Arthur's royal birth. Thus, King Arthur *was crowned with the aid of Merlin*, after all, but Merlin inexplicably did not attend the actual coronation?

The continuators of the story review Merlin's actions to date, recalling that he carried the newborn child to his foster father, that he predicted Uther's death, that he presided at his funeral, that he officiated at the initial election of Arthur as commander, that he appeared in person to Arthur and recited his genealogy for him, that he foresaw the collapse of Arthur's realm because of Modred, that as "Merlin" he openly named himself to Arthur, that he finally "discovered" Arthur's geneaology "to the people," and that he more than once saved the young king's life in battle. Merlin excused Arthur: "Vos estes jovenes et tenres" (you are young and tender), meaning you have only half your strength. Wait another five years and you will see a great difference.[5]

Dressed as a husky commoner, Merlin then has letters of gold "written" on the tombs of Lancelot and Tristan. He predicts that King Loth and the others will attack Arthur, but that he Merlin can slow them down for a time to allow the young king to arrive at his mighty, powerful maturity.

As provision for the approaching war, Merlin takes the young commander Arthur to a deep lake. Standing on the shore and looking over the dark loch, they see an arm clothed in white samite rise out of the water, holding a sword. Then they notice that they are no longer alone on this shore. Not far away is a young damsel mounted on a small, black palfrey. "You can't get it," she says to them.

"I know that," said Merlin, "for if I could get it I would know it and how to get it. So as a favor to me, will you hand it to my lord the King? It could not be better used anywhere else in the world."

"I know that surely," she said. She gets it, but Merlin has first promised to grant her first request. She walks dry shod on the water to fetch it. She grasps the sword. The arm sinks. "Sire," she said, "here is your sword."

Of course, the sword was Excalibur, and the damsel was "Marvelous," Merlin's own pupil, the Lady of the Lake. The fascination with Arthurian literature may stem from its disinclination to explain. Its readers must either collaborate or stay with

• • •

[5] *Huth-Merlin*, edited by Gaston Paris and Jacob Ulrich, Vol. I, p. 186.

another illusion, another mystery like that of Merlin's roles and his disguises. Reading the above passage, some scholars have responded "Magic!" while others have spoken of optical illusions. Perhaps one should remember the passage simply as a beautiful visualization in tones of gray: peat-filled, still waters like those of Loch Ness as a middle ground, with the blue coasts of Wales and Ireland as the background, and the three stark figures, Merlin and the magnificent Arthur with their backs to the observer, the haughty damsel sideways, ready to slip down from her saddle.

In second preparation for the war that he foresees from the proud chieftains who have spurned Arthur, Merlin commences to line up supporters for the young king among the sub-kings nearest the theater of action. Noteworthy among these are the brothers King Ban and King Bohort, who rule adjacent coastal territories, the former probably at North Berwick and Berwick Law. Merlin in the company of the Lady of the Lake will visit King Ban just before King Ban is struck down in retaliation for his support of King Arthur. King Ban's young wife is named Elaine (or Helen). She is seen once when she is expecting her first child, who will be the wonderful Lancelot later adopted by Lady of the Lake, whose name he will bear. The third king Merlin woos is Guinevere's father Leodagan of Carmalide, whom first Merlin and Arthur must defend. The wedding of King Arthur and Guinevere will re-cement this third alliance. The *Auchinleck* manuscript has Merlin explaining the situation:

> Merlin com the king to   v. 3604
> And to them seyd "Bieu sengours"
> [Good Lords]
> Ye ben yswore to King Arthours
> Ye mot bothe with him ride
> To Leodagan of Carmalide
> For by my rede he shall espouse
> Gvenour his daughter precious . . .

King Leodagan has been attacked by King Rion (Urian) and fifteen kingly allies. King Arthur rides up to the rescue with his honor guard: Ban, Bohort, Antor, Ulfin, Bretel, and the bachelor warriors who are his sisters' sons. Merlin leads the way, or enchants them (that is, casts dread enchantments upon the foe, so feared is he).

The *Auchinleck* then begins a list of King Arthur's forty-two allies, or names of ancestors, as follows:

1. Agrauel,

2. Aigilin,

3. Amandan,

4. Antour, foster father of Arthur,

5. King Ban of Benoït (that is, Berwick),

6. King Belias of "maiden castel," that is, *maidan* = mustering place,

7. Blehartis,

8. Bleherris, godson of Bohart,

9. Bleoberiis,

10. Bliobel,

11. King Bohort of Gaines,

12. Bretel, Tintagel's cupbearer, and so on.[6]

So essential was it for Englishmen of John Leyland's day to know these noble warriors that they were listed in his "Assertion of King Arthure": 166 nobles of whom 15 or 16 were kings, 1 was a duke, and 149 were knights.[6]

• • •

[6] EETS, Original Series 165 (1925). John Leyland or Leland (c. 1506–1552) was a celebrated librarian, scholar, and antiquarian, chaplain to King Henry VIII.

Kings

1. Le Roy Meliadus.
2. Le Roy Ban de Benock.
3. Le Roy Boort de Gauues.
4. Le Roy Karados.
5. Le Roy Lac.
6. Le Roy de Clares.
7. Le Roy Vrien.
8. Le Roy Lottho de Orchany.
9. Le Roy Ryon.
10. Le Roy Pelinor.
11. Le Roy Baudemagus de Gorre.
12. Le Roy Pharamondo.
13. Le Roy Galganoys de Norgalles.
14. Le Roy Aguifant d'Efcoffe.
15. Le Roy Malaquin d'outre les marches de Gallounne.
16. Le Roy Claudas.

I

1. *Le Duke de Clarence.*

Knights

1. Meffier Lancelot du Lac.
2. Boort de ga[nn]es.
3. Gawain d'Orchany.
4. Meffier Triftran de Lyonnoys.
5. Lyonet de Ga[nn]es.
6. Helias le Blanc.
7. Hector des Mares.
8. Bliomberis de Gauues.
9. Gaherriet.
10. Keux le Senefchall.
11. Meffier Yuaine.
12. Bruor le Noir.
13. Baudoyer le Coneftable.
14. Agruall de Galles.
15. Segurades.
16. Patris le Hardy.
17. Efclabor le Meffoniez.
18. Saphar le Méfcognieu.
19. Sagremor le defree.
20. Gyron le Curtoys.
21. Seguram le Brun.
22. Galehault le Blanc.
23. Le Morholt de Ireland.
24. Danayn le Roux.
25. Amilan de Seffougné.
26. Brallain.
27. Brallain que lon difoit le Cheualier a[ux] d[eu]x efpees.
28. Gallehaulte.
29. Lamorat de Lyfthenoys.
30. Brunor de Ga[nn]es.
31. Le bon Cheualier de Norgalles.
32. Henry de Ryuell.
33. Meffier Gullat.
34. Gueherres.
35. Aggrauaine le Orguilleux.
36. Mordrec de Orchany.
37. Gyrfflet.
38. Dodynel le Sauaige.
39. Yuain le Auoutre.
40. Ozement Coeurhardy.
41. Gualegantine le Galloys.
42. Gaherriet de Lemball.
43. Mador de la porte.

44. Bamers le forcene.
45. Dynadam de Eftrangor.
46. Herret le filz de lac.
47. Artus le petit.
48. Cinglant Rochmont.
49. Artus lesbloy.
50. Guallogrenant de Winde-
zores.
51. Kandelis.
52. Merangis des portz.
52. Gauuaine le franc.
53. Gnades le fort.
54. Pharas le Noir.
55. Pharas le Roux.
56. Iambegues le Garruloys.
57. Taulas de la mountaine.
58. Abandam le fortune.
59. Damatha de foliment.
60. Amand le bel Ioufteur.
61. Ganefmor le Noir.
62. Arphin le Dire.
63. Arconftant le adures.
64. Le Beau courant.
65. Le laid hardy.
66. Andelis le Roux ferré.
67. Bruyant des Ifles.
68. Ozenall de Effraugeé.
69. Le Cheualier de Efther.
70. Le Varlet de Gluyn.
71. Heroys le ioyeux.
72. Fergus du blanc lieu.
73. Lot le Coureur.
74. Meliadus del Efpinoy.
75. Meliadus a[u] noir [œ]il.
76. Ayglius des vaux.
77. Iamburg du Chaftell.

78. Meffire Clamorat.
79. Surados des fept fontanes.
80. Le Varlet au Circle.
81. Kaedins de Lonizein.
82. Lucane le Boutellier.
83. Brumer de la fountaine.
84. Lenfant du pleffies.
85. Perfides legent.
86. Sibilias aux dures mai[n]s.
87. Sinados le Efile.
88. Arphazat le groz cœur
89. Le blonde Amoreux.
90. Argahac le Beau.
91. Normaine le Pelerin.
92. Harmaine le felon.
93. Tofcane le Romane.
94. Landone le Leger.
95. Le fort troue.
96. Le Noir Perdu.
97. Le fortune de lifle.
98. Le fee des Dames.
99. Le Forefter de Dennewich.
100. Le Chaffeur de o[u]tres les
marches.
101. Ieyr & Landoys de Rufe.
102. Geoffroy le Lancoys.
103. Randowin le perfien.
104. Froyadus le Gay.
105. Rouffelin de la autre
monde.
106. Gurrant le Roche dure.
107. Arm. on. ouuerd ferpent.
108. Ferrand du tertre.
109. Thor le filz de Arez.
110. Iupin des croix.
111. Ydeux le fort Tyrant.

112. Bolinian du Boys.
113. Le bon Cheualier fans paour.
114. Brouadas le Efpaignoll.
115. Brechus fans Pitye.
116. Malignain.
117. Le Cheualeur de Scallot.
118. Melias de l'Efpine.
119. Agrœr le fel Patrides au Circle d'Or.
120. Mandius le noir.
121. Perceuall de Gallis.
122. Aeuxdeftraux.
123. Lamant du Boys.
124. Melianderis de Sanfen.
125. Mandrin le Sage.
126. Kalahart le petite.
127. Sadoc de Vencon.
128. Perandon le pauure.
129. Verrant de la Roche.
130. Le Brun fans ioy.
131. Bufterin le grand.
132. Le Cheualier des fept voyes.
133. Gryngaloys le fort.
134. Malaquin le Galoys.
135. Agricole Beau grand.
136. Gualiandres du Tettre.
137. Margondes le Rongo.
138. Kacerdius de la Vallee.
139. Nabon le fel.
140. Talamor le Voland.
141. Alibel de Logres.
142. Dalides de la Ryuier.
143. Arain du pinen.
144. Arganor le riche.
145. Melias le Beau Cheualier.
146. Meliadus le Blanc.
147. Malaquin le gros.
148. Meffier Palamides.
149. Alexander le Orphelin.

ANGLO-SAXON HOLDINGS from the end of the Sixth to the Eighth Century
(from Maps II and III of Francis Palgrave)

THE
PROPHET

· · · · · · ·

For he by wordes could call out of the sky
Both sunne and moone, and make them him obay;
The land to sea, and sea to maineland dry,
And darksom night he eke could turne to day;
Huge hostes of men he could alone dismay,
And hostes of men of meanest thinges could frame,
Whenso him list his enimies to fray:
That to this day, for terror of his fame,
The feendes do quake when any him to them does name.

The Fairie Queene
(Book III, chapter 3, stanza 12)
Edmund Spenser

• • • • • • •

In order to read the Merlin Prophecy sympathetically, and as submitted by Geoffrey of Monmouth to the Bishop of Lincoln, England, about 1134, it is necessary first to review modern ideas about prophecy as a form of oratory. This art is often presented as a dream, as divine inspiration (Merlin must first "inspire," or draw in the breath, of prophecy). A frame of reference might well be either the Book of Daniel in the Old Testament or the Book of Revelation, also called Apocalypse, by Saint John the Divine, in the New Testament. The choice of examples is countless, for prophecy as a means of oral communication that is divine utterance has been practiced for ages and continues today.

Certain features of this great and noble art remain constant, a given fact that holds true for all universally accepted literary types. The prophet warns, as did Saint John at Patmos, of things *that will shortly* come to pass. The prophet places himself in the past so that he can look forward toward events to come. He speaks in the future prophetic tense. Thus, apocalyptic utterance becomes, by its first rule of procedure, a philosophy of history:

1. these disasters shall come,

2. they shall unfold toward some awful climax,

3. our troubles and terrors shall cease,

4. man shall be allowed to die,

5. we shall go to heaven.

When reading Merlin's *Prophecy*, one must bear in mind that the story that he says *will come*, has already come.

Not to understand Merlin's art here is to debunk both him in particular and prophecy in general; and this is precisely what many modern Arthurian scholars have done, with great learning on their parts, and with considerable delight. They have succeeded in this line of attack because Merlin almost never mentions the names of individual kings. Instead of particularizing, he uses clan names or symbols.

For example, Merlin speaks of a "stag," whom he does not identify since his readers in the Dark Ages would have known which king was a stag, or which one wore a stag's head as a crown, or belonged to a clan whose totem animal was a stag. In Scotland today, the stag is still worn as a crest badge by the clans of Maxwell and Scott. The more ancient pagan god of the Celts, Cernunnos, was represented as an old man accompanied by a stag; but Merlin's *Prophecy* was composed in Christian times, which had been around for a few centuries. The anthropologist Anne Ross has explained that the stag was long considered by the Celts as the holiest and oldest of their animals, and that it led heroes and others to the underworld. However, by Merlin's day, the stag had also become a symbol of Christ Himself, for like Him, the stag was powerful enough to kill the evil serpent, the fiend from hell.

Merlin often speaks of the royal dragon, by which creature he openly designated Ambrosius, Uther, and perhaps Arthur, but here some king belonging also to Welsh royalty, more precisely to the Men of the North (that is, the Royal Caledonians around Edinburgh, who were the ancestors of the modern Welsh). In any case, the dragon symbolizes this premier tribe of Britain. He speaks of that fiercer warrior, the boar, once designating the XXth Legion, but later the totem beast of the Orcs, one of the Pictish peoples of the far north. Their capital was at Inverness, Scotland. In the same breath Merlin refers to other warriors and to some champion of theirs as a lynx (or bobcat), which again was the totem and badge of the Catti, another tribe of the northern Picts, reports Frank Adams (*The Clans, Septs, and Regiments of the Scottish Highlands*, Edinburgh, 1908, 1965).

In fact, the Twenty-seventh Hereditary Lord High Constable of Scotland, Countess of Erroll and Chief of the Hays, wrote in her foreword to *The Clans and Tartans of Scotland* by Robert Bain, that these badges indicated a "brotherhood within clan or Name" (p. 7), by which custom Merlin refrained from using any specific king's name. Each champion was replaceable by another named "Stag" or "Wolf" (crest badge of the Clan Macqueen) or "Bear" (clan badge of Matheson). When Merlin says "Fox," the badge is not necessarily recognizable since the Celtic *madadh* might have meant fox, wolf, or even dog (wolfhound, or shepherd, perhaps). As already seen, the Celtic *buachaille* meant not only "herdsman," which was one of Merlin's disguises, but also "coastguard," or "sea guard," says a Welsh poem of the fifth century. Some of these "names," like that of the Clan MacArthur, are considered "older than the hills." The lion seems to have designated the King of Alba (Scotland).

Merlin's detractors opened their campaign against the *Prophecy* as soon as its discoverer Geoffrey of Monmouth, who was Welsh and a teacher in the Cistercian Order, died in 1150. Three clergymen of influence in that century defended Geoffrey and Merlin: William of Newburgh, John of Cornwall, and Gerald of Wales, who was said to have owned an original copy of Merlin's *Prophecy* and to have translated it. Their controversy centered on whether or not Merlin had written the *Prophecy*.

Opponents claimed that Geoffrey wrote it all and that the savage kings who fought by leaping naked upon their enemies' backs were meant to portray lords and sovereigns of early twelfth-century England: William Rufus, William the Conqueror, Henry I, William II, as well as Duke Robert II of Normandie, King Stephen (to whom Geoffrey of Monmouth had dedicated his *History of the Kings of Britain*), and last, the red-headed, clever diplomat King Henry II. Geoffrey of Monmouth would have had to be insane to think that the Bishop of Lincoln, to whom he formally dedicated his *Prophecy*, would have been pleased to see King Stephen depicted as a frenzied, naked, utterly fierce highland clansman in battle.

The Irish epic of Cuchulain explains as graphically as one could wish how these ancient heroes—dedicated to war and *trained for war from birth*, knowing themselves expendable, as Merlin reminded King Uther Pendragon—entered into the frenzy of combat. They foamed at the mouth. Their faces became disfigured like those of raving maniacs. They could run at the top speed of a deer or a horse. They could leap heights like a dog. They could run all day long, a distance of thirty miles and more, without halting once for food or water. Lancelot frequently leaped from his horse upon the back of another rider. He never felt pain. King Arthur's honor guard were gigantic men, the tallest in the land. Their names are still remembered.

Next to such giants, King Henry II would have resembled a country gentleman, and a dwarfish one at that. Persons warned him not to set foot in Wales because Merlin had prophesied that were any foreign king to do so, he would fall dead on the spot. King Henry II dismounted at the frontier, perhaps on the right bank of the Wye River, and then advanced that fatal step into Wales. With a laugh he turned to his attendants and quipped, "Your Merlin is a liar."

Needless to say, in the Merlin *Prophecy*, there is no such story. But other pseudo-prophecies attributed to Merlin decided medieval politics, altered events, caused wars, and shaped the lives of the powerful for at least three hundred years, at least from their presence, as presented by Geoffrey in 1134, to the treaty signed at Cadillac, France, which ended the Hundred Years War in 1453.

Unfortunately, Merlin in the *Prophecy* does not talk about Druids, and lamentably not about magic either. Because he was a prophet, however, he doubtless came to be known and admired universally as a magician. Because he was an astronomer and a proto-scientist, he also came to be known as an astrologer. Had he lived another few years, he probably would have been excommunicated on either charge, since both astronomy and astrology—any science at all, in fact—were soon to be sternly forbidden. To consider the consequences of this trend toward abolishing learning altogether, which had accelerated by the year 600, is to begin to understand why Geoffrey of Monmouth translated Merlin's *Prophecy* in the first place.

Learning, scholarship, *and science* had all come into favor again by Geoffrey's twelfth century, and the Dark Ages were suddenly being explored. Astronomy in particular had been brought into France and England from the Arab schools in Spain, Africa, and the Middle East. Geoffrey must have been thrilled to the core to read the *Prophecy* of an early astronomer named "Merlin," who had written before the year 536.

Gaining perspective also explains why the early texts claimed that Merlin delivered this *Prophecy* in one breath, during one exhalation, when he was seven years old. He was supposed to have sat down on a boulder, either near Edinburgh, Scotland, or else on the promontory of Great Orme's Head in North Wales, and spoken it to King Vortigern. However, this theory of literature fails to explain any work, much less Merlin's *Prophecy*. Such are not delivered in one exhalation, even after a long breath of air (the Latin "inspiration"). Great works of art require an immensely long preparation, years of education in the best schools of the time, long decades of maturation, and weeks of dedicated work. Robert de Boron visualized Merlin prophesying at the age of seven because he knew that all prophets stood in the past predicting events in the future which had, of course, already taken place. Merlin's *Prophecy* is by way of a history of his own lifetime. His *Prophecy* is a unique document for any age and land.

Merlin does not teach or explain that ancient Roman augurs were still reading the sky for the flights of birds, although he does mention the heron. Every great lord of his time kept a heronry on his estate possibly for the entertainment of gaming guests. He says nothing of the augurs' tents, like the ones outside Rome, where those officals inside their square temples faced the four quarters of the sky to predict according to the flights of birds, as the pseudo-prophetic work called "Life of Merlin"

(*Vita Merlini*) implies, with its long list of non-Hebrew, nonbiblical, unclean birds. Merlin never speaks of looking to the summer part of the sky, or, in Roman, the *antica* (ancient), *postica* (posterior), *dextra* (right) or *sinistra* (left and sinister) part (*pars*) of heaven. His gaze is entirely and devotedly Christian.

Margaret Enid Griffiths, the Welsh scholar, agreed in her thesis on *Early Vaticinations in Welsh with English Parallels*, which was presented at the University of Cardiff, Wales, in 1937. There she emphasized what is perhaps the best, if not the only comparison of the Merlin *Prophecy* to the Book of Daniel in the Old Testament. Merlin actually belongs, in her prudent analysis, among the twenty-one prophets of Judah, notably after Isaiah, Jeremiah, Ezekiel, and Daniel. Or he follows closely the traditional compositions of the eight prophets of Israel, among whom are Elijah, Jonah, Hosea, and Amos. In 1929 even the hostile French Arthurian scholar Edmond Faral admitted that the *Prophecy* showed traces of Isaiah, Ezekiel, Daniel and the Book of Revelation. Griffiths also pointed out how dangerous was the role of prophet, recalling for us the case of a near contemporary of Geoffrey of Monmouth: Joachim of Fiore (1145–1202).[1]

Merlin portrays in graphic detail a period of uncontrollably dominant evil, of cowering fear, and of terrible suffering, during which the anguished spirit of man and his human dignity remain somehow elevated, as the Church has always elevated them. According to apocalyptic theory, which had also become Mer-

• • •

[1] His prophecy, and that part written by John of Parma, preached the four ages of the world:

1. past time: the Age of the Father,
2. present time: the Age of the Son,
3. late, present time: the Age of the Church, and
4. time now about to dawn: the Age of the Holy Ghost.

The work also preached poverty and humility, which would lead to the perfect world envisioned by Saint Francis of Assisi. This work caused

lin's view of history, in his days, human destiny must be consummated. The only way out of the maze is through it. With this eschatological solution the reader, too, must accept being lured down into unspeakable horrors and the darkest night of chaos.

In Merlin's pages, war is portrayed in unbelievable horror as women are corrupted, mountains are uprooted, and the ruts cut by the chariot wheels of a warrior run with human blood. There is no relief. All men are plainly seen; they have reverted to animals, to brutish beasts, where one lone woman in vain passes the cup of truce. She is the Northern Crown, the "peace-weaver" to the Celts as she was in *Beowulf* to the Anglo-Saxons. Thus, certain set symbols appeal to deep emotional centers of our being. Or, says the contemporary philosopher C. S. Peirce, what we have in prophecy is a closed or semiotic structure, apt to trigger responses from all and automatically to cause instant recognition.

The writers of prophecy usually bring readers out of their dire prospects and fainting state by inviting them at last to look up to the sky. The human heart needs splendor, say the twentieth-century prophets. Humans shall turn away from a society corrupted by greed and wealth and look toward the New Jerusalem. Our own century will understand Merlin's cosmic glance into outer space. Although the sun will be darkened here, as Matthew predicted (24:6–7), there are other worlds.[2]

* * *

such a scandal in the Church that *any person possessing the book* was instantly excommunicated. Fortunately for himself, the profane author of *The Life of Merlin*, a work ascribed to Geoffrey of Monmouth, actually remained safely anonymous. No wonder the pseudo-Merlin was called Silvester, a name reminiscent of the ancient pagan god at Rome called Silvanus.

[2] Both Griffiths and Zumthor (see Bibliography) between them give such complete lists of *Prophecies*, both Christian and Sibylline, that it seems unnecessary to cite them again here.

The following translation is original. The *Prophecy* I have translated here I believe to be Merlin's *Prophecy*, as first translated by Geoffrey of Monmouth from Old British. This ancient form of P-Celtic was reportedly very close to the Welsh now spoken in North Wales. And Bangor and the University of North Wales continue as the most active and probably the largest of all centers of Celtic and Arthurian studies in the world. The original school at Bangor was also renowned as a world center of learning in Merlin's day. The scholars and teachers at Bangor–Iscoed were not massacred until after Merlin's death—so that he personally was spared that persecution of the Christian Celtic Church. In Merlin's day there were over three thousand scholars at Bangor alone.

Two English translations of the *Prophecy* currently available were made by Sebastian Evans in 1903 and by Lewis Thorpe in 1966 and form a part of Geoffrey's *History of the Kings of Britain*. At every critical point, these two translators agree, or Thorpe sometimes follows Evans. Both translate dispassionately, usually selecting from the variety of meanings for each Latin word that is preferred by their dictionaries.

I have pondered their translations for decades and come away not only mystified but greatly discouraged. Were we to stay with these excellent scholars, we might not have a clue as to what Geoffrey of Monmouth meant. Thus, there comes a point in the study of a document or a work of art—for the *Prophecy* is both—when one must select from among a dozen or so possible meanings in classical and medieval Latin dictionaries the one word that makes most sense. When none makes sense, then one must turn to the etymological dictionaries.

After studying Merlin's *Prophecy*, one finally decides that his is not a strictly literary Latin but in many places a technical Latin. Merlin seems more used to handling administrative responsibilities involving thousands of acres, thousands of lives, and huge revenues from vast estates. He speaks a litigious, legalistic language such as a corporation president, a university president, or an investment broker might speak.

What did Geoffrey of Monmouth, a humble and obscure monk and teacher, think of all this? Had he any idea who Merlin was? Did he suspect that someone very important loomed behind that childhood appellation, "Son-of-the-Nun"? If so, he carried his suspicions to the grave. He spent his last years editing and correcting his world-famous *History*. No other distinguished and contemporary Welsh scholar, neither Gerald of Wales nor Caradoc of Llancarvan, breathed a word. Nobody in Wales felt at all tempted to reveal knowledge. Why do so? For what reason?

The reader will find footnotes along with the new translation in the hope that they will reveal those points at which the previous translators disallow further claim by Merlin or Geoffrey that (1) this is an authentic text of the Dark Ages, (2) that it was written by a Christian, and (3) that its author could have been King Arthur's Merlin.

This new translation is also edited into sections, given titles, separated into paragraphs, and even identified by genre. Otherwise, in the welter of Latin sentences, page after page, the reader would lose track almost at once. After years of trying to grasp what his text really meant, I decided that it had to be studied piece by piece. The text sometimes gives sections of separate, discursive prophecies, usually written as compound sentences connected by an ampersand. These connected phrases resemble the composition characteristic of ancient epics such as *Beowulf* and *The Song of Roland*. The words Merlin uses, or Geoffrey uses, are often odd, lofted about the air like tennis balls out of reach of one's racquet; and this is especially true of abstract nouns, which often float about indefinitely from one century to another. For example, people love to write books to explain what "charity" means now, or "grace."

Whatever else this attempt at a new translation may or may not have achieved, at least the geography is largely unscrambled. The original author, who I also believe, with Geoffrey of Monmouth, was the "magician" thought of as "Marvelous Merlin," at last finds himself in ancient Britain, and not in the Middle Ages where Merlin could never have resided and needed his various disguises as he went about his business. One correction returns the text to Merlin, who when he spoke of "my garden," which he did at several crucial points, was indulging in a legal joke: "ea hortus, in horti vero heredium," laughed Pliny in Rome. He can call it "my garden," but more accurately it means an inheritance, the territories that he administered and that extended along his side of the Wye River and included the Golden Valley of Wales.

The reader is now invited to hear the *Prophecy* of Merlin, without more introduction, especially without any longer discourse as to how it relates or might relate to King Arthur's wars. After having read this *Prophecy*, which may be taken to consist of Merlin's history of these wars until his death, the reader might then be more interested to read the French and English accounts of those wars. Merlin may have wanted as his epigraph the words of Ezekiel (2:5):

And they, whether they will hear, or whether they will forbear (for they *are* a rebellious house), yet shall they know that there hath been a prophet among them.

. . . .

. . . .

"THE PROPHECY
OF MERLIN"

. . . .

from
The History of
the Kings of Britain
(Historia Regum Britanniae)
WRITTEN IN LATIN BY
GEOFFREY OF MONMOUTH
(OXFORD, ENGLAND, C. 1134)

(retranslated and edited by the author, 1987)

I

GEOFFREY OF MONMOUTH'S
INTRODUCTION

I had not yet reached that point in my History[1] when
the rumor concerning Merlin's *Prophecy* was so spread
about that my contemporaries from near and far drove
me to produce it for them. The man who asked most
compellingly of all was Alexander, Bishop of Lincoln, a
man the highest and wisest in Christendom. There was
not either in the Church nor among the people such a
man, waited upon by so many noblemen attracted to
him by his accustomed reverence and by the kind gen-
erosity he showed to petitioners. Since I had long since

[1] Griscom and Jones, p. 383: "Von dum autem ad hunc lo-
cum historie perueneram." Geoffrey uses the word or title
Prophecy in the plural, "prophetias," for which reason this
text is often called "The Prophecies of Merlin," or "The Va-
ticinations of Merlin." The Welsh translator fails to follow
Merlin here, and has stopped after Merlin explains the two
dragons that cause Vortigern's tower to fall.

chosen to meet his pleasure, I translated this *Prophecy* of Merlin for him and sent it to him along with a letter that ran as follows:

Alexander, Bishop of Lincoln:

The delight which I feel for thy nobility compels me to translate from British to Latin the *Prophecy of Merlin* even before I have finished my *History*, which I had commenced to write concerning the epic deeds of the Kings of the Britons. For I had planned to have completed that work first and then to have explicated this *Prophecy* subsequently; I worried lest encumbered with a dual workload I should prove inadequate in ability to handle the shorter text. But since I feel very secure as well in thy forgiveness as in the subtle discreetness of thy brilliance, I have lifted up my own rude shepherd's pipe now to my lips and have re-interpreted this vaticination of Merlin from its tongue foreign to thee. Even so, I wonder that thou hadst committed this to my meager pen when the rod of thine office could have commanded so many men more learned than me, so many more distinguished, who could charm thine ears, as Minerva's were charmed, by the sheer ecstasy of a sublimer oracle.[2]

• • •

[2] Geoffrey here is paying Merlin the greatest, noblest compliment when he compares the Bishop to Minerva and Merlin's *Prophecy* to the Delphic Oracle and her *carmina* (charms), which soothed the savage breast of the Greek goddess of war. Like Merlin, Minerva possesses many names (*Minerva* from *mind* or *intellect*, *Athene* from *lightning*, *Pallas* from *storm*

And leaving aside all the philosophical theologians of the entire island of Britain, thou alone art he whom I blush to confess could sing such prophecies more beautifully than my audacious lyre, had not the weight of highest honor called thee to thy many administrative functions. Since therefore it has pleased thee that Geoffrey of Monmouth should blow his reed-pipe in this vaticination, may thou condescend to favor his modulations & if he should strike a discord or sour note, may thou rap thy stand with thy baton and bring him into consonance again.

· · ·

and *thunder*). Her shield or *aegis* bore the image of the ocean goddess Medusa, long a symbol of Britain's sea-blue waters and her Roman temple at Bath, England (*Aquae Sulis*). Minerva protected Athens, Sparta, and Troy just as Arthur and Merlin stood to the death over Edinburgh, Stirling, and the "wild country" of "Northumbria."

. . . .

II

. . . .

MERLIN'S INTRODUCTION
KING ARTHUR

DIVERSE PROPHECIES POLITICAL & ECCLESIASTICAL
. . . .

MERLIN'S INTRODUCTION

And thus, while King Vortigern of the Britons was still seated upon the bank of the pond that had been drained, two dragons issued forth from its deep, one of whom was white and the other, red. As soon as the one had approached the other, they locked on to each other in combat to the death & breathed fire as they blew out each breath. However, the white dragon soon won over the other, driving the red dragon all the way to the far extremity of the lake. But this great red one, when, feeling himself expelled, bellowed, launched an attack on the white, pushing the same backwards. Then, while they were fighting each other in their fashion, the king ordered Merlinus Ambrosius to say what the battle of the dragons portended. Then that personage, bursting into tears, drew into his lungs the spirit of prophecy & said: [3]

. . .

[3] Geoffrey wanted no break here but only a period after "said." For the purpose of studying the prophecy, we will set each

126

"Woe to the red dragon for his extermination comes fast.

"The white dragon shall inhabit his caverns, for he is the Saxons whom you have invited.

"The red dragon in truth signifies the British tribes, who will be oppressed by the white.

"And so his mountains and his valleys shall be levelled & the rivers in the valleys shall flow bloody.

"The practice of religion shall decline & the ruination of churches shall spread.

"Finally the one who was vanquished shall rise again and resist the barbarism of the outsiders.

"Moreover, the boar of Cornwall shall send his aid and shall trample their necks under his feet.

"The isles of the ocean shall be given unto his rule & he shall possess the pastures of Gaul (Wales?)

"The dynasty of Romulus shall tremble at his power and its issue shall remain in doubt.

"He shall be celebrated upon the lips of peoples, & his deeds shall be as a nourishment for authors.

"Six of his descendants shall bear his scepter after him, & then shall arise the German worm."

·   ·   ·

prediction separately. We commence on Acton Griscom's page 385, 1.5: "Ve rubeo . . .

"The ocean-dwelling wolf shall finish off the great one whom the African groves shall accompany.

"Once more religion shall be destroyed & a transmutation of archbishoprics shall be made.

"The dignity of London shall adorn Canterbury & the seventh shepherd of York shall be sought in the kingdom of Brittany.[4]

"Meneuia[5] shall wear the pall of Caerleon, and a churchman of Ireland shall be dumbstruck on account of an infant growing in the womb.

"A rain of blood shall fall and a dire famine shall arm mortals.

"When these calamities overcome men, the red dragon shall grieve, but after his labors are done, shall he again grow strong.

"Then shall misfortune hasten upon the white dragon & the buildings on his estates [gardens] will be demolished.

• • •

[4] "Canterbury" seems correct, the Romans calling it "Durovernum" (Geoffrey spells it "doroberniam"); but this whole sentence still seems incorrect from what we know of twelfth-century politics. He gives "Brittany" as "in armorico regno," by which Stuart Piggott thought was meant "armonico," or North Wales.

[5] Saint David's in Wales.

"Seven bearing scepters shall be slain & one of them shall become a saint.

"The mothers' abdomens shall be cut open & their infants aborted.

"There shall be a great torturing of men so that their progeny may be reinstated.

"He who shall achieve this shall be known as a bronze man & through many eras upon his bronze horse he will safeguard London's gates.

"Thereafter the red dragon shall turn back into his own customs & shall labor to save himself.[6]

"A plague shall strike the populace, and shall decimate the tribes.

"The survivors shall abandon their native soil and sow foreign fields.

"The blessed king shall prepare a navy & shall be numbered twelfth in the vestibule of saints.

"The desolation of the kingdom shall be pitiable & the bare threshing floors shall re-grow into fruitful forests.

• • •

[6] "& in seipsum seriure," but the *Harlech* manuscript gives "seruire." It seems that this passage, especially the reference to the "bronze horse" means that Constantine, Arthur's ancestor, will safeguard the gates of Lothian (not London); for the man on the bronze horse, the equestrian statue of Marcus Aurelius in Rome, was thought then to have been a statue of Constantine and thus was spared destruction by the early Christians.

"Then the white dragon shall arise once more and invite the German daughter.

"Again our estate [garth or yard][7] will be filled full of foreign seed & the red dragon shall languish in the far corner of the pond.

"Thereafter shall the Germanic worm be crowned & the bronze prince shall be interred.

"A terminus has been imposed upon him which he cannot overstay.

"For a hundred fifty years he shall remain in unrest and subjection, but for three hundred shall he sit there.

"Then shall sweep upon him the north wind & shall tear out of his hands the flowers which zephyr [the west wind] fertilized.

"There will be gold work in the temple, but the sting of swords shall not cease.

"Barely shall the German dragon reach its caverns because vengeance for its treason will overtake it.

"It will grow strong for a while but a plague in Neustria[8] will decimate it.

∙　∙　∙

[7] Merlin uses the word "ortulus," which the translators call "little garden," and it makes no sense. Merlin is not referring to a garden plot before a row house in London. He implies an ecclesiastical domain: "enclosure," "womb," and therefore monastery. Arthur had Merlin make gold work for him: statues of gold and silver.

[8] Geoffrey consistently uses—and his other manuscript copiers follow him—the word "Neustria," that is, "neustrie." There

"For a people in wood and iron tunics will come, who will exact vengeance for his villainy.

"It shall restore the mansions of the original inhabitants & the ruination of the alien folk shall be visible.

"The seed of the white dragon shall be scraped from our barnyards [garths] & the remainder of his generation shall be wiped out.

"They shall bear the yoke of perpetual servitude, and they shall wound their own mother [earth] with spades and ploughs.

"Two dragons shall succeed them of whom the one shall be suffocated by invidious envy, and the other shall remain hidden under the shadow of a name.

"The lion justificer shall succeed them, at whose roaring the towers of Gaul & the insular dragons shall tremble.

"In his days gold shall be extorted from the lily and the nettle & silver shall drip from the hooves of the lowing herd.

•   •   •

is no reason for his translators Sebastian Evans and Lewis Thorpe to have translated "Neustria" as "Normandy," which denies Merlin authorship of this *Prophecy* since the Normans invaded northwestern France hundreds of years *after Merlin's death*. "Neustria" appears in maps of Europe and the Roman Empire in the years 533–600, or within Merlin's lifetime. Then it included parts of what *much later* became Brittany and Normandy.

"Sheep shall be clad in hides of many colors & their outer garments signal what wolves are inside.[9]

"The feet of dogs shall be truncated; the wild animals shall have peace; humans shall learn to beg for their lives.

"The round of commerce shall be halved, that half rounded.

"The hunger of the hawk shall be dulled & the teeth of wolves, blunted.

"The cubs of the lioness shall be metamorphosed into deep water fishes & his eagle shall nest on Mt. Arauius.[10]

.   .   .

[9] The text says: "they that go crisped and curled," and I have decided Merlin means "sheep." "What is inside," or "exteriora" I have taken to mean "wolves." This seems an allusion to pagan priests.

[10] Unidentified. Other translators give *Aravius* or *Aravia*. The Latin is in the accusative: "Arauium." The reference is not biblical, neither to Mt. Abarim in Palestine, nor to Mt. Ararat in Armenia. Therefore, it seems to refer to a *dunn*, a Celtic fortress, that would have been no longer inhabited as a result of this war, and where the eagle could then nest safely. But we shall meet it again and finally recognize it as Mt. Snowdon in North Wales.

· · · · · · ·

III

THE CELTIC REALM

· · · · · · ·

NORTH WALES SOUTH WALES
SCOTLAND IRELAND
CORNWALL BRITTANY

· · · · · · ·

"North Wales [Gwynedd] shall be red with mother's blood & six brothers shall slaughter the line of Corineus.[11]

"The island shall be wet with tears at night because of which all shall be provoked to all deeds.

"Their descendants shall climb up to fly over the lofty summits, but public favor of these new men shall be disappointing.

"Our patriotism shall scorn the man owning land from the pagans, until he adopts the habits of his ancestors.

"Then, girded with wild boar's teeth, he will climb over peaks of the mountains and the shadow of the helmeted man.[12]

· · ·

[11] The *Bern* manuscript gives "corrinei," and this chief's name is well known from Geoffrey's *Historia*.

[12] The previous translators had thought: (1) Evans: "The shadow of him that weareth a helmet," and (2) Thorpe: "the Helmeted Man." I believe with Thorpe that Merlin

"Albania [Scotland] shall become angry & having mustered her clans ["collateralibus," or "colleteralibus"] shall devote herself to spilling blood.

"A bit which shall be cast in the Breton gulf[13] shall be put in her jaws.

"The eagle of the broken treaty shall gild it & shall be happy in his third nesting.

"The roaring cubs shall stand watch & when the forests have been passed shall come hunting inside the walls of the citadels.

"They shall make not a little slaughter among their foes & shall cut off the bulls' tongues.

"They shall load with chains the necks of the bellowers & renew the days of their ancestors.

"Thereafter from the first to the fourth, the fourth to the third, the third to the second the thumb shall be rolled in oil.

•   •   •

here is indicating a well-known peak, perhaps like the tallest of the triple Eildon Hills, the Roman *Trimontium* where Uther Pendragon died, or which he could not ascend in his litter. It would seem that it designates even more probably a well-known Celtic *dunn*, whose clan chieftain (Mars) was called "The Helmet," as King Arthur was called "The Grizzly."

[13] Now the *Golfe de St.-Malo* (Armorica), between Normandy on the north and Brittany on the south. Within this gulf are the Channel Islands, unless Merlin is referring to Colwyn Bay to the east of Great Orme's Head, in *Armonica* (North Wales). Thus, Breton-Briton?

134

"The sixth shall tear down the walls of Ireland & level its forests into a plain.

"He shall reduce the holdings into one & shall be crowned with the head of the lion, i.e., he shall be crowned King of Scotland.

"His beginning shall bow to an unstable following, but his end shall fly to the heights.

"For he shall restore the seats of the saints throughout their native lands & he shall establish pastors in suitable communities.

"He shall robe two cities in the pallia [of archbishops] & he shall endow the virgins [nuns] with virgins' rewards.

"Thus, he shall deserve well the favor of the [Roman] Jupiter and shall be placed among the saints.

"From him will step forth a lynx penetrating all things, which will threaten the ruin of his own people.[14]

"For through this ruin Neustria shall lose both islands and shall be despoiled of her pristine honor.

"Then [our] citizens shall be returned into the island [of Britain], for a tearing apart among those foreigners shall arise.

• • •

[14] Thorpe translates "a She-lynx" where Merlin said "linx" (lynx), a common clan totem. It is true that the Greek word "lynx" (a bobcat) is usually feminine, but it also occurs as masculine, specifically in the Latin of the poet Horace. Merlin gives Thorpe no reason to think specifically here of a famous or notorious woman; the lynx is the totem of a northern Pictish clan near Inverness.

"A white-haired old man on a white horse shall divert the river of Periro [15] & with his white divining rod shall measure out a mill upon it.

"Cadwallader [or Galahad] shall call Conan [Duke Conan of Brittany] and shall receive Albania [Scotland] into the confederacy.

"Then there shall be a massacre of the foreigners; then shall the rivers run blood.

"Then the mountains of Brittany [16] shall burst and it shall be crowned with the diadem of Brutus.

"Wales [Cambria] shall be filled with joy & the oaks of Cornwall [cornubie] shall leaf out.

"The island shall be called Britain from the name of Brutus & the swearing of the oaths of the foreigners shall be abolished.

"A warlike boar [Pict] will proceed from Conan who will cut his teeth on the oak groves inside Gaul.

"For he will cut down only the full-grown oaks and leave protection for the young trees.

"The Arabs and Africans shall tremble for he shall extend the onrush of his march into farthest Spain.

• • •

[15] Or River Periron, as Evans and Thorpe decided.

[16] He probably meant "Britain." Brutus founded "Britain," as we shall soon learn, and as Geoffrey of Monmouth said in his *Historia* I, 16. There are no mountains in Brittany, but there are high mountains in Wales, Cambria, and Scotland.

"A ram from the Venerean Camp shall follow, having golden horns and a silver beard, and shall blow such a fog from its nostrils as shall cast a shadow over the whole island, however wide.

"Peace there shall be in his time & harvests shall be multiplied.

"Women shall glide like snakes & all their steps shall be filled with pride.

"The camps of Venus shall be renovated nor shall the arrows of Cupid cease to wound.

"The fountain of healing water[17] shall be turned into blood & two kings shall fight in single combat at the ford of the scepter.[18]

"All the soil will be fertile, and humanity will fornicate without ceasing.

"Three generations will see all this, until the kings buried in the city of the Londons.[19]

•   •   •

[17] We have a choice: *ague* = water in the *Harlech* manuscript, or Amne(?) = Anne(?).

[18] Evans and Thorpe called it "ford of the staff," or "Ford of the Staff." They shall fight "propter leenam," which the translators think should mean "for (for the sake of) the Lioness." If there were a Latin feminine word for lioness, the accusative would still be "leonem." The whole sentence is unclear. The combat may be between Lancelot and Tristan, which Merlin elsewhere predicted.

[19] "lundoniarum," or "londoniarum ": Merlin may have meant "Lothians" and not "Londons," Scotland and not England.

"Famine will return again, death on a large scale & citizens will mourn the desolation of their citadels.

"The boar of commerce shall come over them again, and he will call back the herds from their last pasture.

"His breast shall be food for the hungry & his tongue shall give drink to the thirsty.

"From his mouth shall issue rivers which will water the dry throats of man.

"Next a tree will be grown on the tower of the Londons (Lothians), which will shade, content with only three branches, the whole surface of the island with the breadth of its leaves.

"Against this shall come its enemy the north wind & moreover it will tear off its third branch with a great blast.

"Truly the last two remaining branches will fill up the extent of the torn limb until one annihilates the other by the multitudinousness of its foliage.

"Finally it will occupy the place of the other two branches & will sustain the migratory birds from foreign parts.

"It shall be considered harmful to native birds, for by fear of its shadow they shall lose their freedom of flight.

"A wicked ass shall follow, swift to attack the goldsmiths [bankers], but slow to curb the greed of the wolves.

"In these days oaks shall burn in the forest depths & their acorns shall be born on the branches of the lindens.

"The Severn [20] sea shall flow through seven channels & the Wye shall boil for seven months.

"Fishes shall die from this heat & serpents shall be born from them.

"The baths of Bath [21] shall grow icy cold & their salubrious waters shall cause death.

"London shall weep for twenty thousand dead & the Thames shall be turned into blood.

"The cowled [22] shall be called forth to the nuptials & their clamor shall be heard on the Alps."

• • •

[20] "Severn" in Geoffrey has replaced "Solway."

[21] "badonis" for Bath, but Mt. Badon is also a Celtic dunn, Dumbarton on the Clyde River, near Glasgow.

[22] The Latin word for "monks" which Merlin uses here, "cucullati," shortened to "cuculli" appears in the late verse prophecies attributed to Merlin that give the Latin numerals for 1428, the year that Joan of Arc, the Celtic maiden from Gaul ("puella gallica") was to appear out of her forests in what was in Merlin's day still eastern Gaul.

. . . .

IV

. . . .

THE CALL
TO ARMS

. . . . . .

"Three springs of water will burst forth at Guintonia
[Edinburgh],[23] the channels of which shall divide the
island into three parts. He who drinks the one shall en-
joy a lengthy life, nor be burdened with any heavy ill-
ness. He who drinks of the other shall die of continuous
hunger & the pallor and horror of it shall sit upon his
face. He who drinks of the third shall tumble down into
sudden death, nor shall his body be in condition to
undergo entombment.

"Those who wish to escape such a hideous fate will
try to hide this third water with various coverings.
Whatever structure is placed above it, however, will take
on another body. For if thrown over it earth will revert
to stones, stones to liquid, wood to ashes, ash to water.

"To this spot a damsel from the white grove[24] to

. . .

[23] Usually translated as "Winchester" in southern England.

[24] "canuti nemoris," and not the later Danish King Canute.

140

take care of healing. After she shall have tried her arts, by her breath alone, she shall dry up the injurious springs. Then as soon as she shall have refreshed herself with the healing water, she shall bear in her right hand the Caledonian Forest, and truly in her left hand the warrior walls of Lothian. Wherever she shall set her feet down, her footsteps will burn with sulphur and smoke with two flames.

"The fumes shall excite the Ruteni [in southern Gaul] and make heat for those who live under the sea. She herself shall shed tears for those suffering, & she will fill the island with horrid screaming.

"The stag with ten branches shall slay her, four of his antlers crowned in gold. The other six shall be turned into the horns of wild oxen, which shall arouse the three islands of Britain with their bellowing. The Danean[25] grove shall become aroused & bursting out with a human voice will shout:

> Advance, Wales & add Cornwall to thy side
> & tell Winchester:
>
> The earth shall swallow thee!
> Transfer the shepherd's see
> where the ships come to land
> & let the rest of your limbs
> follow your head!

•   •   •

[25] Evans took "daneum nemus" to be the Forest of Dean in southern England, and Thorpe disagreed, calling it "Daneian forest" without identification. In my opinion this refers to Ireland, originally settled by the *Tuatha De Danann*, or gods of the Gaels. The maiden herself could be the goddess Dana, or else Erin.

'For the day draws near when citizens who have per-
jured themselves shall perish for their crimes.

"The whiteness of wools has hurt thee, Wales, and
even more so the diversity of their colors.[26] Woe to a
perjured people, because of whom their celebrated city
shall crumble into ruins.[27]

"The ships shall rejoice at so much expansion & one
[business center?] shall be made out of two. Our ancient
heritor whose endowment was loaded with fruit trees
["pomis"], rebuilt this city; towards the perfume of its
varied flowering orchards the winged creatures shall fly
back together.[28] He shall erect nearby a huge [archie-
piscopal] palace & a circumvallation with six hundred
towers. In consequence, London shall envy her and shall

•   •   •

[26] The *Harlech* manuscript omits these last two sentences, per-
haps because they refer directly to the quarrel with Rome
over the longed-for archbishopric for Wales. The arch-
bishop wears a pallium (Webster's: "a circular band of white
wool with pendants") and so did Saints Germanus and Lu-
pus, Gallic ambassadors from the Pope, who went to Wales
to chastise the Celtic Church. See "vestments" as illus-
trated, in Webster's.

[27] Caerleon-on-Usk (Wye River) where Geoffrey says King
Arthur was crowned, which makes it in Welsh eyes of the
twelfth century a celebrated city ("urbs inclita"). It was also
a Roman harbor.

[28] Acton Griscom, p. 391, l. 16: "Reedificauit eam hericius
. . ."; Evans translation: "The Hedgehog that is loaded
with apples . . ."; Thorpe: "A Hedgehog loaded with ap-
ples. . . ." Evans and Thorpe translate *hericius* as hedgehog
probably because the genus *Erinaceus* names this Old World

increase her own walls threefold. The Thames River shall encircle her on all sides & the rumor of this construction shall cross the Alps. The heritor shall conceal his fruit trees inside her [walls] and shall find ways and means to excavate tunnels.

"In that celebrated time stones shall speak & the sea men who navigate from here to Gaul shall withdraw into a narrow channel. A man will be heard from one shore to another & the island soil will be extended outwards. Those things hidden under the sea shall be revealed & Gaul shall tremble for fear.' "

. . .

mammal. My Latin etymological dictionaries persuade me that *hericius* is a technical term used only in church Latin, as by Saint Irenaeus, a Greek Father (c. 125–c. 202), in legal land transactions, as *heres, heredito, heredifico* (inheritor, inherit). Dictionaries also suggest similar usage of these roots in ancient Scots law.

V

A Fable

"After this from the Calaterian [Caledonian?] Forest shall proceed a heron, which shall fly around the island over a period of two years.[29] By her nightly cries she shall assemble the birds of the air & all winged creatures ally to herself. On the cultivated fields of mortals they shall swoop down & devour all sorts of harvests. A famine among the peoples shall ensue, and moreover a horrible epidemic shall follow that famine. But when so great a disaster shall have ceased, that detestable bird shall fly

[29] The generally pseudo-Merlin prophecy in the Latin poem *Vita Merlini* reaches an authentic note and high point in the prophecy Merlin makes concerning birds:

Mox Merlinus eis, 'Volucres, ut cetera plura, naturia ditavit   *v.* 1298
conditor orbis.

(The Lord God gave to birds, as to many other creatures, their own special nature.)

up to the "galabes" valley, [30] and more than that, shall lift it up into a lofty mountain. On the summit of this same mountain she shall plant an oak tree, and then moreover shall build her nest inside its branches. Three eggs shall be procreated in the nest from which eggs a fox & a wolf & a bear shall emerge. The fox shall eat her mother and wear an ass's head. When she has put on this disguise, she shall terrify her brothers, and drive them in flight into Neustria. But these same shall awaken the toothy boar in that wood & brought back in a ship they shall contend with the fox. Who, when the battle commences, shall feign to be defunct & shall move the boar to pity for herself. Soon she shall go look at her eyes & face. But she, not oblivious at all of her old cunning, will bite on his left foot and rip the whole foot out of his body. And when she has leaped upon him, then she shall tear off his right ear & his tail & go hide in the caverns of the mountains. The boar who has been tricked will therefore demand that the wolf and the bear restore his lost parts. Who, when they espouse his cause, promise him two feet & two ears & a tail & from these they will make him pig's parts. He agrees and will await the promised restoration. Meanwhile the fox shall de-

· · ·

What Merlin says here about the heron (sign of rainy weather) differs completely (v. 1341ff.). See Basil Clarke's *Life of Merlin* (Cardiff, 1973). We should also note that the heron is a "clean" bird and mentioned in Deuteronomy, while those birds cited by Merlin in this pseudo-prophecy are for the most part considered "unclean" by the Old Testament writers.

[30] Unclear, but we shall meet the word again soon.

scend from the mountains & change herself into a wolf and pretending as if she was about to enter into a colloquium with the boar, she will approach warmly & will devour all of him. Thereupon she will transform herself into a boar & pretending as if she were without her parts, she will await her twin brothers ["germanos"]. However, & after they shall have brought themselves there, with a swift tooth she shall slay them, and what is more, she shall be crowned with the head of the lion.

"In her days there shall be born a serpent that shall threaten the death of all mortals. He shall encircle London with his coils & shall devour all those who are passing by. The mountain ox shall put on the head of a wolf and shall whiten his teeth in a workshop on the Severn. He shall make a federation for himself of shepherds from Scotland & Wales, who shall drink dry the Thames River between them."

VI

WAR

"The ass shall call the heavily bearded goat & shall change shapes with him. The mountain bull shall consequently become furious & shall stab them both with his horn. Once it shall have vented its cruelty upon them, it shall gulp them flesh & bones, but it will be cremated on the summit of (Mt.) Urian. The ashes of his funeral pyre shall be transformed into swans which shall swim as well upon dry land as upon the river. They shall gulp down [even to] the fishes within the fishes and the men within men. When old age shall truly have crept upon them, they shall be turned into underwater wolves[31] and there shall they plot their underwater stratagems. They shall sink navies & shall amass no small amount of silver.

"Once more the Thames River shall commence flowing, having collected its tributaries, it shall proceed

[31] The handwritings here are unclear: *lupos* (wolves), *luces* (lights), or *duces* (leaders).

to overflow its banks. It shall smother neighboring city states, overturn mountains in its way. It will make use of the water sources in Wales; [32] they are replete with trickery and prodigality. From this shall arise rebellions provoking the Venedotians [North Welsh] to battles. The oaks of the groves shall converse & fight with the rocks of the Gewissi [Gwent in Wales]. A crow will fly over there & with a kite bird shall devour the bodies of those who have perished. Above the walls of the Chesters Fort [on Hadrian's Wall] an owl will build his nest & in her nest an ass will be hatched. A serpent in Malvern will foster him & make him expert in many stratagems. Having assumed the diadem, this ass will transcend the lofty & with his horrid braying will terrify people.

"In his days the mountains [33] will topple & the provinces will be stripped of their forests.

"For there shall come along a fire-breathing worm which will burn up the trees as he blows on them. There shall step out of him seven lions crowned with the heads of goats. By the stink from their nostrils they shall corrupt virgins & they shall turn their own wives into com-

• • •

[32] See Note 30 for the unidentified "galabes," which here is repeated with the alternate spellings we needed for identification: "galahes," and the correction "galaes" (from the *Harlech* manuscript again): "galaes" = "Wales" (g and w are often interchangeable).

[33] Unidentified unless it means Pictish, or the central range of Scotland. Other translators spell it "Pachaian" in English.

148

mon property. The father will not know his own son because they live in common like brutish beasts. But a giant of iniquity shall tower over them, who shall cow men universally by means of his piercing eyes. The dragon of the Chesterholm Fort [on Hadrian's Wall] shall rush forth against him & attempt to exterminate him. After the battle is fought, however, the dragon shall have been overcome & he shall be oppressed by the evil of his conqueror.

"For he shall mount upon the dragon & when he has taken off his clothing, he shall sit naked upon him. The dragon shall carry him up into the heavens; with his tail held erect, he shall beat him on his naked body. When his strength has come again, the giant shall pierce the dragon through the throat with his sword. The dragon shall be caught, however, under the coils of his own tail and shall die of poison.

"The boar of Totnes [*totonesius*] shall follow that great one & shall oppress people with hateful tyranny. Chesters Fort [on Hadrian's Wall] shall send forth a lion which in diverse skirmishes shall harass the raging boar. He shall tread him under foot, and frighten him with his yawning jaws.

"Then finally the lion will feud with the kingdom & climb upon the backs of the noblemen. A bull shall come in the midst of the turmoil & shall strike the lion on his right foot. He shall expel him throughout the corners of the kingdom, but he shall smash his horns against the walls of the Welsh Fort Exonia [*exonie* = Wye River].

"The fox from the Irish Fort of the Dark Bailey [*caerdubali*] shall conquer the lion & chew him all up, with her teeth.

"The adder of Linden Colony [*lindocolinus*] shall coil about her and shall signal his presence to many dragons by his horrible hissing.

"Then dragons will combat & the one will tear the other to pieces.

"A winged dragon will best one lacking wings & will stick his poisonous claws in the other's cheeks.

"Others congregate around the battle & one of them will kill another one.

"A fifth will replace the slain & will break into pieces the rest by means of various wiles. He will climb on the back of one & separate his head from his body. When he has put off his clothes he will climb upon another & seize its tail in his right and left claws. Naked he will overcome him when he shall do nothing clothed. He shall torment the rest from the rear & drive them before him all around the kingdom.

"Afterwards a roaring lion shall intervene, horrifying all by its monstrous cruelty. He shall reduce fifteen holdings into one & alone shall possess the people [therein].

"A giant shall shine in snowy white; he shall beget a purely white people.

"The princes shall grow enervated with self-gratification & their subjects[34] shall be changed into overgrown animals.

* * *

[34] "& subditi" is repeated = "and their subjects."

"A lion shall be born among them, turgid with human blood. A reaper of his shall be placed in the crops, who, while he shall labor, shall be troubled in his brain by that monster."

VII

The Last
Battle

"A charioteer from "York" [or Stirling in Scotland] shall quell them; having driven off the lord, he shall mount the vehicle, which he shall drive. Having unsheathed his sword he shall menace the east & he shall fill up the ruts of his wheels with blood. Next he shall become a fish in the sea, who, called back by the hiss of a serpent, shall mate with it. From this union shall be born three bellowing bulls, who, having consumed the grass in the meadows, shall be turned into trees. The first shall wield a whip made of vipers & shall turn his back upon the second born. He [in turn] shall try to seize the whip from him, but it shall be carried away by the third born. They shall turn their faces away from each other until they shall have tossed away the poisoned goblet.

"His successor shall be a harvester from Scotland on whose back a snake [whip?] shall hang. This one shall work at turning over the soil so that his fatherland shall grow white with the harvest. The snake shall work at spraying its venom so that the sprouts shall never ripen into a harvest. The people shall be decimated by a fatal slaughter & the walls of the cities shall be desolate. The city of Claudius [Chesters Fort on Hadrian's Wall][35] shall be given assistance, which shall introduce the foster daughter of [the bull with] the whip. For she shall bring a cup of truce[36] & the island shall quickly be renewed.

"Thereafter two males shall hold the scepter, in whose reigns the horned dragon shall govern. The first shall arrive in iron & he shall be mounted upon a flying serpent. His body stark naked, he shall sit upon its back, and grasp its tail with his right hand. The seas shall rise up at the sound of its battle cry & shall instill fear into the second. And so the latter will ally himself to the lion, but as soon as a quarrel comes between them, they too shall war. They shall succumb each one after many wounds, but the beastliness of the beastly one shall triumph.

"Another shall come then with a harp and a tympanum[37] & shall soothe the lion's cruelty. The na-

·   ·   ·

[35] Formerly thrice translated as "Gloucester," in England.

[36] Literally a "dish of medicine."

[37] The manuscript reads "tympano," which, according to musicologist J. A. Milliman, most likely referred to the Greek "tympanon" or Latin "tympanum," a handheld frame drum of ancient Rome that originated in ancient Greece and would have come to Wales through the Roman occupation of that country during the Dark Ages. Later the word is applied to kettledrums. Also, the "harp" of this time was probably a triangular lap harp whose strings varied in number. It is

tions within the kingdom shall be pacified & they shall call for the lion & call for the cup. When his citadel has been settled, he shall turn to [other] considerations, but he shall send palm branches into Scotland.[38] The ensign-bearing wolf shall lead the companies & shall encircle Dumnonia [Rhinns of Galloway] with his tail.[39]

"Therefore the northern provinces shall be saddened & will unlock the Eucharistic host of the temples.[40] A

. . .

now thought that the Irish cruit, a triangular psaltery mentioned in literary sources from the 7th to the 14th centuries, existed at the same time; therefore, the instrument mentioned here could have been either the lap harp or cruit. Geoffrey of Monmouth may not have known the instruments Merlin referred to and therefore may have used later medieval equivalents whose "ancient sources" were probably based on scripture, that is, the timbrel and harp (Psalm 150, for example).

[38] War parties in Scotland traditionally bore or wore palm fronds.

[39] This is Cornwall inside Scotland, of course, or what was later called the "Rhinns of Galloway." There were originally three areas named by the Greek geographies as Cornwall (Dumnonia): Brittany in France, Cornwall in southwestern England, and our Cornwall here, or the promontory of southwestern Scotland, that is, the north shore of the Solway Firth. The next sentence will send us to the Severn estuary in southwestern England, but we are still near the Solway in Scotland.

[40] Formerly translated: "throw open the gates of the temples." The Latin *hostia* originally meant sacrificial victims and later came to mean "host."

154

soldier in a war chariot shall oppose him, who shall change that people into the boar. Thereafter the boar shall lay waste provinces, but he shall hide his head in the deeps of the Solway Firth. Someone shall enfold the lion's head with a wreath of grapes, the blaze of gold so strong it shall blind those present. Silver shall glow all about & shall arouse envy among the diverse [personages wearing] torques [*torcularia*]. Those mortal men shall become drunk with wine and having put the sky behind them shall look down on the ground."

VIII

The Cosmic Conclusion

"The stars shall turn their faces away from them & shall quit their usual tracks across the sky.

"In the wrath of the stars crops shall wither & the rain from the vault of heaven shall be withheld.

"Roots and branches shall exchange places & the novelty of this shall seem a miracle.

"The shining sun shall dim under the amber of Mercury & this shall be visible to those who see it. The planet Mercury from Arcadia shall change its shield & the helmet of Mars shall call to Venus. The helmet of Mars shall cast its shadow; the fury of Mercury shall pass the bounds. Iron Orion shall draw his naked sword. Oceanic Apollo shall whip up the clouds. Jupiter shall emerge from his established bounds & Venus shall abandon her statutory tracks. The star of Saturn shall rush forth in lead-colored [rain?] & with a crooked sickle shall kill mortals. The twice six houses of the stars shall weep that their hosts jump their tracks. The twins shall depart from their usual embrace & shall call the bowl to the water-bearer. The scales of Libra shall swing free until Aries shall place his crooked horns under the balance. The tail of Scorpio shall ferment lightning & Cancer shall contend with the sun. Virgo shall rise on the back of Sagittarius & shall forget her virginal flowers.

The chariot of the moon shall disturb the Zodiac & the Pleiades shall burst into tears. None shall return to their appointed course, but Adriana[41] behind a closed door shall seek refuge in her causeways. At a stroke of the wand the winds shall rush forth & the dust of our forefathers[42] shall blow on us again.

The winds shall collide with a dire thunderclap & their blast shall echo among the stars."

•   •   •

[41] Probably Ariadne, or the Northern Crown.

[42] The texts are garbled: *uentu*, or *ventorum*, or *ueterum*. I have chosen the last or the *Bern* manuscript reading.

THE
WARRIOR

Nobeles the clerk Merlyn sais certeyn, That Bretons at the last salle haf this land agayne, . . .

(The noble cleric Merlin says: "For [it is] certain That Britons at the last shall have this land again, . . .)*

Chronicle
Peter de Langtoft and Robert of Brunne,
edited by Thomas Hearne, 1725.
Vol. I, Chap. XXII, p. 7.

· · · · · · ·

Merlin's Prophecy foreshadows the last desperate wars that peaked in his lifetime and continued during the centuries that Saxons and Scots, Picts and Welshmen fought over borders and territories. Reading Merlin, one can hardly escape recalling the better known eras of defeats for Wales, as when "Glorious Athelstan" (925–940) established forever the border of the Welsh at the Wye River and expelled all Welsh people from Exeter, and when Harold son of Godwine (d. 1053) ordered every Welshman found east of the border, as established by Offa's Dyke, to have his right hand cut off. Offa had established the Kingdom of Mercia south of the Humber River in the eighth century. After considering three other major battles in which Merlin participated personally, it should be possible to visualize the geography for northern and western Britain as he knew it. It has long been known that all the names of the rivers of Britain are Celtic, as well as most of the other place names.

The primary text up to now for considering the history of the late fifth and early sixth centuries is Geoffrey of Monmouth's *History of the Kings of Britain.* However, in the case of the three or four last battles, which are given in some greater than usual detail in another group of texts, Geoffrey has been thought to have remained silent.

One always suspects, in dealing with history of the age, that one will eventually fall into a dark hole, and it probably is here. Thus far, the efforts of scholars have only drawn the veils of concealment tighter and tighter, thereby deepening the mystery surrounding Merlin.

KING ARTHUR'S
BATTLEGROUND:
BORDERS (Scotland)

The three major texts that offer the benefit not only of three
authors, or three groups of authors, but also the great benefit of
various editors for each text over the last two hundred years,
are as follows:

1. The *Prose Lancelot* in Old French (also called the "Vulgate"), as
   edited here by Paulin Paris in 5 volumes (Paris, 1868–1877),
   specifically Vol. 2, "L'Estoire de Merlin" ("Merlin's His-
   tory/Story");

2. *Merlin*, a Middle-English Metrical Version of a French Ro-
   mance (about 1450), by Henry Lovelich (Louelich the Skin-

ner), edited by Ernst A. Kock from the unique manuscript called *Cambridge* 80, EETS in three parts, Extra Series No. XCIII (1904–1913). The *Cambridge* 80 manuscript ends at v. 27, 852;

3. *Of Arthour and of Merlin*, 2 volumes, EETS (London, etc., 1973 and 1979), edited by O. D. Macrae-Gibson. Vol. I = text; Vol II = notes. Six manuscripts are collated here, or this is a diplomatic text that has translated and added to the *Prose Lancelot* of about 1330. The primary and best text is the *Auchinleck* manuscript, in the National Library of Scotland.

It is both remarkable and gratifying to have three texts—*Prose Lancelot, Cambridge* 80, and *Auchinleck*—upon which scholars for several hundred years have spent their lives, and with such a trove it is easy to learn more about both Merlin and Arthur.

The first text narrates three major battles following King Arthur's coronation, explaining that six rebel kings, who added several allies to their number as they prepared for war, have repudiated King Arthur because at his coronation ceremony no ascertainment of his right to the throne was made. Merlin proceeds after the fact to ascertain this right, and he even brings forth witnesses. Afterward, he rushes off into "Northumberland" to enlist two major kings: Ban and Bors. These kings are brothers occupying adjoining kingdoms. The former is King Ban of Benoïc, seemingly the northern Berwick, near Berwick Law, on the south shore of the Firth of Forth where the coastline turns south as it meets the North Sea. King Ban will sire the greatest Arthurian hero, Lancelot of the Lake.

Battle 1 is the siege of Carlisle, won when Merlin sets the hostile kings' tents on fire. The *Cambridge* 80 manuscript closely follows the misadventures of these "Syxe Kynges" who abandon their goods and possessions and "fly" from King Arthur and Merlin. The *Auchinleck* manuscript also agrees that six British kings vigorously opposed the coronation, that they besieged "Cardoil"

(vv. 3201–3371), that Merlin sent wild fire into their tents (v. 3203) and that there was offered a feast in London (*Londonesia* once more probably mistranslated for Lothian, or Edinburgh), at which Merlin delivered an oration beginning, "Listen to me now . . ." (v. 3403).

Eleven kings and dukes by now, he said, have conspired to kill King Arthur, and among the conspirators is King Loth (Gawain's father). Merlin will send word, he says, into "Lesser Britain," to two kings, Ban and Bohort (Bors), who were formerly sworn to Uther Pendragon, saying that Uther has died and that they should now pledge allegiance to his son. At once, all should set out for a parliament and pledge support to Arthur.

Turning to the king, Merlin continues: "They will come soon, I think, and help thee against King Loth" (vv. 3425–3426). The "clerk" Merlin chooses two noble messengers and sends them off with his Godspeed, "Now heaven help you for love of Jesus!"

Battle 2, says the *Prose Lancelot*, takes place at the "meadow" of "Bredigan," which extends near Merlin's Font or Fountain of "Bellenton," and this location, furthermore, is situated in western Northumberland, *on the frontiers of Scotland.* Or the "meadow" was called "Broceliande," near Merlin's Stone ("Perron"). [1]

The *Cambridge 80* manuscript comes to the rescue here, repeating the original Celtic place name "Bredigan," which is reassuring, but adding reasonably that it is five days forced march from Berwick, which is already sending reinforcements post haste. King Arthur meanwhile has captured the allies' supplies. Merlin bears King Ban's ring as he asks for more men. Now while the Saxon foes are starving, Merlin escorts reinforcements by night

• • •

The author of the *French Grail* manuscript called the *Grand-Saint-Graal*, knew "Broceliande" was not French meaning "Brushy Swamp," and boldly called it Celtic in phonetics and English in meaning: "Brookland."

to the seashore. The return trip takes him five days since Berwick and Bredigan lie some one hundred fifty miles apart. (The country is not called *Bretagne,* but "Britain," from its founder Brutus, who came from Troy. They also call it "Blue Britain," adds an enquiring author, because there was once a plague there that turned all their sorrowing hearts black-and-blue.)

The Arthurian forces finally see an aged man approaching. Around his waist he wears a girdle of game birds, which he offers to sell to King Arthur. It was Merlin. He can assume, "by necromancy," six or seven shapes, adds our author; because he has so many foes, he must use multiple disguises. [2]

Meanwhile, the defeated foes continue to starve, sorrow, and thirst. King Arthur's sister (here called Blasine) sends her son as a recruit. King Loth's wife, called now a "stepsister" of Arthur, also sends her oldest son, whose name is Gawain. She asks that Gawain reconcile King Arthur and her husband (vv. 11,473–11,789); Blasine asks her son Galathin to do the same, or to win over his father King Nanters of Garlot.

The *Auchinleck* manuscript lists eleven rebellious sub-kings who have fought King Arthur and Merlin (vv. 3725–3770):

1. King Clarion of Northumberland,

2. King Brangore of Strangore,

3. King Cradelman of North Wales,

4. The King of a Hundred Knights,

5. King Loth of Leonis (Lothian) and Dorkaine (the citadel of Orcanie),

6. King Carodas of the Round Table,

. . .

[2] Malory thought these game birds might have been geese, but David Palladini says that is hardly likely: "Geese would have been too large."

7. King Nanters of Garlot,

8. King Urian (Urien),

9. King Yder,

10. King Anguisaunt of Scotland, and

11. Duke Estas of Cambernic.

Merlin instructs Arthur specifically, notes the editor (note to v. 3859), that King Ban and his brother will take their armies quietly behind the forest so that they can attack the enemies from behind while Arthur storms them from the front.

The various scribes, revisors, and translators who together have given us the *Auchinleck* manuscript worried about the site of this second battle, going so far as to suggest: Rokingham? Brekenham? They suggest that "Borceliande" is not only Merlin's Fountain, his special health spa, but also a new construction of some sort, a "neue werke."

The third battle again unfortunately fails to produce a clear winner. What seemed a short war has by now, says the *Prose Lancelot*, gone from bad to worse because of a new Saxon invasion upon the east coast. It will develop into a "long war." King Rion (Urian) of Gorre, Ireland, with allies among the northmen, has now launched from the west a full-scale attack upon King Leodagan of Carmelide, whose daughter King Arthur had been advised by Merlin to wed.

Here, finally, is the background, otherwise lacking, of the Queen Guinevere story. King Rion is Arthur's oldest and most committed foe; he is this same King Urian of Gorre who refused to move in the procession at the coronations of King Arthur and Queen Guinevere. Guinevere had first been promised to King Urian.[3] Her territories must have been vast, for this war

* * *

[3] See Norma L. Goodrich, *King Arthur*, Part II, Chapter 5.

pits King Arthur against King Rion for possession of "Carme-
lide." This battle will be fought on the Field of Carmelide (Tar-
melide), confirms the *Cambridge* 80 manuscript, and the place
was "long shown." The translators all understood how important
it was to pin down the site: Carmelide (Tarmelide), Caroise
(Taroaise), or perhaps Carmalide. All Arthur's young bachelor
nephews take part. Merlin stops on his way to Carmelide to
visit a young lady who he has been told is the most beautiful
girl in the world. She lives near the kingdoms of King Ban and
Bors, in eastern Northumberland.

Merlin reaches Carmelide before the betrothal ceremonies
of King Arthur and Guinevere; but the lady, according to Geof-
frey of Monmouth, was already wed and crowned. On the day
after the Whitsuntide Feast the battle is joined, Merlin himself
bearing the banner and blowing on the war horn so hard that
he shook the forest for half a mile on every side. Then Merlin
raised a tempest with "a marvelous wind" that roared and gusted
like thunderclaps. Through all this wind he bore the *flaming* dragon
banner, which set the banners of the "heathens" afire with red
flames. Arthur followed Merlin's lead closely. The king engaged
Rion in a long single combat. As the enemy tried to escape,
Merlin sent flood waters along the plain, thus surrounding the
combatants. The issue was therefore not decided.

King Arthur and his warriors still aim for Merlin's flaming
banner through the mêlée and try again for a victory. When
they are needed, reinforcements are sent into combat by Mer-
lin's orders. One is left with the impression that Merlin has been
in charge not only of the elements but also of some of the ac-
tion on the field.

That night Gawain is elevated to High Constable, Merlin
shows Arthur a buried hoard, and the other young bachelors are
graciously received by the king. Then they hear that the Saxons
are threatening Berwick, and Merlin calls, "To arms!"

What else he may have said on that occasion is repeated by
James A. Murray among the *Prophecies* of Merlin found in Scot-

land centuries later, one of which is "specially directed to Berwick-on-Tweed, formerly the first of the four great burghs of Scotland:

> *'Though thou be subject to the Saxons, sorrow thou not,*
> *Thou shall be loosed at the last, believe thou in Christ!?'* "

Merlin proved very "worthy" in this battle, says the *Cambridge* 80 manuscript (v. 27,496ff.), showed much prowess, rode very strong of limb, stood of a stature surpassing long, "but Brown he was, an sclendre in growenge,/Thereto more heery [hairy] thane ony man lyvynge," gentle on his mother's side of the family.

When he bore his flaming dragon banner, which reddened the sky above them, the warriors took it as a sign of God's wrath. Merlin's chief foes generally fell weaponless and breathless to the ground after seemingly endless alterations of hoarse exultings and quiet despair. Not so, King Rion. The editors and translators at this point seem to look at each other in mystified astonishment, agreeing that King Rion seems incredibly to have survived even Carmelide.

The *Auchinleck* manuscript continues (from v. 2164–9938), having commenced a list of the forty-two "companions" who came to aid King Leodagan: Agrauel, Aigilin, Amandan, Antour (the foster father of Arthur), King Ban of Benoît, King Belias of "maiden castel" (that is, *maidan,* or mustering point), Blehartis, Bleheris (godson of Bohort), Bleoberus, King Bohort of Gaines, Bretel (Tintagel's cupbearer), Cologreuand, Canode, Claries, Craddoc(k), Cristofer of the "roche" north, and so on (vv. 3605ff. and 5353ff.). It then reiterates the story (vv. 5585–6430).

Four giants began the war by ravaging the countryside and by slaughtering the inhabitants up to the very gates of Carohaise. Merlin led the first charge against them. He rode before his company, carrying the pennant aloft, which had a small dragon on its tip, the dragon having a forked or barbed tail that streamed in the wind behind him. The dragon's tongue shot fire, and Merlin did a marvel by opening and closing the gates by himself:

> *With the banner dashed Merlins*[4] v. 5686
> *Among two thousand Saracens . . .*

Merlin performs the more ancient Roman duty, acting proudly as the dragon-bearer, *Draconarius.* He has already exhorted the forty-two bravest men to follow him:

> *So said Merlin, "Mine knightes free* v. 5917
> *Pricketh your steeds and follow me."*

King Arthur fought. King Ban fought. The losses were terrible. Other great warriors performed deeds of great note. Merlin then urged King Arthur on to an even better performance by showing him the lady spectators:

> *Guinevere sat on the citadel wall* v. 6375
> *And she was over her ladies all*
> *Of Arthur she sees the jousting of this*
> *On him she lay all the prize.*

Despite his enormous personal deeds of valor, King Rion is finally felled. He flees and seems to have escaped. He was that king who wore on his clothing the beards of those whom he had slain. He had also wanted King Arthur's beard as an ornament, and when he was again refused, he had again declared war.

Merlin's actions during these battles earned him such renown as a warrior that many still exclaim at the very mention

· · ·

[4] "Heathens," "Saxons," or "Saracens," it makes little difference to the epic poets whose hearts are full of ire. "Merlins" is the nominative, as in "Merlinus."

169

of his name: "Ah, Merlin!" It was he alone who swore a holy oath concerning Arthur's antecedents and birth (v. 3571) to maintain the royal line of Constantine. It was Merlin who personally organized Arthur's allies and who, at the risk of his own life, passed in and out of camps and battles, as well as friendly and foreign kingdoms, in order to recruit warriors, organize war bands, and enlist raw youths into companies under heroes such as Gawain. In every emergency Merlin strode to the podium to clarify the situation, to advise as to strategy, to calm nerves, and to instruct the unready. He taught King Ban how to plan his embassy to King Leodagan, whom Merlin desired to defend so that he could enlist his help. Merlin encouraged Arthur and Leodagan to agree to Guinevere's marriage—or to break her betrothal, if betrothal there was, with King Rion. Finally, Merlin did not hesitate to upbraid Gawain's three younger brothers for having turned tail and left him to fight alone. To them, Merlin spoke:

> Sure you be brave men, you be!　　　　　　　v. 7218
> Where were you going to during combat?
> In such as you there is little real hope
> Who your brother left among his foes
> While you three took to cover somewhere . . .
> By your fault he now may lie slain.
> No, I say! You lot aren't worth a pea!

By the same token, it is Merlin who chastises Gawain when that youth, now a full-fledged officer of the crown, neglected to rush out in defense of his mother Belisent. That lady had been kidnapped by King Taurus while she was traveling with her baby son Modred. King Taurus had wounded King Loth, whose men-at-arms all lie dead around him. Merlin seems here to be speaking in a very low key:

> Gawain, he said, verily　　　　　　　　　v. 8464
> Her name is said: Belisent.

170

Thou ought to amend her state
For thou sucked at her tit.

So Gawain took heed, defeated King Taurus after a fierce fight, and showed everyone that his love for his mother and his baby brother remained overwhelming (v. 8497ff.).

In addition to these deeds, Merlin bore messages over long distances, kept his tutor Blaise informed so that he could record the war for posterity, kept his finger on the nation's pulse, and constantly judged men in situations of national emergency. He also found time to recruit King Arthur's honor guard, all of whom pledged to die before the king himself came to blows. Always Merlin continued to prophecy a victory after the present trials.[5]

The author of *Huth-Merlin* recounts the end of the rebellion, although he is much less interested in war than in psychological drama. For this reason perhaps he caught the situation leading up to the three major battles of Carlisle, Bredigan, and Carmelide with an unmistakably droll wit: King Rion of North Wales (Norgalles) had sent word for Arthur's beard. After having already vanquished eleven kings, he now needs Arthur's beard, he claims, to use as the clasp of his cloak. When he hears of the demand, King Arthur bursts out laughing. He is still too young to have a beard.

The next thing King Arthur knows, King Rion is besieging Carlisle, to which reinforcements are rushed from Camelot (from the fortress of Stirling two days distant). Merlin reacts quickly, sending his master Blaise and his precious archives to safety in Camelot. Toward the end of this war, Merlin dispatches a war party to lie in ambush on a mountainside.

This final scene concerning King Rion's war is so vivid and memorable that it is rarely matched in today's literature. King Rion will ride along a mountain path with his escort. He will

•   •   •

[5] Zumthor always stressed Merlin's humanity, saying that his *Prophecy* expressed a providential and predetermined view of human history.

approach during the night and dressed in red will be easily recognizable. (Note that in the far north there are few hours of total darkness in midsummer, which is the campaign season.) The ambush succeeds as Merlin's men catch the invaders by complete surprise. The chosen heroes rush upon the mounted party, attempting to knock them from their horses. Most members of Rion's elite guard turn instinctively and succeed only in tumbling off the path and down the steep mountainside in their abrupt retreat. Out of forty, only twelve men and the charmed King Rion himself remain alive. The survivors are rounded up and taken prisoner, but spared when they submit on their own recognizance. They are ushered as prisoners into Arthur's presence and apparently released after honorable payment of the stipulated ransom, the swearing of oaths, and the promise of peace.

Thus, the rebellion fizzles out after the capture of the leader, King Rion, and the reported death in combat of King Loth. The ladies of the dead king's household were received with all honor by King Arthur at Camelot. Arthur had statues of the twelve rebellious kings made in gold and silver, and also had his own image made but much larger than theirs. Each king was holding a candlestick and was placed over the crenellations of Arthur's major fortress so all could see them. Arthur's own statue stood, holding a sword, in the center of the group, and menacing them, they bowing toward him and begging for his mercy. Despite wind and rain Merlin devised the means to keep the twelve tapers lighted until the day he would die. After the funeral ceremony for King Loth, Merlin prophesied the date of his own death.

The mystery of where these two battles, Bredigan and Carmelide, took place must be solved, for here Merlin and Arthur performed wonders. The series began with the siege of Carlisle, which suggests a starting point on the west coast of Britain, at the westernmost ending point of Hadrian's Wall. Here stood a major fortification in Roman Britain for five hundred years. (Although this fortification was a permanent station for a Roman legion, the raiding parties of Picts from the north were unhindered.) Carlisle was in Arthur's day, a major route junction, as it is today the major rail junction where roads and rails branch off to northeast Edinburgh, to the west and Ireland, and to the northwest and Glasgow. Obviously, King Rion from Ireland and the Isles had only to approach Carlisle along the Solway Firth. If he failed to breach the walls of Carlisle, he could perhaps have had the Solway as a retreat by water, or the Rhinns of Galloway as a westward retreat over land.

Battle 2 takes place, then, at Bredigan, which lay five days distant from Berwick, on or near a large meadow that was to become the field of battle. Nearby was Merlin's healing baptismal spa, called the Font or Fountain of Bredigan/Broceliande. A stone church stood there beside the fountain and the sea.

Astonishingly, the etymology of the place-name "Bredigan" proves simple. It is composed of three Celtic words descriptive of that geographical site:

> *Bre* = promontory,
>
> *di* = at,
>
> *gan* < *llan* = meadow, or enclosure (ancient church).

The Welsh word for promontory is *rhyn*, as in the *Penrhyn* near Bangor in North Wales, that "head promontory."

The word *llan* indicated first of all a meadow, a particularly distinctive and unusual geographical feature in a land of cliffs, highlands, forests, and mountains. Meadows were almost always sites for ancient churches, which were usually unroofed, stone squares, or enclosures. Thus, *llan* came also to mean chapel or stone church. Furthermore, the word is classed as enchorial or as familiar usage usually employed in demotic writing such as in wills, deeds, and the inheritance of religious property. This church is probably the "neue werke" or church built about 400, on the promontory or *rinn* of Galloway called Whithorn, by Saint Ninian, the premier Christian saint. It faces the northern tip of the Isle of Man. At Ninian's other church near Camelot (Sterling, Scotland), King Arthur, Perceval's father, mother, and sister, and Lancelot worshiped.[6]

Thus, King Arthur and Merlin pursued King Rion as he fled toward Ireland and the Isles along the only road west, by way of Castle Douglas, to the site and meadow of Whithorn and its prominent, famous peninsula that extends south toward Irish territory, the Point of Ayr on Man. There, on that rare meadow and renowned *llan* on its tongue of land is the second site in the war against King Rion. He must have fled overseas afterward, with the remnant of his forces, but, knowing Arthur, without his siege machinery, treasure, hoard, horses, arms, materials, and foodstuffs.

King Rion must have prepared for war the next time at Carmelide (with its variant Tarmelide), based on the following reasoning: King Arthur has had Rion on the run after the initial victory of Carlisle, where Arthur and Merlin had compelled him to raise the siege and decamp. After the second resounding defeat in pitched battle at Bredigan, King Rion must have assessed his properties in the Irish Sea and whatever out-isles he administered to fund new goods, build ships, and recruit men. If he decided against another frontal attack at Carlisle, where Arthur and Merlin had proved strongest, perhaps he would hurt them most by knocking out their foremost ally. This relative of Arthur was mentioned several times by Geoffrey of Monmouth as Duke Hoel of "Brittany," whom we can less anachronistically identify as Hoel of *Gallia* (Wales) and not from *Gallia* (Gaul, or France); from *Armonica* (North Wales) and not Brittany (*Armorica*). Either way, Arthur's near ally and kinsman Hoel turns out

. . .

[6] Merlin's Fountain of fresh water, probably similar to others near the Irish Sea, had apparently been a place famous for healing properties and sanctity.

to have come to his aid from somewhere nearby, such as from across the Irish Sea, North Wales to Scotland being only a short distance.

Bredigan on the southernmost Rhinn of Galloway stood within sight of the Isle of Man. In turn Man rises within sight both of Ireland and of North Wales at Great Orme's Head and of the Isle of Anglesey to the west of it. All seagoing ships cruising south on the Irish Sea must pass the massive plateau of Anglesey Island. "Carmelide" now proves easy to spot, being most likely the northwestern promontory of Anglesey that juts out into the Irish Sea. This point upon which mariners take a fix is today called Penrhyn Carmel in Welsh, or Carmel Head in today's English. Ships passing Carmel Head, our Carmelide, coast along Anglesey, come on their port side to the old Roman fort that once guarded their silver shipments down the Irish Sea, or to the Welsh ruin of Caergybi on the small rocky island now called Holy Island.

When considering King Arthur's arrival along the western coast of North Wales, two other similar stories that he went ashore there must be taken into account. The *Prose Lancelot*, the *Cambridge* 80 Manuscript, and the *Auchinleck* manuscript from Scotland were not sure he did. First, Geoffrey of Monmouth (Book X, No. 3) has King Arthur leave Carlisle after his coronation and proceed to "Gaul," landing at Barfleur (Bar + fjord, a Norman or Viking seaport), an exploit and a place that plunge him into a lamentable anachronism. Geoffrey follows these blunders with a story about Arthur's ally Hoel, who had just made a speech (Book IX) endorsing Arthur's excursion overseas to the continent of Europe.

From Duke Hoel's home (in Brittany, or in Gaul), his niece named Helena, has been abducted by a huge giant named Ritho. She had been hauled up on the Mont-Saint-Michel, ravaged, and killed. King Arthur is persuaded to slay the giant, and the Arthurian heroes embark. Their route is not to Gaul but to Carmel Head in Wales, past the large island of Anglesey, where at night the mariners glimpse a fire or a beacon burning, past the

small or Holy Island, upon which another beacon burns, warning ships to stand off the red rocky coast. The hero Bedevere spies out Helena's tomb on Caergybi, rather than upon Geoffrey's site, the French *Tombelaine* (which in any case does not mean Helen's Tomb, as Geoffrey had supposed). The "Great Tomb" is not on the Mont-Saint-Michel but on Mt. Snowdon in North Wales, visible from Anglesey.

176

King Arthur's combat with the giant Ritho took place upon Mount Aravius, says Geoffrey, and this is the same name and place given in the Merlin *Prophecy* as an Arthurian battlefield. Merlin followed the name in the next sentence by "North Wales." Thus, there is confirmation, albeit small, that Merlin's *Prophecy* dealt with his own days and not necessarily with royal personages in the twelfth century, the time of Geoffrey of Monmouth. The Merlin *Prophecy* may not be a forgery after all. Moreover, there is evidence that after his coronation King Arthur proceeded to the *Gallia (ad Galliam)*, which is Wales, and not to the *Gallia (ad Galliam)*, which was Gaul. By Arthur's day King Clovis ruled Gaul, which he had already renamed France after his own tribes, the Franks.

The *Prose Lancelot* and the two English manuscripts brought King Arthur only down to North Wales, where he fought King Rion, not at a Barbe (Beard) River, but to save his own beard *(barbe)*. Geoffrey's account finally elucidates the situation, that Arthur is rescuing his ally Hoel's family and province from King Rion's depredations.[7]

These four or five sources give an excellent idea of how the Arthurian contingent approached the coast of Wales, glimpsed the bonfires on the cliffs, and possibly caught sight of the most famous view in Wales, lauded today for its gorgeous scenery: "the view of Yr Wyddfa, or Snowdon, the highest mountain in Wales "seen from the waters of Porthmadog Bay" and mouth of the Glaslyn River.[8]

• • •

[7] Rion has become in folklore a Welsh prehistoric giant Ritho. And Helena is a very common Welsh name for a noblewoman. The prehistoric Welsh are still referred to as the "giants" who once dwelled in Tre'r Ceiri. Their moorland descendants in the Tywi Valley of Wales are even today recognizable by their long heads, distinctive gait, and prevalence of the B blood group.

[8] See Jan Morris's *The Matter of Wales: Epic Views of a Small Country*, pp. 11, 47, 51 passim.

Of course, King Arthur personally took Ritho's beard and also his hair cloak. Ritho must have been Rion, and this final man-to-man combat was the fourth in that campaign. One must turn a blind eye to alternate versions, which claim that it was Lancelot who killed Urian. That may have been another king of the same name, son of the first giant whom Arthur killed in North Wales.

Furthermore, Queen Guinevere may have come from North Wales after all rather than from York, England, where Geoffrey had placed her. She has a Welsh name, she is mentioned in Welsh *Triads*, and she was given by one *Triad* a father in Wales. This "father" was the mythical giant Ogrvran, who presumably also resided on the Isle of Man. Her other "father" linked her to royalty in "Cornwall" (Scotland) and Wales, but Thomas Pennant in *A Tour in Wales* (London, 1773) mentioned seeing Ogrvran's seat when it was pointed out to him in North Wales in the late eighteenth century.

No mention in these texts is made of Merlin either on Anglesey or on the heights of Mt Snowdon; but the poet Taliesin, who lived later than Merlin by a century or so, is reported to have greeted the mad Merlin:

All hail, Myrddin, whose primary abode is in
the western high region under King Maelgwyn.[9]

The "western high region" referred to here could have been Mt. Snowdon, and Maelgwn is the king who ruled North Wales (Gwynedd) after Merlin's death and after King Arthur's death at the battle of Camlan. The Welsh say that event occurred in 542. King Maelgwn Gwynedd's chief seat was on Anglesey it-

•   •   •

[9] Merlin is called "Myrddin" by Welsh people but it was not his Welsh name. I am much indebted in these pages to two recent books on Wales: Chris Barber's *Mysterious Wales* (see p. 141 for the lines from Taliesin), and Jan Morris's *The Matter of Wales*.

self. He was also reported to have fought Arthur at Camlan, and it is known that he founded a major Welsh dynasty.

Thus, one suspects that some of Arthur's twelve wars were fought for the sovereignty of North Wales. But Merlin seems to have belonged to all Wales and all Scotland rather than to one kingdom alone. He has strong ties to Carmarthen (Caerfyrddin) in Dyfed, where he was perhaps born, as well as to Powys and the Brecon (Brycheiniog) area, which was settled by his ancestral tribe, that of Brychan.[10] On the other hand, the "Myrddin" to whom Taliesin is said to have referred was one of Merlin's self-styled heirs. Such a famous man has followers, especially among the mad.

In his *Prophecy* Merlin himself shows knowledge of prehistoric Wales and her mythical kings when he speaks of the "blessed king" as a naval conqueror and future saint, who once built a fleet to invade Britain, an observation recounted by Geoffrey of Monmouth concerning Brennius in Book III of his *History*. Merlin called him the blessed king: "Rex benedictus parabit nauigium" (*Prophecy*, p. 386, 1. 10). "The blessed king will prepare a navy," and so on. The "blessed king" of the Welsh people is Bran, brother of Queen Branwen of Ireland, whose grave (*Bedd Branwen*) and the urn holding her ashes were discovered on Anglesey in 1813. In her day she was considered one of the three most beautiful women in Wales.

Welsh legends tell many stories of Bran and Branwen, as Merlin would certainly have known.[11] In Wales today Arthur

• • •

[10] See the index in Wendy Davies's *Wales in the Early Middle Ages*.

[11] See the *Mabinogion*, a collection of Welsh tales first translated by Charlotte Guest, who learned Welsh so that she could devote her life to this translation. Her notes are still the most extensive written on the subject. See also a more modern work such as Charles Squire's *Celtic Myth and Legend*. Squire retells the *Mabinogion*'s tales, recounts how Arthur feasted Bran's Wonderful Head, and points out what Geoffrey of Monmouth and Sir Thomas Malory added.

himself is still revered as a stone-carrying giant, like the terrible giant he killed there. Arthur's grave in the mountains of Dyfed is still shown to visitors, and some of the stones of Stonehenge came from these same Preseli Mountains. Other stones he hurled are also shown to visitors in North Wales and in Dyfed, or South Wales, and the stones his sons threw also. The greatest preponderance of Neolithic and other sites named for him and associated with Arthur are in Scotland. However, it is Welsh popular tradition that confirms the ancient texts in both French and English that King Arthur once fought and conquered a terrible giant in North Wales.

In his book *Mysterious Wales* Chris Barber explains the necessity of another look on the Bwlch-y-Groes Pass (Gr 914230 [125]), the road from Dinas Mawddwy-Bala in Powys, and the "highest road in North Wales," where Arthur met the giant, whom the Welsh today call by the same name "Rhitta," or Big Rhitta, the one who wanted Arthur's beard for *a collar to his cloak.* After Arthur had killed Rhitta, he threw the body down the hillside toward the Twrch. This giant is probably the "Boar" of Merlin's *Prophecy.* Rhitta's grave can still be seen today, says Barber (p. 131), who also explains that others in Wales locate this same battle site differently, or on Merlin's Mount Aravius (in English, Snowdon). Geoffrey of Monmouth's "Tombelaine," or what he called Helen's tomb, also once was visible, *not in Brittany,* France, but on the summit of Snowdon. It was a cairn or pile of ancient stones such as was usually placed over the body of a great personage. An Arthur Cairn (Carnedd Arthur) rises nearby (p. 135).

In the opening pages of her eloquent book *The Matter of Wales,* Jan Morris explains that because Wales was never conquered, as England was, by the Angles, Saxons, Jutes, or Normans and Franks, the small country became the trustee of a lost Celtic civilization . . . "that became part of the world's consciousness" (p. 3). The same is true of Scotland, from where the Celts migrated into Wales in Arthur's lifetime, while as many Welsh were even then migrating back into Scotland. Edinburgh was once captured by the Angles, it is true, but was soon liberated by the Picts.

"Imagination," said Henry V. Morton, "is part heredity and part environment," for which reason the legends that the Welsh people remembered from time immemorial resemble the lofty, stone landscapes of Wales itself:

> On Snowdon lived the most powerful of all giants, Rhitta, who wore an unpleasant garment made of the beards of kings whom he had slain. The act of cutting off a man's beard was the most deadly insult that could be offered in the old days (p. 143).[12]

The sanctity of the warrior hero's beard continued through the epic poetry of the Middle Ages, as seen in Charlemagne's beard in *The Song of Roland* and El Cid's beard in his *Song*. "Snowdon is haunted by both Merlin and Arthur," Morton adds (p. 144), for which reason King Henry II had to destroy the memories of Arthur in both Wales and Scotland. He first arranged to have Arthur interred and reinterred in Glastonbury, England, and the evidence destroyed so that nobody could question it. But all failed, and today "the very winds of Snowdon still breathe the name of Arthur . . ." and the name of Merlin also. Near Beddgelert in the Snowdon range stands the rock of Dinas Emrys (Fort of Ambrosius), a presumed seat of Vortigern's citadel, where the young Merlin could have delivered his *Prophecy*. An adjoining rocky mass is still called "Merlin's Cell."

•   •   •

[12] See Henry V. Morton, *In Search of Wales* (London, 1932), pp. 142–48.

7

MORGAN
LE FAY

. . . .

BOOK XIV

LXX

An isle that with her fellows bears the name
 Of Fortunate, for temperate air and mould;
There on a mountain high alight the dame,
 A hill obscur'd with shades of forest old,
Upon whose sides the witch by art did frame
 Continual snow, sharp frost, and winter cold;
But on the top, fresh, pleasant, sweet, and green,
Beside a lake a palace built this queen:

LXXI

There in perpetual, sweet, and flow'ring spring,
 She lives at ease, and 'joys her lord at will . . .

Torquato Tasso's *Gerusalemne Liberata*.
Translated by Edward Fairfax, 1600.

• • • • • • •

It always comes as a surprise to learn that no account of the most celebrated of Arthurian women, Morgan le Fay, has survived. Virtually all the accounts of the Arthurian male heroes mention her name only in passing. Thirty-seven major texts before 1500 give some anecdote or repeat the half dozen principal anecdotes taken as facts: that she was a sister of King Arthur, that her reputation preceded her, that her crimes had earned her a considerable notoriety during her lifetime. People knew that she was somehow special, certainly prominent, that she was influential and a royal power to fear in those days. Lucy Allen Paton's *Studies in the Fairy Mythology of Arthurian Romance* lists the thirty-seven medieval texts that report some incident where she demonstrated her absolute power over somebody, everybody, Merlin excepted. When other means presumably failed, Queen Morgan raised the knife in her own hand, as once against King Urian. She was at that time married to him. [1]

Paton listed the queen's names as shown on page 186.

The queen's name, it now appears, was *Morgue*, pronounced in two syllables: Mor-gue. [2] This nominative form is only rein-

• • •

[1] See the Excursus of Paton's 1960 survey, p. 255ff., edited by Roger Sherman Loomis. Paton considers Morgan a fairy, an otherworld being, as she first makes clear by the title of her scholarly book.

[2] The author of the possibly spurious text called *Life of Merlin* (*Vita Merlini*) called her *Morgen* (morning in German) as another joke, spoofing both Merlin and Geoffrey of Monmouth to whom, in an effort to blacken his name, he probably attributed his comical text.

Names	Number of texts in which each name appears
1. *Morgen*	1
2. *Morgue (Morgue la fée)*	13
3. *Morghe*	2
4. *Morge*	5
5. *Morgain*(s)	9
6. *Morgan*(s)	2

These (3 and 4) may be variants of 2

+

Morgua (Danish), Morgna (Icelandic), Murena (Swedish), Morguein (Swiss German), and Morgayna (Spanish), among others.

forced by the adoption, often in the same text, of the accusative case, *Morgain*, which the scribes, who were themselves often illiterate, mistook for her name in the nominative case. The name *Morgan* is not possible, for it is a man's name in Celtic and was, in fact, the name of King Arthur's physician. It is still a man's name in Welsh. Twenty-nine texts call her Morgue; two non-Celtic, non-Arthurian texts call her Morgan; and the man who called her *Morgen*, which also means "morning" in German, was having a laugh all by himself, for in Arthurian mythology she is no morning but the hideous black Queen of Death.

The twenty-nine authors and co-authors who correctly called her *Morgue*, and who added "la fée" in proper French (not "le Fay," as Malory incorrectly called her), represent her as the black, vile, hideous hag of death personified. This is clearly illustrated in what must be the most beautiful Arthurian text in Old English, *Gawain and the Green Knight*. In the following passage, Gawain sees two ladies being ushered into the castle hall, the older escorted by an honor guard of candidates, the younger lady becoming on sight Gawain's heart's desire:

Another lady led her by the left hand v. 947
A matron, much older, past middle age,

. . . .

For if the one was winsome, then withered was the other.

. . . .

The other was swathed with a wimple wound to the throat

. . . .

Trellised about with trefoils and tiny rings.
Nothing on that beldame but the black brows,
The two eyes, protruding nose and stark lips,

. . . .

Her body was stumpy and squat,
Her buttocks bulging and wide; . . . [3]

The poet returns to this great lady, saying later in the translation of the poem that she is "Morgan the Goddess," or the poet has her host "Bertilak of the High Desert" say so, and that she is a witch. With this picture of a Pictish queen in mind, of a queen who in old age looks like the Loathly Damsel of Arthurian letters, decorated with royal peacock feathers and sitting, one leg draped over the pommel of her saddle, and one hand holding the head of a newly slain foe, blood running down her fingers to the ground, one begins to reach some notion of who Morgan was.

First of all, she was Queen Morgue. Second, she was "the goddess," which is precisely what the earliest and best manuscripts recording ancient information from the Dark Ages called her, *"Morgue la fée."* "Fée" in French means Fate; hence, she was equated with the Third Fate, from the Latin *fatum,* or Fate, or

· · ·

[3] This marvelous translation was made by Brian Stone in 1959 and revised in 1972. Stone used the text of the poem as established by Israel Gollancz in 1940 and 1967, with the collaboration of J. R. R. Tolkien and E. V. Gordon. I take these lines from the edition I taught at least 25 times, 1973–1982: *Medieval English Literature,* edited by J. B. Trapp, pp. 310–11 and p. 346.

Destiny. In earliest and best Arthurian texts, Morgue la Fée is a mythological personage. It is impossible to get any closer to her as a real queen of the Dark Ages until this shroud, these mythological winding sheets that veil her from the light of day, is stripped away.

Greek scholars like E. R. Dodds in his books on pagan Greek and Christian practices write that there were Three Sisters under the direct supervision of Jove. Their names were Lachesis, Klotho, and Atropos. The eldest sister, also called *Nona* (Ninth), measured out the thread of every human being's life, or "assigned the portion thereof." The middle sister, also called *Decima* (tenth), twisted or wound the thread on her spindle. The third sister, called *Morta* (Death), who is the legendary Morgue, wove the thread on her loom and either bit it off with her teeth or cut it with her shears. Atropos, or Morta, always turned her back away from her fellows and her victims.

The Three Fates later appear in Dante's *Divine Comedy*: "tria sunt nomina Parcarum, *Nona, Decima* et *Morta*." They belong among what Hesiod and Ovid would have considered The Lesser Divinities of Heaven. They were always present in the most tragic stories (including, long after Merlin's time, Shakespeare's *Macbeth*).

The Roman poet Catullus in his wedding poem for Peleus and Thetis, the future parents of Achilles, describes the Three Fates, who were guests at the wedding. They came wearing *white robes* and uttering prophecies that were incontrovertible truths: a son shall be conceived and he shall be born, and he shall never turn his back on the foe, and he shall outrun the deer in the forest. Their song sounds like the text that inspired the authors of *Perceval*. The Fates were not beautiful like the young Morgue, but old, ugly, and yellow, even in Catullus's time: [4]

• • •

[4] *Epithalamium*, translated by Horace Gregory (New York, 1931), but see also Charles Mills Gayley's translation from *Classic Myths in English Literature and in Art* (Boston, etc., 1893, 1911), pp. 269–73.

Whilst the decrepit Sisters of Fate, their tottering bodies
Solemnly swayed, and rehearsed their soothfast vaticination.
—Lo, each tremulous frame was wrapped in robe of a whiteness,
Down to the ankles that fell, with nethermost border of purple,
While on ambrosial brows there rested fillets like snowflakes.
They, at a task eternal their hands religiously plying,
Held in the left on high, with wool enfolded, a distaff,
Delicate fibers wherefrom, drawn down, were shaped by the right hand—
Shaped by fingers upturned—but the down-turned thumb set a-whirling,
Poised with perfected whorl, the industrious shaft of the spindle.
Still, as they span, as they span, was the tooth kept nipping and smoothing,
And to the withered lip clung morsels of wool as they smoothed it—
Filaments erstwhile rough that stood from the twist of the surface.
Close at their feet, meantime, were woven baskets of wicker
Guarding the soft white balls of the wool resplendent within them.
Thus then, parting the strands, these Three with resonant voices
Uttered, in chant divine, predestined sooth of the future—
Prophecy neither in time, nor yet in eternity, shaken　　　(pp. 271–72).

Robert Graves brought all this up to date in his 1961 book *The White Goddess.*[5] He claimed that the Three Fates are also the Three Graces, Nymphs, and the Grey Ones who helped Perseus kill Medusa. The three are daughters of Phorcus or Orcus, and one of King Arthur's legendary palaces was *Orcanie,* whose symbol was the crane or swan. Orcus was god of the underworld to whom the boar and the pig were sacred, as they were to the Death Goddess, Morta herself. Orcus was also said to have fathered a beautiful African queen named Libya, or Medusa. The

•　•　•

[5] See Robert Graves, *The White Goddess* (London, 1961–1971), pp. 229–33, but see also Chapter 26, "The Return of the Goddess" (p. 480ff.); and see also his *Greek Myths,* 2 vols., (London 1965–1975). See also James Frazer's *Golden Bough* on the rites of Demeter, Vol. II, Part V passim.

Death Goddess became the Great Queen (*Mawr Regan*) of Ireland, as the Irish still have Morgue la Fée as Morrigan.

In the newly studied mythology of Ireland, Morgue has become the goddess from the western island of Avalon, which lay in Gaelic territory, at the navel of Britain: the Isle of Man in the Irish Sea. There Morgue bears the high sprigs of alder in her hand, like Diana Nemorensis, the waning moon. The alder, which yielded a crimson stain for the Celtic kings, grows along the riverbanks to shield the temples of the pagan goddesses. The Death Goddess, Atropos, was said to rise from the western sea, whence her name in Gaelic: Muir-gen, or Sea-born. Her later appearance as Queen Morgue has her taking King Arthur on a funeral barge for burial to this same Avalon, beside the Isle of Man, but on its western or Irish side.

There seems little doubt but that Queen Morgue's worldwide celebrity as a pagan deity derives to some degree (as does Celtic mythology, which along with Greek was studied in ancient Ireland), from the Lesser Gods of the Greek Pantheon. Or else the Greek Pantheon, particularly its divinities of sea horses and the sea, were borrowed from the British Isles.

The Anglo-Saxons who sported boar's head helmets cannot have felt out of water in a Britain speaking of "awful Wyrd" in other words, when she urged them on to battle and wove their destinies, in a cult perhaps already six thousand years old. For their part, however, they showed and felt none of the Greek fear of the sea. No such correlation existed to them: death and sea, or sea = death.

We can almost put our hands on Morgue la Fée in the following list of the sea gods.

DIVINITIES

Ceres	-	goddess of earth whose daughter was *Proserpina*
Cronus	-	the ruler of the Fortunate Isles
Pluto and		
Proserpina	-	gods of the underworld

Phorcys and Ceto	-	rejoiced in the dangers and horrible deaths at sea.
Neptune	-	created the horse, horse races, drove a chariot over the sea.
Triton	-	the trumpeter of Ocean, who aroused or calmed the waves.
Graeae	-	three witches who had only one eye between them.
Gorgons	-	three monsters whose glance caused icy death.
Sirens	-	mermaids, muses of the sea and death.
Scylla	-	a monster, serpent/dog/wolf of the churning abysses of the sea.
Proteus	-	an old man of the sea, a prophet, and wearer of disguises, or other shapes.
Harpies	-	ravenous creatures with bodies of birds and heads of old maids.
Water Nymphs	-	Oceanids, fifty Nereids, Naiads.
Atlas	-	father of the nymphs who guarded the golden apple tree on the Fortunate Isle far to the west.

(*Hecate* was on both sides descended from Titans and doubly a granddaughter of Uranus and Gaea.)

Morgue and her mysterious Christian Church or "chariot," which, Malory believed, was her castle of the chariot, link the pagan world of ancient Greece during the five-hundred-year occupation of Britain by Roman legions to the Christian world of Merlin and King Arthur. Not only did Merlin have to be summoned from his studies with Blaise to "suppress" Morgue, but King Arthur had to conquer the Isle of Avalon, where Morgue resided as queen, ostensibly to re-Christianize and reconsecrate it. Through the enchantress Morgue la Fée, then, the Arthurian world descends from its even more distant past, the secondary gods of antiquity: Sky, Sea, and Earth.

In the mythology of the Arthurian age, Morgue herself and

the maiden Lunette figure openly and subliminally as the three phases of the moon, the ancient hag Morgue impersonating the abducted, imprisoned moon for whom Earth mourns. She sometimes rides resplendent in white on a white horse like Lady Godiva at Coventry. At the new moon, once in every few centuries, there occurs a period of terrible and total darkness and silence at noon when the eastern moon has eclipsed the rising sun, so powerful is the antique sorceress Morgue.

In her human relationships with the powerful heroes of Arthur's realm, Yvain, Gawain, and Lancelot most remarkably, Morgue turns to murder, sequestration, and enchantments. She puts them to sleep, drops them into dungeons, and drives them mad so that they lose all notion of time, often raging naked in the forest like primeval savages. Then she rides away astride her ambling mule or "old gray mare" of the silken gait. Morgue turns to premeditated murder when she deals with the kings, her brother Arthur and her husband Urian, for Morgue is finally handed over to Urian as a *pis-aller*, a sop, a poor substitute for the gorgeous Guinevere he intended to have and finally had in death after he abducted her twice.

Some people might have favored clemency for her even then, offering in her defense extenuating circumstances: she was young, she was not asked to state either her preference or her objection to marriage, and she did not bring her plots to actual murder. Such a defense argues from weakness, or worse, from the religious belief that all women are, by nature, inherently evil, seductive, and prone to adultery and murder. Such arguments would miss the point.

Morgue depicted as a murderess probably comes from the ancient Greek tales and dramas of the notorious, tragic murderess Medea. The greatest writers of Greece and Rome labored mightily to explain her crimes but still could not understand them. Like Morgue she too has puzzled people for ages.[6]

• • •

[6] Both Medea and Morgue were prophets, for prophecy among holy women seems even older than the prophetic gift in men. On the

In the Arthurian text *Didot-Perceval*, priestesses still dwelled near Arthur's Perilous Ford at the confluence of the River Nith and the Solway Firth, on the Rhinn of Galloway near King Arthur's birthplace. They inhabited or presided at an oracular cave identifiable, as at Delphi, because of a mysterious noise like falling water that issued from it. Perceval killed their champion, and them, too, probably; the Welsh text *Peredur* says that a hero (Perceval) killed his women teachers because they were "witches."

Unlike Morgue, whose reputation suffered such attacks as being called "bastard," Medea was a descendant of Jupiter himself and therefore belonged to the primary gods of heaven, the major gods of Greece. She was a niece of other priestesses now much maligned, Circe and Pasiphaë, daughter of Hecate, and granddaughter of the sun Helios. She escaped from vengeance by borrowing his Sun's chariot.

Both Medea and Morgue are able to change their appearances from old to young, hag to beauty, crone to damsel. The

. . .

north shore of the Bay of Naples, the Greek Sibyl Herophile moved to a suitable cave at Cumae during the reign of Romulus, who founded great Rome in 753 B.C. Time for the Romans began that year: *Ab Urbe Condita* (from the city founded = AUC). The priestesses/prophets like those at Delphi, long the ancient world's most revered site on earth, its navel, were all women who presided at the Oracle until deposed by male conquest, supposedly by the god Apollo. The Sibyls chose caverns or caves, where pure water flowed, for water was believed to be the medium of oracular speech.

The Greek and Roman oracles were suppressed by Diocletian, reinstalled by Julian the Apostate (360–363), and suppressed permanently by Justinian in A.D. 529, during Morgue's lifetime. It is no wonder she has come down to us as a vile enchanter, and far worse. No women except virgins devoted to the Church could be educated after A.D. 529, when the dark curtain of the hateful and ignorant peasant Justinian fell upon the world of women. For centuries they had been educated at the oracular centers. Pomponius Mela, Strabo, Sophocles, and Plutarch, who was himself a priest of Apollo at the Delphic Oracle, speak of colonies of educated, exalted priestesses.

two women described in *Gawain and the Green Knight* both seem to be Morgue, young and old depending upon these two phases of the moon deity. The Green Knight performs at Morgue's oracular shrine, from which issues the same horrible noise, and it is near their palace. Both priestesses are marvelous healers, or one could say, doctors of medicine. Both hate their husbands. Medea sends a burning garment to kill her rival, and Morgue sends another such garment to destroy her brother Arthur. Medea succeeds. Morgue fails, thwarted by the worshipful Lady of the Lake.

Huth-Merlin tells the long story of Arthur's Hunt, which Malory repeats, much shortened and somewhat softened, in *Le Morte d'Arthur* (Book IV, Chapters XV and XVI). When the hunters are two days distant from Camelot, they are beguiled into entering a lovely ship. There twelve ravishingly beautiful young girls feast and entertain them. When Arthur awakens, he finds himself in Morgue's dungeon. A dwarf who brings him the wrong sword hands Excalibur to his enemy. That foe is one of Morgue's lovers, Accolon. King Arthur is almost defeated by Excalibur in the hands of his foe, but again the Lady of the Lake saves him in the nick of time. King Arthur is forgiving enough to send Accolon's body to Morgue at Camelot. What she is doing there is never explained.

In his treatment of Medea (*Myths*, Vol. II), Robert Graves first noted the connections between the myths of Medea and Arthurian literature, between the Argonauts and the *Mabinogion* of Wales. Morgue's chariot, like Medea's, is mentioned in the Welsh *Triads* as the property of these triple deities, Hecate–Demeter–Persephone, and related to the Women's Eleusinian Mysteries, which were never revealed in Greece and are still unknown today. Graves solves the problem by saying Medea killed her children possibly because the gods had promised her they thus would not be tortured by the Corinthians but would become immortal. When the ancients called Medea a Hyperborean, they meant that she was a British goddess, Graves concluded. Her husband Jason had been raised by the Centaur

Chiron, or Sagittarius, the most illustrious teacher of his ancient day, while Arthur, Lancelot, Perceval, and Gawain were taught by Merlin, one of the greatest intellectuals of his day. Both Medea and Morgue rise vengefully from a man-dominated warrior society, which had little place for women except as menials and breeders.

The ancient Greek hero Jason performed the ancient rain-making ceremony by throwing water upon the sacred stone near the healing well or fountain, which is the later Arthurian hero Yvain's chief adventure. There the Moon Goddess, called Lunette, officiates. Earth's daughter is always some Helen of Troy from whom the Trojan British are said to have descended, and "Helen" is the most sacred name of Welsh and Arthurian women— mother and wife of Lancelot, for example.

Queen Morgue is known to be the sister of King Arthur, the wife of King Urian, the mother of the older Yvain who fought so long and heroically by Arthur's side after having stayed the hand and knife his mother thought to plunge into her husband's heart. She can be found, aside from her roles in the Arthurian world, in literary borrowings from classical mythology. The question has yet to be answered: Who was the real Morgue? Was she not Merlin's student, the Morgue who was a doctor of medicine?

The Morgue encountered thus far looms far too large, far larger than the life-size of any human lady, even of a great queen. In other words, what has been gleaned belongs not so much to her as to a pagan antiquity by Morgue's time considered quaint and romantic, survivals of a world already outmoded and almost forgotten after some five hundred years. Jerusalem, and not Rome, where the Church was not yet fully organized, loomed in the Middle East as the center of her universe. One can credit from informative narrators their statement that Morgue was King Urian's queen and the mother of his older son Yvain, perhaps also of a daughter.

Morgue herself doubtless blushed to have been born under

the stigma of "bastard," but even that, given their almost total lack of knowledge of human sexuality and reproduction, may be subject to question. These narrators write that noblemen of those days entrusted to an attendant the recording of their orgasms. They dignified only those infants born after some calculated number of days or periods of some sort. With the same skepticism one may hesitate to credit the reports that Morgue herself gave birth to a daughter who was Yvain's twin, since mothers of twins were routinely killed along with the second-born. The second birth proved adultery on the mother's part, or what was worse, seduction by an incubus, it was thought.

The evidence of Yvain's loyalty to King Arthur, which falls into the same pattern as that of his cousins, all children of Arthur's other sisters, argues rather convincingly against the Medea-type crimes attributed to Morgue. It seems accurate that people believed these allegations in the case of Morgue, for even pronouncing the name of the notorious, evil Morgan le Fay was forbidden centuries after her brother's death.

On the other hand, Morgue's description from the wonderful *Gawain and the Green Knight* strikes one as accurate in each detail except for the line about her having been a "goddess." The same racial characteristics attributed to her often appear in other Arthurian descriptions of Pictish royalty, including the dwarf who attended her. Gawain himself is also characterized as a Pict because their princes possessed that awful surge of physical strength that assisted them in combat, peaking toward the middle of the day and subsiding in the afternoon. It is medically interesting. That Morgue and Gawain did not necessarily look like the royal persons described in the poem is not the point; the point being that they probably were Pictish.

One notices how over wide areas of our world and throughout long ages, conquered peoples are frequently so described: dwarfish, dark-skinned, misshapen, beetle-browed, grotesque, and despicable. When the blond, handsome Aryans conquered India, and drove the Dravidians into the distant south, dispossessing them of their ancestral lands, they then called them dwarfish, blackish, unworthy, thus rationalizing their conquest. The Hawaiians, or conquering Polynesians, said the same about the Menehune, who labored so hard at constuctions of stone but who supposedly lived in dark caves underground, like the "fairies" of Ireland. Whenever the word "Pictish" is used today, the wide-eyed reaction is too dogmatic to be entirely innocent: "Oh! the Picts!" Anthropologists have taught readers to suspect that gnomes like Grendel and his dam in *Beowulf* also fall among the dispossessed and unfortunate primitive peoples of prehistoric Denmark.

The point is that for King Urian to have accepted her real property and her person, Morgue was more likely the highly admired Irish royal type, an auburn or red-haired beauty.

Another charge against Morgue results from one of the stumbling blocks of the Old French language, a trifling point that still presents a certain peril to foreigners speaking French today. This is the exact meanings to native speakers of the words "friend" and "woman friend": *ami, amie.* They may mean "concubine," "lover," or even "spouse." Thus, when indexes of Arthurian names mention Morgue's connections, they state that she was the "amie" of Accolon, Guiomar, Queen Sebile, the Ladies of Norgalles, and of Avalon. And so she has also come down to us as notoriously nymphomaniacal. The medieval authors also add another connection that seems likely to explain their bias and hard allegation of adultery and other sexual misconduct. Morgue was notably Merlin's pupil, *"who lost her beauty because of her learning,"* as Arthurian authors repeat with delight. It is the common fairy-tale injunction aimed at girls.

Morgue was more apt to have been an anomaly, an educated woman in a world that rarely saw one, and that was prejudiced against women of all degrees into a fury of suspicion, jealousy, and hatred at the very mention of that connection: female and intelligent.

The earliest Arthurian texts list King Arthur's sisters at the time when at the age of fifteen he was crowned for the first time by Archbishop Dubricius, who later became Saint Dubricius of

Wales. Then after all the other young girls have been more or less named and assigned husbands, the chroniclers came to the last one, namely Morgue, who was too young yet for marriage. At that time the narrators commented that she was "in London," or Lothian, at school, and that she was curiously fond of learning, and, in fact, already eccentric, that is, "brilliant." Brilliance is, of course, an unusual characteristic, even among young males, but Merlin consented to educate her, said Chrétien de Troyes in *Erec et Enide*. Later on, in a desperate circumstance, she was brought forth to wed King Urian.

Merlin reportedly protected his pupil Morgue, who often astonished him, said the *Prose Lancelot*, by her great beauty, "grant biaute," as by her "marvelous intelligence," and the "subtlety" of her mind. After she had progressed far enough, she also learned "astronomie" from him, "ingremance,"[7] and "other great marvels." One of the other great marvels Merlin practiced at his Healing Well of Bredigan (Broceliande) was medicine, and here Sir Thomas Malory demonstrated Morgue's knowledge of that art, which has since become a science. But medicine and prophecy were once closely related skills.

Morgue once heard of a valiant warrior named Alisander. "Well, said Morgan le Fay, I shall meet that knight or it be long time, an he dwell in that country."[8] After his next duel Morgue "laid Sir Alisander in an horse litter, and led him into the castle, . . . for he had sixteen great wounds, and in especial one of them was like to be his death." First she anointed him with such a medicine "that he should have died. And on the morn when she came to him he complained him sore; and then she put

. . .

---

[7] I think this means prophecy, but the dictionaries think it meant necromancy (communication with the dead), or augury. Merlin was a Christian prelate who would not have taught pagan practices to a favorite pupil, or to anyone else.

[8] *Le Morte d'Arthur*, Vol. II, Bk. X, Chaps. XXXVI, XXXVII.

other ointments upon him, and then he was out of his pain.
. . . Then came Queen Morgan le Fay to Alisander, and had
him arise, and put him in an horse litter, and gave him such a
drink that in three days and three nights he waked never, but
slept; and so she brought him to her own castle. . . ." She
made him promise, since he wished to be cured and made "whole,"
that he would stay there and convalesce for "twelvemonth and
a day."

Usually Morgue is found near Merlin's Fountain, a recogniz-
able locale in most Arthurian romances, identifiable when Mat-
thew Arnold repeats its features in his *Tristram and Iseult*:

> *All round the forest sweeps off, black in shade,*
> *But it is moonlight in the open glade:*
> *And in the bottom of the glade shine clear*
> *The forest chapel and the fountain clear.*

In Celtic tradition the precious fountain of pure spring water is
guarded by a woman, whose charge is to keep the covering
stone in place.[9] Whether Merlin's Fountain was used only for
healing the sick or used also for baptism still seems unclear.

In her books on mythology Augusta Gregory often ex-
plained that in Ireland the fountain represented the well of
knowledge, the location of which was one of the world's best
kept secrets. Perhaps this is why the Merlin texts about Bredi-
gan, or Broceliande fail to explain its whereabouts. Three mys-
tical fountains dated from the creation of the world, the Celts
believed:

1. salt water rose up into the sky whence it descended on earth
   as rivers,

* * *

[9] See also "The Folklore of the Wells" in *Celtic Folklore Welsh and Manx*,
Vol. I, Chapter VI, by John Rhys, p. 354 ff.

2. rain was also a fountain, the water falling from the limitless atmosphere, and

3. a fountain itself arose miraculously from the flinty mountains, springing out of the very veins of the rock strata, furnishing a refreshment, indeed a nourishment for man from the Almighty.

Thus, Merlin's Broceliande figures repeatedly in the Arthurian archives as such a hidden, sacred place that readers may fail to recall it from one text to another. It is sometimes referred to allusively as near a forest in northern Britain, or beside an ancient church, or vaguely as "on the way to Scotland." Merlin was seen there once in his disguise as a loutish herdsman. Lunette officiated there in rainmaking ceremonies on behalf of her mistress Laudine, the eponymous queen or sovereign of Lodonesia (Lothian). But Laudine's story reads as if it once may have been a play or a masque remembered, so little realism does it convey. The sacred well is otherwise located at the Forest of Darnantes, where Morgue once resided, which makes better sense. It also lay near the enchanted forest "which (road) went straight" to the sea of Cornwall (Galloway) and to the "Kingdom of Sorelois" (Upon the Water?). It was again Morgue's Forest, near her Valley-of-No-Return, so named because the people who journeyed there were healed and remained there forever "carolling" (dancing) enchantedly.

Springs such as Merlin's boil up out of the rock or bubble into a pool in the forest until they are contained inside walls and covered so that forest animals will not fall in and drown. Most such "holy wells" and "healing waters," as the Welsh call them, are related to miracles performed there by saints.

One strikingly typical example is the case of the Welsh virgin Saint Winefred at Trefynnon, Gwynedd. This highly beloved princess of Wales was a ward of Saint Beuno. She refused to wed a certain Welsh prince, who then in his wrath pursued her and cut off her head. At that, the earth opened and devoured him. Her severed head rolled down the hill to the chapel near a dry riverbed. Where it came to rest, a spring of water suddenly gushed out of the rock with a huge jet. The moss that grew instantly around the rocks smelled very sweet. The drops of blood from her severed head turned to tiny red Adonis flowers. Saint Beuno reunited the maiden's head to her body so cleverly that for the rest of her life only a thin red scar along her neck betrayed her sad past. [10]

Morgue seems more prominently remembered on Avalon, the Isle of Man in the Irish Sea, through their vivid folk tales of mermaids, all stemming originally from the Gaelic or Irish folktale that records for Ireland the life and death of Morgue. In real life, they say, she was a girl named Liban, who was saved when a holy well was left uncovered and flooded the plain. Liban lived for ages under the water with her pet dog, and then for more ages swam as a salmon (of knowledge) in the sea, her dog beside her as an otter, for more hundreds of years. When she was caught, she was offered a choice by the Church: baptism and heaven, or baptism and a human life on earth before heaven. She chose baptism and heaven. She was baptized either

·   ·   ·

[10] See Chapter 5 for this story illustrated and told by Chris Barber in *Mysterious Wales.* A similar story is told in France of their patron saint, Apostle of the Gauls, who is remembered particularly at Montmartre (Mountain of the Martyr), where he was decapitated. Saint Denis (Dionysien) carried his head in his hands as he strode in triumph from the Place du Tertre in Paris to his Abbey Church, which rises dark and somber over the northern skyline at the Paris suburb named for him. A Saint Adelbertus, after being similarly martyred, swam the Vistula River, carrying his own head.

The Holy Wells of Wales still exhale beneficent airs that promote healing, and there are dozens of such spas in Wales today. While none is named for Morgue, who seems to have practiced healing at Merlin's Well, Bredigan on the Rhinn of Galloway, many such wells in Wales are associated with the Lady of the Lake, about whom toddlers are warned if they tend to stray too near the water.

as "Murgewn," that is, "Sea-born," or as "Murgelt," that is, "Mermaid." She died a holy virgin and still works wonders of healing in Ireland.[11]

The Manx tell a particularly haunting story of a mermaid who lived in a creek on Man. She brought good luck to a boatman who took apples down to her and who planted an apple tree first for her use by the seashore. When he left for foreign parts, she grew so lonely that she wandered in search of him. Neither ever returned to Man.[12] This story is unforgettable for two reasons: first, because it again demonstrates that the fairy tale originated, like the chronicles and histories of Merlin and Morgue, in the Dark Ages, and second, because the tale associates Morgue with apples, the food of the otherworld. The Isle of Man, which is Avalon, where stood the Castle of the Holy Grail, was often called Island of Apples. For centuries scholars believed that even the name Avalon derived from the Welsh word for apple.

The apple moves the search back again to Avalon as an oracular center and Isle of the Dead, to which King Arthur was ferried by Queen Morgue and her sister queens after his fatal wounding at Camlan. It also returns us to another of the ancient prototypes in the world's treasure chest of ancient mythology.

• • •

[11] But see Patrick Weston Joyce for a much superior, a superb translation of "Liban the Mermaid," *Old Celtic Romances*, pp. 97–105.

[12] See "The Mermaid of Gob Ny Oyl" in *Manx Fairy Tales* (Douglas, Isle of Man, 1929, 1971), pp. 75–78.

8

NINIANE/
VIVIAN

OBERON: *Thou remember'st*
Since once I sat upon a promontory,
And heard a mermaid on a dolphin's back
Uttering such dulcet and harmonious breath,
That the rude sea grew civil at her song,
And certain stars shot madly from their spheres
To hear the sea-maid's music.

PUCK: *I remember.*

OBERON: *That very time I saw, but thou couldst not,*
Flying between the cold moon and the earth,
Cupid all arm'd: a certain aim he took
At a fair vestal throned by the west,
And loos'd his love-shaft smartly from his bow,
As it should pierce a hundred thousand hearts;
But I might see young Cupid's fiery shaft
Quench'd in the chaste beams of the wat'ry moon,
And the imperial votaress passed on,
In maiden meditation, fancy-free, . . .

A Midsummer Night's Dream, II, i.
William Shakespeare.

Concealed beneath the shape of an ugly old man, Merlin once went to Camelot in search of Gawain. It was for Merlin a new semblance: crooked legs, bent head, hoary beard, broad shoulders, other disfigurements, a great staff hanging from his neck. He drove beasts ahead of him: food for the camp.

Gawain hears this noisy arrival. Merlin is so weary that he falls fainting to the ground. He moans and weeps. Awakening, he taunts Gawain. What he wanted he finally receives, namely Gawain's consent to follow Merlin that very day and reenter the battle. Sometime later he finds Gawain at Bredigan. This day Merlin has donned assorted garments. In reality he is tall and dark. He wears a wide beard. He has a crooked nose. His hat hangs far down his back. Again he dispatches Gawain, this time on a rescue mission.[1]

When Merlin hears that a savage King Claudas plans to ravage Berwick, he prophesies darkly of a lion and a leopard, then of a serpent and a leopard. There will come a leopard, Lancelot, that will be all black, that will be particularly robust and fierce, a panther, a cougar, a jaguar, a catamountain that will leap from horseback onto King Claudas, that will hunt alone and spring upon the unwary as easily as upon those who stand impatiently waiting for battle. The ward of the Lady of the Lake will kill King Claudas: Lancelot of the Lake.

• • •

[1] *Cambridge* 80 manuscript, Part III.

Merlin has already recommended Gurneval, despite his previous capital crime, as a suitable tutor for another hero: Tristan. He has thoughts about who could gentle the future leopard, Lancelot of the Lake. That person will be the Lady of the Lake.

Merlin has been promised the first daughter of a noble vassal who resides near Berwick on the east coast. Gossip said the father's name was Dionas, but who knows? Some said the family resided at Berwick itself, and others said that they lived nearby and not in town because Merlin when he visited them went to a forest rather than inside the town walls where someone would be apt to recognize him. In this connection some people have speculated about the old Roman goddess Diana. Some said she had promised Merlin a female child. Others said Diana had promised Dionas a female child (v. 21, 189 ff.). If the goddess Diana was godmother to Dionas, or if a great lady named Diana was godmother at his christening, then one of them promised Merlin a beautiful first daughter.

Dionas often visited King Ban and King Bors at their two citadels named Berwick on the east coast of Northumberland.[2] From them he frequently carried messages to King Claudas. People subscribing to the romantic notion of Dionas and the ancient pagan Diana were those who recorded their theory: his godmother Diana promised Dionas that his first daughter should be coveted by the wisest man on earth and that she should subse-

• • •

[2] Lest he be impugned by readers centuries after he wrote, the author of *Huth-Merlin* wished to set them straight (Vol. III, p. 143):

> Nor do not suppose, between you all who hear these accounts, that this (that that is) "Norhomberlande" of which I speak be the kingdom of "Norhomberlande" which was between the kingdom of "Logres" and that other of "Gorre": . . . for this "Norhomberlande" was in the little "Bretaigne," and (in) [the other] "Norhomberlande" in the great.

quently be taught by him *as a reward for her subjection.* Since one good story deserves another, the next storyteller added juicier details: that in Merlin's day there were still Druids who had replaced the olden Roman priests of Vesta, and they enrolled beautiful little girls to tend the goddess's temple in Rome. If one such girl lost her virginity, she was put to death by the male priest, her keeper.

There was born to this nobleman Dionas a most beautiful daughter, whom they named Niniane. Reports of her early childhood were brought to Merlin. They were so favorable that by the time she had reached the age of twelve, he detoured from his journey, doffed his formal attire, and went to see her for himself. That particular day he was dressed as himself, "a fair young man." Niniane used to play in the cool forest near a spring of clear water shaded by lofty trees. It was her favorite spot, where she could rest and watch the deer and other forest creatures come down to drink.

Merlin remained hidden in the trees for a long time as he observed her studying, playing, and dreaming. She was truly the most beautiful girl he had ever seen, tall and willowy, with long golden curls and deep blue eyes. Finally he stepped forward and began to speak with her while, like a teacher, watching her every reaction but seeming not to, listening to her words, to the tone of her voice, studying her accent, modulations, and inflections, testing her responses to certain key words and emotionally charged topics, drawing her out so that he could judge her capacity and the degree of her education. He did not on this occasion reveal his true identity, but said he was the servant to a great man.

After she had unsuspectingly passed the second test, Merlin began to sound her out about her ideas of what her life could be. In this process, either that day or later, he consciously charmed and bewitched her in the same way that the freshness and innocence of her childhood and the brilliance of her intellect had already charmed him. Little by little, he expanded her

207

notions of the outer world. He told her of the magical castle of Camelot, "la chitet de Camailaoth": [3]

> Li grans palais ou li rois tenoit ses neuces estoit en tel maniere assis qu'il seoit el chief de la chité par deviers le grant forest, pres d'un bois a deus archies, et tout entour a la reonde estoit il enclos de gardins et [d'arbres] miervilleus aussi haus et aussi espes comme che fust une fores.
>
> (The great palace where the king held his celebrations was seated in such a way so it should overlook the citadel from across the great forest, away from a wood by about the distance of two arrow shots, and enclosed all around it was by gardens and wonderfully rare trees as high and as thick as if they were another natural forest.) [4]

The more Merlin told her about the outstanding marvels of his kingdom, and of King Arthur's realm, the more Niniane wished to become a part of it. Eventually, after he was satisfied that she could be highly educated, that she could become a valuable contributor to this realm, which was currently being warred upon by King Rion, Merlin asked the lovely maiden if she would "plight her troth." She marveled at all he had told her. She agreed to be his beloved girl in all honor *and in chastity*.

Merlin drew a circle about her small person to prefigure her life for her, to signify she would live henceforth inviolate within a closed, charmed circle. Then he summoned his servants, his dancers, his musicians and surrounded her with the delights of the new world. The maiden marveled at it all. Willingly, Niniane again promised to be faithful, true, and loving. Again she

•   •   •

[3] *Huth-Merlin, Continuation,* Vol. II, edited by Gaston Paris, p. 76.

[4] Manuscript illustrations usually show trees that have all been trimmed to the same height. In other words, we have here the classical "closed garden" as the Romans preferred them.

vowed her absolute devotion. She again "plighted her troth."
Finally, Niniane heard about Merlin's prophetic powers. She
longed more than anything in the world to become his student
and to learn everything that he knew about all subjects. Before
he left for Carmelide, Merlin taught her how he caused a wide
river to flow across a dry plain.

However, Merlin's Master Blaise was not pleased to learn
that Merlin had recruited this girl, less so that he had chosen
"the most beautiful girl in the world." Blaise put no trust in women:

> *Cambridge* 80 manuscript
> *but whanne Merlyn tho spake of his paramour,* v. 25, 976
> *thanne abasched hym sore blasye that our.*
> *For evere he dredde in his herte*
> *that hym sche scholde deseyven, aperte,*
> *lest that he hire tawhte so moche konnenge,*
> *that hit sholde ben his distroyenge.*

Blaise upbraided Merlin, telling him in no uncertain terms what
this relationship with Niniane would look like in the eyes of the
world. He stressed the way the world's eye would probably see
it despite all truth and lack of evidence. Niniane would un-
doubtedly be called his "lover." She would "deceive him" and be
said to have done so. He would teach her so much knowledge
that she would be his undoing, and all this was reported as true
long before Alfred Lord Tennyson retold it. In his "Vivien" he
is an "Enchanter," and she is a "wily" enchantress:

> *And Vivien ever sought to work the charm*
> *Upon the great Enchanter of the Time,*
> *As fancying that her glory would be great*
> *According to his greatness whom she quench'd.*

Tennyson in 1859–1885 uses her alternate name, which comes
from later versions of the Merlin-Niniane affair. Perhaps Ten-
nyson had read Hersart de la Villemarqué, the distinguished

Breton scholar who in 1862 wrote the first book on Merlin, whom he called *Myrdhinn*. That might have been his name in Old Breton (if he was ever named in Old Breton). Villemarqué had noted in 1862 that the earliest manuscripts called the girl Niniane, adding that it was a "Chaldean" name. Her name is, of course, neither Chaldean nor Semitic, but Old British. Villemarqué hypothesized that "Niniane" came from another hypothetical name, Chwiblian, which he said could have been Old Celtic, or Hwinleian in ancient Gaulish, perhaps. In 1891 the distinguished Welsh scholar John Rhŷs published his famous *Arthurian Legend*, in which he corrected Villemarqué. The later name "Vivien," he said, results from a series of scribal miscopyings (*m* to *n* to *v*): Niniane to Vivian, or Vivien (Chapter XII).

Tennyson's visualization of Niniane/Vivian corresponds to the famous painting of Merlin and her by Edward Burne-Jones, where Merlin looks up at her, hollow-eyed and supplicating, like Dante in the *Inferno*. Niniane/Vivian stands looking not at him but at the artist. She is sinuous and sexually attractive, a grown woman with long dark tresses. In her hands she holds a large open book, one too large for any such temptress or any woman to master, implies the artist. Niniane would have held a small British archive or some Chaldean treatise on astronomy from Babylon or the Middle East.

A hundred years later the mythologist Robert Graves saw Niniane as another moon-goddess named Phoebe, or Virginia, or Gloriana. Or she was in his vision a love goddess from the more ancient Eleusinian Mysteries in Greece, a loving dove whose temples were always at the seashore, a mermaid. Tall and golden-haired, as he more accurately pictured her, she was an exact icon of Botticelli's *Birth of Venus*, rising rosy and nude from her scallop shell, later to be dressed in a flowery robe for the myrtle groves about her shrine, or wrapped like the three Fates in a purple-fringed mantle.

Dark-haired temptress like Queen Morgue of Man, or sunny-haired nymph in her virginal cell, Niniane/Vivian has enchanted readers and scholars ever since the first archivists entered her name in their copies. Merlin's twelve-year-old girl captivated him and his world too from the first day he set eyes upon her in the woods of what must today be northeastern England. She became the celebrated, much esteemed Lady of the Lake.

The medieval author of *Le Roi Artus* (Vol. II, *Continuation*) says Niniane and Merlin had made a bargain, the end of which he knew. He says Merlin had three secrets that Niniane wished to learn: (1) how to raise a castle in the air, (2) how to walk dry-shod on water, and (3) how to divert a river over a dry plain. This author's theory of human love is an old one, that it commences in affection and joy but finishes in sorrow:

> *Voirement comence amor*
> *En joie, et fenist en dolor* (p. 178).

Niniane said to Merlin. "Teach me all, and I will consent to everything you desire." Merlin agreed. So she learned how to make him fall asleep and how to make him impotent. "Merlin never knew a woman anyway," adds the author, who concludes on his own that Merlin must have been crazy. Meanwhile "Vivian" like Morgue became a scholar and learned the seven liberal arts, as well as all of Merlin's lost secrets. At the least she knew more than any woman before her ever knew, except for one secret: the secret of how to bind and keep a man without enclosing him in a stone tower or walls of any kind, without tying him with ropes of any kind, but, even so, holding him forever bound only by means of a magical spell, which only she could cast.

When he heard her long to master him also, Merlin sighed a deep sigh, said the author of *Le Roi Artus*. But Niniane/Vivian pointed out to him that she had left her home and loving parents for his sake, and she cushioned his head in her lap until he fell sound asleep. Then she rose quietly and traced a magic circle about him, enclosing him, and afterward she often went to look at him in it.

Merlin at first took Niniane from her forest home to King

Arthur's court, now a place of medieval and courtly love. While she resided there, he always went willingly to spend time at her court with his dear "Damsel Chasseresse," or "Diana the Huntress," as she was then called. He loved her then with "too great a love because she was of a too great beauty," and because in those earlier days "she had no more years than about fifteen summers." She feared that he would forget and shame her or that he would take her virginity while she slept. But during the four months she spent learning the ways of the court, he never angered her. He went to call on her each day, as one would call on a lover. "I shall never love you more," she told him, "unless you swear to teach me the enchantments that you know I shall ask you for. Since you love me so dearly, I want you to swear with your bare hand (raised) that you will never work any enchantment upon me, nor by any other means you know I would be enraged at." And Merlin swore.

However romantically these interpreters have argued the facts of their texts, the impression of strong emotions still comes through. In just such a way, with an equally hysterical hope and abject fear, the ancient lady saints of the fifth and sixth centuries dreaded marriage, loathed the loss of their virginity, and prayed to reach peace and safety in the Church. In his book *Pagan and Christian* (p. 29ff.) E. R. Dodds writes about this passion on the part of ancient women.[5]

Such hysteria did not infect the sisters who married Kings Ban and Bors, the first giving birth to Lancelot, and the second

. . .

[5] They read in the *Acts of Paul and Thecla:* "Virginity was the supreme, crowning achievement," and that "only virgins would be resurrected." All other women would remain in hell throughout eternity. They read in the *Gospel of the Egyptians:* "Christ came to destroy the works of the female . . . to put an end to sexual reproduction." It spoke in the *Apocalypse of Peter* about the "malice of the chaste vs. the unchaste . . . and of the post-mortem tortures inflicted routinely upon the corpses of adulterers, fornicators, and homosexuals." But

to two sons, Bors and Lionel. Merlin and the Lady of the Lake traveled through Northumberland after a sea crossing of one night with Merlin at the helm. After this passage, probably over the Firth of Forth, from north to south, they journeyed to North Berwick near the peak called Berwick Law and saw Elaine's baby boy, who was then one year old. Both agreed with the doting young mother that her baby son was "la plus bele creature del monde."

As they continue their journey, Merlin and the Lady of the Lake come upon two harpers seated under ivory palanquins near two large elm trees. Between them stood a stone cross under which were more than one hundred tombs. Merlin at once stops his ears so as not to listen to the harpers who might cause him to fall into an enchanted slumber, "as asps do, so as not to fall prey to snake charmers." Indignantly Merlin puts the harpers to sleep, seated as they are among the groves, and then sets them afire with chemicals containing a sulphur that, he says, will burn but preserve the harpers just as they are as long as King Arthur reigns. After his death, Merlin will be considered "the wisest of the wise," for he tolerated no other magic in his jurisdiction.

They are soon informed that King Ban of North Berwick has been beseiged by King Claudas, who intends to seize his territories. Queen Elaine, who is a descendant of Saint Joseph of Arimathea, might lose her husband, her infant son, and her kingdom. Her husband is killed evidently upon Berwick Law. This steep sugarloaf of a mountain east of Edinburgh stands alone near the coastline of East Lothian and rises from the level farm-

. . .

they knew, first and foremost, that their beloved Saint Paul had attached a "fantastic value" upon virginity.

Nobody seems to know to this day, despite all the progress in linguistics and anthropology, why in this ancient world of King Arthur young married women were so frequently beheaded by their husbands as soon as they became pregnant.

lands to a conical point some seven hundred feet in elevation.[6] According to the story told in the *Lancelot* manuscript (Vol. I), the queen, hearing the news of her husband's death, picked up her son in his blanket, ran out of the gates, and threw him into the (arms of the Lady of the) Lake. Then she ran distractedly up a mountain peak to hold her dead husband in her arms. She and her sister, King Bors's widow, became nuns, but a local legend seems to recall this young Queen Elaine:

> There's a green grave on North Berwick Law,
> And a maniac comes and sings,
> And with the burden of her song
> The valley 'neath her rings.

This story represents the Lady of the Lake's first official act of her majority, to take charge of the infant Lancelot, whose guardian and tutor she has become. One can assume that she was chosen by Merlin for that purpose, and so trained and educated. It is also possible to suggest that she kept her virginity, not because she feared marriage but because, unlike Morgue, she had taken holy vows. Her title, by which she is generally known, indicates her rank, apparently that of a mother superior of an important educational institution to which she brought the young sons of King Bors after his death. In fact, she had them abducted or brought to her by force. Her accusation of mistreatment of these little boys by King Claudas seems to have silenced his protests at her high-handed deed.

When she is called "Lady of the Lake," the place indicated is the Irish Sea where Lancelot is said to have been raised and

* * *

[6] The Flutre index believes that "Benoïc," land of King Ban, is either a kingdom in western Gaul near the village of Saint-Just or a corruption of "Ganoric" (a misreading for "Genewis") = Gwynedd ((North Wales) from its Latin name, "Venedotia." Thus, if Flutre is correct, Lancelot was born, and grew up, and spent his life in France and not in Britain.

trained by mermen (?) or sailors (?). Castle Rushen on the southern coast of the Isle of Man was for centuries and until very recently a private school for the education of princelings. Lancelot's son Galahad was raised there by Lancelot and his queen, the Grail king's daughter Elaine.

The Lady of the Lake wept easily whenever she encountered her ward, the baby Lancelot. She sheltered him in her castle hidden by the "lake," down a valley, where at low tide one could enter freely through a great portal. People said, "My heart tells me this child is Lancelot, who was said to have died on the same day as his father died."

"The child has no name," the Lady always replied.

"Be blessed, Lady," Lancelot told her, "for having allowed me to aspire to great nobility, even if I do not yet know who I am."

"The greatest noblemen of the world before now," the Lady taught him, "were John the Baptist, Judas Maccabeus, Simon brother of Judas, King David, Joseph of Arimathea, his son Galahad who was king of Hofelise (Wales), Pelles of Listenois (the Grail Castle) and his brother Helain the Great (Alain le Gros)."

Lancelot was sometimes called "Handsome Foundling" and "Noble Orphan," but the Lady called him "Fitzroy" (king's son). Queen Guinevere said, "If I had been Our Heavenly Father, I could not have put one thing more or one thing less in Lancelot." When he was twelve, he beat his tutor for striking his hunting dog, at which the Lady granted him his majority, having judged that he already possessed a king's heart. One curious detail usually identifies him: his torso was so much out of proportion to the rest of his body, so much larger that it constituted a physical defect or imperfection.

After the sons of King Bors had been rescued by the Lady, they ate from the same dish as Lancelot, and all three slept in the same bed. Lancelot repeated his lessons to them:

1. A king's son must show no mercy to those who have despoiled him of his kingdom.

215

2. A king's son must surpass all others in prowess.

Lancelot carved at table before the Lady did, and although it was August when roses no longer bloom, he always wore a crown of roses on his head. The Lady had these flowers laid at the head of his bed each morning before he was awake. He divided them at once between himself and the two other king's sons so that each princeling had a hat of flowers to wear during each day. If Lionel burst into tears, Lancelot repeated for his benefit:

3. Never weep for estates, for if you take heart, you will regain them.

4. Gain a kingdom for yourself and hold it by means of your own prowess.

When Lancelot was eighteen years old, the Lady of the Lake escorted him to King Arthur.[7]

Their departure took place on the Friday before Saint John's day. The Lady insisted that Lancelot wear her armor and ride her horses. Her last advice to him was that he not use his own name until others had addressed him by it. She told him she knew that he would complete many deeds of high adventure. However, he would fail to finish one of them. Dressed all in white, her head covered with a white veil, and mounted upon a pure white horse, the Lady escorted Lancelot up to the king, bowed low to Arthur, and presented Lancelot to him. Before she turned to leave Lancelot forever, she said: "Adieu, my beautiful one, my gracious one, my long desired, the beloved of all men and of all women!"

•   •   •

[7] See Madeleine Pelner Cosman's *The Education of the Hero in Arthurian Literature* (Chapel Hill, N.C., 1965–1966).

Afterward the Lady dispatched maidens as messengers who communicated frequently with Lancelot, took new weapons to him, and brought news to her. She sent one of her famous red-and-white horses to Gawain also, and it was branded with the turtledove, emblem of the Grail Castle. She sent Lancelot a gold ring that helped him cross the dangerous Sword Bridge. She sent Tristan his dog from the kingdom of the dead, for only the dog can find the ruler's grave. She sent healing medicine to Queen Morgan's son Yvain when he was suffering from a bout of insanity. She once exculpated Queen Guinevere of charges levied against her. After Merlin's death, the Lady for a short while replaced him, first by warning King Arthur that Accolon held Excalibur, so saving the king's life.

While there is little doubt that she was the greatest and most powerful female personage of her time, except for women saints, the Lady of the Lake still eludes absolute identification, especially because the name, many have remarked, was severely tabooed. It is not certain that she was named either Niniane or Vivian. Sometimes she is called Elaine, and even Helaine, and is said to have married late in life one of the Grail kings, perhaps the one called Pelles. Or Niniane may have replaced an earlier mother superior because celibacy was not enforced for a full lifetime in the Celtic Church. As the famous archaeologist W. M. Flinders Petrie told the British Academy in a paper he read on November 7, 1917, this is a much neglected area of British history.

The name "Niniane" is undoubtedly Celtic. It closely resembles that of the premier British Saint Ninian who founded (c. 397) the great monastery of Britain ("*magnum monasterium*") on the peninsula of Whithorn (*Witerna*).[8] There the Rhinn of Galloway faces south toward the Isle of Man. Fragments of sculpted

. . .

[8] The names "Ninian" and "Niniane" are connected, but how? Neither Merlin nor Niniane has told us.

crosses and of tombstones found there indicate a Romanized congregation, predating the British kingdom of Strathclyde.

Saint Ninian had been trained in Rome, was an admirer or student of Saint Martin of Tours, and settled in Britain in an attempt to convert the southern or Galloway Picts. His stone church was called The White House (*Candida Casa*) in his day but Bredigan (*Broceliande*) in Merlin's day. Saint Ninian's Cave, where he was interred, is still there on that finger of land, still surrounded by the Irish Sea on three sides: the east, the west, and the south. Biographers and church historians know all this perfectly well and also connect Saint Kentigern (*Mungo*) to this cave. King Arthur has been connected also, and said to worship there during a service that was originally written by Saint Ninian himself.

The Welsh still tell stories of a marvelous blonde mermaid who dwelled in a "lake" and of her many adventures with mortals; and Chris Barber recounts several such stories in *Mysterious Wales*. The beautiful blonde messenger's tales, from the western isle where the dead heroes go for burial are told in memory of the Lady of the Lake by the Irish as by Marie de France in her Arthurian poem "Lanval" (Sir Launfal). The Irish tales call her Fand and say she seduced the young son of a king of Ireland. The prince followed her, as did King Arthur; neither was ever seen again.

Until recently the Lady of the lake could have claimed direct descendants in Wales. Relics drawn from her Welsh lake, Llyn (Lake) of Du'r (Black) Araddu in the same Snowdon range where Arthur killed the great giant Rhitta (Rhitta Gawr) include bronze axes, symbols of ancient royalty and of Merlin himself. Sickles, chisels, and two cauldrons are all preserved in the National Museum of Cardiff, Wales. Elsewhere in Wales her legend calls her one of three sisters, which confuses her life with that of Queen Morgue. Her legend in South Wales has her appear from another lake to wed her earthly lover in the Welsh village of Myddfai; but her husband accidentally touched her with metal, causing her to return to the lake. Her earthling husband drowned while trying to bring her back.

At this point in the story, the ancient Arthurian material surfaces like a modern fairy tale: the Lady of the Lake reappeared just long enough to instruct her eldest son. There at a place still called "The Doctor's Gate" in her memory, she commanded her son and his son's sons to become forever the healers of mankind. Welsh people, says Chris Barber (p. 169), customarily go up to her lake on the first Sunday of August in hopes of seeing her drawn out of the black, peat-filled water by her oxen or to glimpse her seated on a stone, like the mermaid in Copenhagen, Denmark, combing her long, blonde hair.

The village of Myddfai, Wales, where the Lady was wed, says her legend, in fact, claimed her descendants in the famous medical men, the physicians of Myddfai, whose cures are recorded in the ancient Welsh text, the *Red Book of Hergest*. This is one of the several revered, ancient books of Wales. The *Red Book* contains medical prescriptions dating from ancient Britain, and doubtless from Merlin and two of his most famous pupils, Morgue and Niniane/Vivian. [9]

Among the Welsh families claiming descent from the Lady of the Lake are the following: Jones, Williams, Owen, and Bowers. Several garden plots in Myddfai still produce medicinal herbs descended from the herb gardens of the Lady of the Lake. Chris Barber says that the last of these doctors of medicine in Myddfai died in 1860 (p. 183).

There is some evidence because of their numerous descendants—Queen Morgue's among the clans of Scotland, and Nin-

• • •

[9] The *Red Book of Hergest* is one of the ancient books Charlotte Guest described as Geoffrey of Monmouth described his source also for *The History of the Kings of Britain* (and Merlin's *Prophecy*): as a "little, small, ancient book." I mention this again, for Geoffrey has always been called a liar by his critics. In my view he was too fine a scholar to have been a liar. He was also named to a bishop's see just before his death. Such a great honor is not bestowed on liars.

iane/Vivian's among the physicians of Wales—that both were real women. Still, other Arthurian mythologists have disagreed, Roger Sherman Loomis concluding that the Lady of the Lake is Queen Morgue in one disguise, and John Rhŷs also concluding that the Lady of the Lake and Niniane "may be taken as different aspects of the one mythic figure, the lake lady Morgan."[10]

· · ·

[10] See Lucy Allen Paton's *Studies in the Fairy Mythology of Arthurian Romance* (New York, 1960), pp. 291, 284 passim.

TESTING

But he held a holly cluster in one hand, holly   v. 206
That is greenest when groves are gaunt and bare,
And an axe in his other hand, huge and monstrous,
A hideous helmet-smasher for anyone to tell of:
The head of the axe was an ell-rod long.
Of green hammered gold and steel was the socket,
And the blade was burnished bright, with a broad edge,
Acutely honed for cutting, as keenest razors are.

Sir Gawain and the Green Knight.
Translated by Brian Stone.

While he counseled King Vortigern, Merlin existed by himself, somewhere beyond the reach and outside the protection, if any, of that ruler. The same situation holds true for Merlin when occasionally he devised strategies and prophesied outcomes for both Kings Ambrosius and Uther Pendragon. In all three cases Merlin's real vocation drew him back to his teacher, Master (*Magister*) Blaise. From his birth about the year 450 until the death of King Uther and the birth of his son Arthur about the year 475, Merlin remained primarily occupied in study. On the other hand, Merlin would have been forty years old and at the height of his physical strength when he had Arthur elected *"dux bellorum"* about the year 490, at which time Merlin said Arthur was still too young and too undeveloped physically to bear the full brunt of battle. Consequently Merlin fought Arthur's battles beside him and bore the dragon staff and banner for what could be more than a decade thereafter.

Although ancient Celtic sources in Britain claim that Merlin began prophesying when he was seven years old, or at the demise of King Vortigern, European Celtic sources put his years of prophecy at the time of or directly following the great British victory of Badon Hill. Geoffrey wrote that it was Saint Dubricius, and not Merlin, who exhorted the Celtic forces to dislodge the Saxons from their mountain fortress (Dunn-Britons, or perhaps Dumbarton Rock on the Clyde River, adjacent to modern Glasgow). Merlin returned to his command beside Arthur at the battles against King Urian, or launched the Island Campaign from the Rhinns of Galloway, south to the Isle of Man, thence to the Isle of Anglesey, thence to the Snowdon Mountains of North Wales. After this series of victories, Merlin must have been fifty or fifty-one, says the *Prose Lancelot*, Merlin commenced his *Prophecy* at about that time. His length of prophecy, calculated the clergymen who together worked on a definitive compilation extended over a period of 1,690 weeks.

After Merlin's victories beside Arthur at Bredigan and Carmelide, or, as discovered earlier, at Whithorn on the peninsula of Galloway, and at Gwynedd opposite Anglesey, King Urian of the Isles was finally defeated. The Isles were re-Christianized. Merlin's pupil Morgue wedded King Urian. Merlin had already enrolled Niniane/Vivian as her replacement and eventually as his own replacement, for Merlin has now only thirty-two and a half more years to live. King Arthur has secured for them a respite and happy period of peace. They can safely leave the coastal areas and return home, possibly to their great Roman-style villas.

By this time Merlin has completed his own formal education and turns his energies to the younger generation. What most characterizes his life now is his relationships to others: Merlin and Niniane/Vivian, Merlin and Gawain, Merlin and Arthur, Merlin and Gawain a second time, Merlin and Arthur again, Merlin and Queen Morgue's son Yvain, and Merlin and Perceval. Merlin's last pupil was Lancelot's son Galahad, who performed so successfully in his examinations and then as a holy teacher himself that he may very well be found under the name and career of the illustrious Saint Samson. Galahad may not be the only one of Merlin's pupils to have been universally acclaimed during his lifetime as a saint.[1]

· · ·

[1] This is how saints were made in those ancient times, according to the mysterious workings of Celtic Christianity. Then the title *"Sanctus"* was apparently bestowed as a tribute to the life and works of the most holy men. They constituted a class of elders (*seniores*), who functioned as isolated "senators" upon whom individuals and groups

As he progressed from one step to another along his way to becoming "king" at the Grail Castle, Perceval encountered various elders or high clergymen, and one by one, passed their tests. Ancient ecclesiastical titles present problems even today:

dominicati rhetorici	=	secretaries (?)
sacerdotes	=	bishops (?),
presbyters	=	priests (?),
diaconi	=	deacons (?),
episcopi	=	bishops (?),
doctores	=	educated persons (?).

The dignitaries who tested Perceval are not identified by any such title, however.

Many Arthurian heroes, including Perceval himself, seem to have passed severe and perhaps final examinations under Merlin personally. First and foremost may have been Arthur himself, whom Merlin had sent out for fostering in some secret, well-forested refuge, perhaps near Loch Arthur on the eastern coast of the Rhinns of Galloway. Nearly everyone knows of the boy Arthur's first test, so celebrated that this mysterious public examination has never been forgotten over a period of some fifteen hundred years. It is common knowledge that in the presence of the various tribes or northern clans, Arthur drew a sword from a stone *where Merlin had placed it*. It could be that Arthur lighted a fire by friction in such a dramatic way that the illumination blazed unforgettably upon the nerve centers of the onlookers. The scene certainly was recorded upon the memory of all present. The western Camelot where this history-making event occurred was subsequently called the Castle of the Dolmen Stone, "le château del Perron." It stood outside both the medieval and modern city of Carlisle and perhaps at the very edge or shore

. . .

of people could call for advice and assistance. Because they lived so close to God, they were held as ultimate authorities on earth.

of the Solway Firth. People embarking there for the Isle of Man are said to have first stepped upon this stone and then into their craft.

Arthur's second test took place in such secrecy that it has not come down through the ages and must only be inferred. This test was his inauguration as "president" of the Round Table Order. Since he established that order, Merlin would have again functioned as examiner. The third test took place in the presence of Saint Dubricius, and it was his coronation, at which high ceremony Merlin inexplicably was not present. However, he did preside later on at a second, subsidiary coronation ceremony, where he performed the ascertainment of Arthur's right to the throne.

One of Gawain's first tests took place at the Grail Castle. There he was commanded to obtain the "head of John the Baptist" by defeating an Albanian King in Scotland. This sacred object had to be wrested from its Albanian owner, carried to the Grail Castle, and presented to the Grail King for his treasury. Although Gawain accomplished this task and brought this assignment to what would appear to be a satisfactory conclusion—for he handed the object to the Grail King during a religious service—he was told to his great sorrow and the reader's puzzlement that he had failed the test. As they recorded this dramatic procedure, the authors assumed that Gawain was subsequently whipped by a fierce cyclonic storm as he departed "along the opposite shore" of the Isle of Man.

One clue suggests that the purpose of these tests concerned the future Grail King's person by determining beforehand who among Arthurian heroes was proceeding satisfactorily toward that high honor. Because of his close association with the Grail Castle, professional scholars and other readers have wondered if Merlin himself in his official capacity could have been a Grail king. In other words, today is not the first time people have suspected that "Merlin" was an agnomen only and not one man's real name when dressed in full honor in the world.

While the genealogy of the Grail Kings remains unclear, it still needs to be looked at because of Merlin's reported connections there with the re-Christianization, with Gawain, with the Lady of the Lake, and with Perceval.[2] The question would be: Was Merlin one of the three generations of Grail Kings called Pelleam, Pelles I, or Pelles II? The Welsh archives do not help to answer the question, for these names of kings come from the French manuscripts:

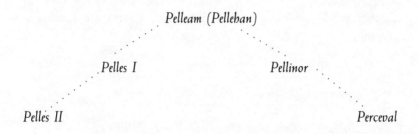

Pelleam (Pellehan)

Pelles I   *Pellinor*

Pelles II   *Perceval*

The French authors were working with unfamiliar foreign names, which were neither Old British (or modern Welsh) nor comprehensible, but only foreign. The king named Pelleam was recorded under at least four alternate spellings as King of the Waste Land, or as King of the "Terre Foraine," or Foreign Land where another foreign tongue was spoken. This tongue was not "Chaldean" (an error presumably for "Caledonian" or Scottish) but most probably Gaelic since Man belonged to Ireland first rather than

• • •

[2] See Arthurian indexes such as Flutre's, or critical works such as Alfred Nutt's *Studies on the Legend of the Holy Grail* (New York, 1965), John Rhŷs's *Studies of the Arthurian Legend* (Oxford, 1891), Roger Sherman Loomis's *The Grail: From Celtic Myth to Christian Symbol* (New York, 1963), and his *Celtic Myth and Arthurian Romance* (New York, 1926). The Welsh sources do not elaborate on the Grail, although their tale of "Peredur" appears derived from the testings of Perceval.

to the mainland of Britain, as its "foreign" King Urian so capably demonstrated by opposing both Merlin and Arthur.

The Lame King Pelleam was father to Pelles, to Pellinor (called Alan of the Isles, or the Alain, who fathered Perceval), and to Lamorat de Listenois (father of Tristan). Pelles had a daughter named Dame Elaine (or Helen), who bore a Lancelot and who married a Grail King's daughter, also named Elaine (or Helen), who bore Galahad (also Lancelot's baptismal name). This Pelles I is called uncle to Perceval and called also the Lame King, the Rich[3] Fisher King, and also "Guardian of the Grail at Corbenic." Loomis points out that these names are Gaelic in origin:

Gaelic	Welsh	Arthurian
Bile	Beli Mawr[4]	Bellinor, Pellinor
	Beli	Belin, Pelleam, Pelles

Galahad greets his grandfather King Pelles at the Grail Castle, where Perceval had previously greeted his uncle King Pelles. It seems probable, therefore, that they are another line of hereditary kings and not connected to Merlin. This may be true despite Thomas Malory's information that King Pelles loved and married Merlin's ward, the Lady of the Lake.[5] Great confusion stems from such lines of royal personages all named either Pelles

·   ·   ·

[3] The name "Alan" means "noble," and so does the French adjective "Riche."

[4] King Beli the Great.

[5] *Le Morte d'Arthur*, Vol. I, pp. 122–23. It seems very possible that the Lady would have been released from her vows at the death of Merlin.

or Lancelot, as the male rulers are named, with Elaine (Elen, Helen) as their queens and mothers.

The *Didot-Perceval* account shows Perceval with his teacher Merlin at the Grail Castle. By that time Merlin was as old as Father Time, recognizable as the Old Year. Merlin wears a long white beard and holds a rolled scroll in his right hand. Thus, Perceval was Merlin's student, and Yvain was another of his students.

Queen Morgue's son Yvain also undertakes what sounds like another of Merlin's deadly examinations at the latter's favorite haunt in his older years: the celebrated Fountain of Broceliande, actually Bredigan at the Whithorn peninsula.[6] After a failure by a first hero, Yvain pursues this quest until its completion by officiating in a rainmaking ceremony at the basin surrounding the spring. He slays its former guardian and marries the widow Laudine (Lodonesia > Lothian), the eponymous sovereign or princess of Lothian.

Although this poem was written by Chrétien de Troyes as a fairy tale, one wonders if it was not originally a masque presented at the wedding feast for Yvain and his bride. Persons of such importance must have deserved such an honor and had either a masque written to commemorate the happy union or an epithalamium in the manner of Catullus's poem for the parents of Achilles. Yvain and the princess of Lothian seem to have been ancestors of Saint Kentigern (Beloved Head) called Mungo, who is the older patron saint of Scotland and who lies today in the Catholic Cathedral of Glasgow. Although Merlin does not appear here, his emissary, the Lady of the Lake, brings medicine to heal Yvain when he, like Lancelot, goes mad and wanders in the forest. Like *The Birth of Merlin*, such a drama would have played very well in an outdoor theater or in the courtyard of Stirling Castle (Camelot).

• • •

[6] See *Yvain, ou le chevalier au lion* in the telling by Chrétien de Troyes. Yvain (Owain) is here called "Knight of the Lion," and the heraldic lion has long symbolized Scotland and its royal families.

229

This Whitsuntide ceremony performed by Yvain—or the initiation and examinations he surprisingly survived—are enveloped in such heavy, mythological implications in medieval French and medieval Welsh texts[7] that audiences may have enjoyed them in whatever form they originally had. The story—but not the characters—is mythological: a midsummer rite to ensure abundant rainfall for crops, fertilization of the earth (goddess), the descent into hell, or madness of the wounded hero, who portrays the god of spring, and a return to fine weather with happiness for all.

The story goes that the princess of Scotland, who is named Laudine in Old French, dwells beside her magical boiling spring, which summons a terrible storm every time a shield is struck or water is thrown upon it. Then birds fly madly about, and the old, red husband, whose tenure of seven years is about over, appears and is killed. The princess becomes an eligible widow. Yvain's horse is cut in two as he passes the portcullis and meets the moon goddess Lunette (Luned), who regulates her mistress's periods of fertility. If Merlin presides, then he is the bullish Old Man of the Mountain, who sports a bearskin. The upshot is that the young hero has supplanted the old, decrepit husband of an earth annually rejuvenated and perpetually renewed. From primitive times people all over the world probably enjoyed such midsummer festivals of the mature Earth. Yvain's adventure appears to coincide with the summer solstice at Merlin's "Perilous Fountain." Fortunate youth, Yvain does not die under the lone pine tree of pan-Celtic paganism but lives to love Laudine the following year.

·   ·   ·

[7] The date of Chrétien's Yvain is c. 1155. The Welsh "Lady of the Fountain" from the three romances, Y Tair Rhamant, as translated customarily in the Mabinogion, is not now considered an adaption of Chrétien. The characters in the Welsh tale of Owain are now considered not only mythological but also historical.

On the other hand, Gawain is the much more glamorous hero of the spring equinox, Easter or Beltane, as it is called in Ireland. Then on May Eve, at places known also as Mayfair or Fairfield, the new fires of spring were lighted in honor of Aries the Ram. This greatest of all joyous ceremonies was performed at Uisnech in Westmeath, once called the navel of Ireland.[8] They were also probably performed at the "foreign" Grail Castle, which stood upon the more ancient oracular center, or navel of all Britain, at Saint Patrick's Isle beside the Isle of Man. In *Gawain and the Green Knight*, the ancient, great queen, Morgue la Fée, appeared to Gawain under her double identity, as a beautiful young princess and as the ugly, black mother hag.

Merlin is thought to be either the "green" or "gray" hero of death or winter, but the color is uncertain. He comes to Camelot on a Christmas Eve to challenge a hero to a test. Dressed in furs and precious fabrics, bearded, long-haired, half gigantic, Merlin bears the holly branch of peace, but as he is green, he symbolizes the corpse-like hue of death. He is called Bertilak, the Giant Herdsman from the land of fairies: Ireland. At his challenge Gawain strikes off his head, which the Green Knight, like Saint Denis of France and Saint Winefred of Wales, calmly picks up and carries away.[9]

Gawain must meet him (at Saint Patrick's Isle off the coast of Man) a year hence. It is the Grail Castle, described correctly here as near a forest and a promontory, within a peel stockade two miles in circumference, opposite a road, across water via a bridge, and as surrounded by a peel or palisaded wall. The Green Chapel is two miles distant, sited perilously upon a hill, probably at Saint John's Church and the present Tynwald Hill on the

. . .

[8] See Patrick Crampton's *Stonehenge of the Kings* (New York, 1968), p. 91.

[9] German scholars, notably Heinrich Zimmer, have long thought so too: He is Merlin.

Isle of Man. There is a ravine for Gawain to cross and a rough path around a cliff for him to climb. He sees a barrow for the dead adjacent to a stream, near a lime or linden tree (sacred to the mother goddess). He hears a barbarous noise issuing from the underground, an ear-splitting din. Gawain is said to be bound in Christmas colors, red and green, with a lady's lovelace, but one doubts it. Early Asian Christians were always so bound, around the waist, at their initiation, says Onians in his history of religious thought.

The high priest of the chapel does not behead Gawain. At this ritual initiation, or final examination, the priest gives him only three dolorous strokes upon the bare neck with his ceremonial ax, and we recall that a "merlin" is a ceremonial Celtic ax. Gawain must forever bear the scar as a token of his failure, construed by the medieval poet as being due to the perversity of his flesh, to grievous sin, and to a temptress to whom he has yielded. She was Morgue la Fée, Merlin's pupil and deputy.

Heinrich Zimmer and others have found thirteen reasons that this Green Knight was probably Merlin:

1. his kingly presence, his size, his mass of hair;

2. his disguise as a green warrior;

3. his further and continual lessoning of Gawain;

4. the presence of his star pupil, Morgue;

5. the location at the Grail Castle on Saint Patrick's Isle, perhaps even then called "Merlin's Isle";

6. Merlin's frequent association with death, as here, himself as the Headless Horseman in person;

7. Merlin's further association with hunting and forest life;

8. the prominence of the ax with its four-foot blade, as a *merlin*;

9. the oak forest, which evokes memories of the hereditary

priesthood of the Celtic peoples (Druids also were "oak-men" perhaps);

10. the holly branch, or golden bough, as an ancient, sacred symbol mentioned elsewhere as an assignment given Gawain (*Parzival*);

11. the chapel, *perron*, hill, mound, barrow, or burial place, a perilous spot, its relationship to Irish fairies (ancestors) and to Ireland;

12. the repetition of magical numbers, such as the three hunts;

13. Merlin's usual association with fire and storm, as here with lightning.

As well as being the colors of Christmas, the colors red and green also symbolize Wales, to which Merlin was certainly connected. The sacred chapel and barrow and cliffs seem a fairly precise description of the world's other revered oracular sites, especially Jerusalem and Delphi.

James Frazer explains in *The Golden Bough*, "The Magic Art and the Evolution of Kings," why Gawain failed Merlin's test here:

> For strength of character in the race as in the individual consists mainly in the power of sacrificing the present to the future . . . [;] the height of heroism is reached in men who renounce the pleasures of life and even life itself for the sake of keeping or winning for others, perhaps in distant ages, the blessings of freedom and truth.

Perhaps Gawain as the lascivious Aries was supplanted by a greater springtime hero, also a mounted warrior as his equestrian statues remember him, who is venerated on April 23. In France the statue of Saint George was (or is) carried through the cherry orchards of Anjou with prayers for a good crop. The French held Saint George to represent, as he still does today, courage meeting death halfway.[10] Gawain as fertilizer of the earth was probably replaced but not forgotten because of this supreme work of art, *Sir Gawain and the Green Knight*. And a new correlation, however tenuous, has been established: Merlin and John the Baptist.

In 1973 Elizabeth Brewer showed the beheading threat where it originated, in Ireland, and followed it through Arthurian literature. She recognized it not as a historical event but as a cherished ceremonial.[11] The initiation and failure or success of the hero go from that of the older Irish hero Cuchulain(n), who was trounced by King Cu Roi but who cut off his head a year later, to Lancelot, and then to Gawain's double adventures. Each text mentions the same sort of castle and the same hairy huntsman with an ax over his shoulder. He portrays the same "green" or "gray" man of death or winter (for in Celtic "glas" may mean either color), the same herdsman called in the Gaelic noun of three syllables "bachlach," later spelled Bertilak. In the original Irish plot, the young heroine, whose name is Blathnat, or Mayflower, is hurled into the sea as a punishment for adultery. In Merlin's realm she actually committed no forbidden act and so apparently escaped chastisement, but Gawain was nicked on the neck, scarred for life, and furthermore refused as king of the Grail Castle. He had yielded to her seduction and had accepted her gift of a sash, which plighted his troth.

• • •

[10] See Emile Mâle's *Religious Art* as translated from *L'Art religieux du XIIe au XVIIIe siècle* (New York, 1949). No credit given or name of translator (Pantheon Books).

[11] In *From Cuchulainn to Gawain*, Brewer traced the incident in four texts: *Fled Bricrend* (The Feast of Bricriu), *Continuation of Perceval*, *Perlesvaus*, and *La Mule sanz frain*. In these four texts the heroes are Cuchulainn, Carados, Lancelot, and Gawain, who appears again in *Sir Gawain and the Green Knight*.

Elizabeth Brewer also related the castle on its peel or stockaded islet to the famous revolving castle of Irish mythology. No one could enter it casually because the doorways would not hold still long enough. They are both castles of death where the apple is held sacred because it is the fruit of the Otherworld. Any mortal who eats one there can never again return to his life on earth. Saint Patrick's Isle seems to be the island of initiation or inauguration where those who failed the test were ritually scarred by a dolorous stroke. The illustrious Welsh poem called "Spoils of the Deep" also speaks of it:

> *Am I not a candidate for fame, to be heard in song*
> *In Caer Pedryvan, four times revolving?* [12]
> *A rim of pearls is round its edge.*
>
> *And before the door of the gate of Uffern* [13] *the lamp*
> *was burning.*
> *When we went with Arthur—a splendid labor!—*
> *Except seven, none returned from Caer Vedwyd.* [14]

One may assume that many candidates in this long period of peace under King Arthur have already established themselves in schools either in Britain or in Brittany, France. The life of Saint Gildas shows how clergymen of those days moved easily from Scotland to Ireland, thence, to Brittany. Saint Kentigern moved, it is thought, from eastern Scotland, where he was born, to North Wales just south or inland from the medieval Flint

• • •

[12] Four-cornered castle, surrounded by white breakers, a dangerous coast, but spectacularly beautiful.

[13] The Cold Place = Hell, then visualized as a place of ice and Arctic cold, for 100,000 miles.

[14] Castle of Revelry, or perhaps place of the Feasting of Bran's Head, as recorded in the *Mabinogion*.

Castle, and then to Glasgow, which he raised to the religious center of Scotland. Holy men were great scholars of Merlin's days also; they spoke Latin, P-Celtic (tongue of Scotland and Wales), and Q-Celtic (the language of Man and Ireland). During Arthur's lifetime when the Irish, who were called Scots, moved into western Scotland, they brought Gaelic, or Q-Celtic, along with them. Their men wrote Latin, and their *Lives* were also written then and later in that once universal language.

Before Saint Patrick had established his churches in Ireland, Saint Ninian (or Ninia) had already built his White House, which the Irish called Rosnat, on the Whithorn peninsula. This same place has already appeared as Bredigan or Broceliande in Merlin's wars alongside King Arthur. By 398, it has been thought, Saint Ninian had founded a prestigious monastic school there beside his stone church, or stone enclosure *(llan)* where Merlin and his pupil Morgue practiced medicine as part of their regular ministry and/or mission. Queen Morgue cured Lancelot of "madness" three times: twice after he had been confined in underground prisons and almost starved to death, and once when he fell ill after the death of his ally Galehaut.

Male babies were then customarily put in the care of a foster mother or nurse until they were old enough to be transferred to a male tutor made answerable for the development of their minds and their bodies. Thereafter the most intelligent students sought teachers in advanced schools—always a difficult undertaking. Just as during these centuries the Christian Church in Rome and its symbolism were being organized, so were the future great schools of the Middle Ages. One can judge the quality of the best schools in Merlin's day by reading what their students were able to write. The greatest, most brilliant theologian of those days, an earlier British clergyman called Pelagius, astonished Rome by the polish of his oratory and writing. Nobody then in Rome could match him for eloquence, it is believed.

Within a century or two the learned teachers and best students of Merlin's day had founded the educational system that was to flower during the Middle Ages. They drew up a plan for teaching the liberal arts, which required the highest degree of intelligence for their mastery. Those able to complete the first group of three disciplines—grammar, logic, and rhetoric—earned the bachelor's degree.

Since many documents relating to ancient Celtic education—which was a Church affair *par excellence*—have not yet even been printed, much less translated, it is necessary to turn the search for Merlin to what has already been learned about the Celtic Church and the educational opportunities it offered those able to learn in Merlin's day. A prime text is *An Essay of the Welsh Saints* (London, 1836) by the Rev. Rice Rees, a fellow of Jesus College, Oxford, and professor of Welsh at Saint David's College, Lampeter.[15] Rees found no Merlin among the Welsh saints of the fifth and sixth centuries. But he found Saint Samson (Galahad) very prominently and that saint who exhorted Arthur's forces at the battle of Mt. Badon and who crowned King Arthur thereafter: Saint Dubricius.

The "Archbishop" Dubricius, says Geoffrey of Monmouth, addressed Arthur's forces in words something like these:

> You men who are here set apart by your belief in Christ, consider what love of our fatherland you owe today, and think how your people have been slain by the pagans. Unless you now close ranks and defend them, you shall be everlastingly disgraced. Then fight for your country. If death should fall upon you today, bow down willingly under it for the sake of your native soil. There is not so much a sting in death as a victory and salvation

. . .

[15] This is a rare book, virtually unobtainable today, despite the fact that encyclopedias of religion refer to it as their authority. I am very indebted to Trinity College, Hartford, Connecticut, for its generosity and courtesy in furnishing me with a photocopy. But see also Charles Thomas's *Christianity in Roman Britain to* A.D. *500* (Berkeley and Los Angeles, 1981), Chapters 10 and 11.

for your immortal souls. In dying for your families, you will offer yourselves as sacrifice to God, and thereby follow the footsteps of Christ, who lay down His own soul for us all. Those among you who shall die in combat today may be certain they do so in full penance, and full absolution from all sin. Therefore receive absolution from me, willingly now, in this fashion.[16]

His words were followed by the victory which ensured the peace in Britain for twenty or so years.

Rees explained that Geoffrey's "Archbishop" really existed in King Arthur's day. The great saint was descended from one of the three royal landed families of Wales, that of Brychan, who was a grandfather. In this third generation the family members irrevocably renounced their vast Roman villas, huge holdings, and all possessions, so hideous had the world of chaos and invasion become, and quietly entered the Church. Those few who continued on in the world, men and women both, finally renounced all their lands and vast wealth also in the next generation. Originally high potentates and royal warriors, they took other names and disappeared from history forever, except for Dubricius, who was too illustrious to have vanished that easily. A second exception must be made for King Urian Rheged of Cumbria, who ruled later in western Scotland after King Arthur's death and who also descended from the common ancestor of these noble people, Brychan.

The church that Saint Dubricius entered was the Celtic, already known from its delegates to synods (Church councils) in Arles (314) and Rimini (359) but especially noted for the articulate, brilliant Pelagius in Rome. The organization of the Celtic Church in his lifetime was monastic, consisting of landed monasteries ruled by abbots, where the clergy were allowed to marry,

• • •

[16] *The History of the Kings of Britain,* IX, 4.

to raise families, and to bequeath their posts to their descendants. The only evidence that the Celtic Church was once ruled by an archbishop, namely Archbishop Dubricius, comes from Geoffrey of Monmouth and other Welsh clergymen and princes of the twelfth century perhaps intent upon reinstating an archiepiscopal see inside Wales, not necessarily proving them wrong.

Their hopes had already been dashed, for Wales was last among the members of the Celtic Realm, as Norah Chadwick called it, reluctantly to yield to Rome and give up its religious freedom:

Ireland	632 and 695,
Northumbria	644,
Scotland	717 (and 1150),
Cornwall	768,
Wales	777.

This great Roman aristocrat and landowner, Saint Dubricius, was born of a royal mother named Eurdila in Latin and Efrddyl in Welsh. She was Brychan's daughter, Rees thought. The father of Dubricius was declared to be unknown, and his birth was miraculous. The mother of Dubricius was sentenced to death by her family because of her pregnancy but allowed to live until her child was born. The baby Dubricius touched the old king who had sentenced his mother to death. This touch cured the patriarch of a terrible illness (possibly leprosy), after which miracle both mother and child were allowed to survive. The infancy of Dubricius, whose Welsh name was Dyfrig, was considered miraculous. Wherever he went, the world bowed down in great respect and awe to this child prodigy.

Although Saint Dubricius has often been called either archbishop of Wales, archbishop of South Wales, first bishop of Llandaf, bishop of Caerleon, and first archbishop of Llandaf, there is no uncontested proof that any such title was his. It is certain, however, that he traveled frequently around Wales and the islands of the Irish Sea and that he functioned like a Roman prelate, an archbishop with power over contemporary clergymen, churches, and monasteries.[17] His prestige was enormous.

Aside from having crowned King Arthur. Saint Dubricius distinguished himself by having founded three colleges in Wales, writes Rees. He founded and during his lifetime ruled:

1. Llancarfan in Glamorgan: cathedral, diocese, and anciently a vast, landed monastery and school.

   Abbot 1 = Cadog the Wise, famous for his aphorisms. Saint Cadog was Dubricius's constant, lifelong companion, often at King Arthur's Court with him.

   They founded several churches (about seventeen) and chapels. (Feast day = February 24).

   Saint Dubricius lies buried there today, at the cathedral dedicated to him by Urban, Bishop of Llandaf, c. 1130.

2. Llanilltud Fawr, or Bangor Illtyd (Llantwit Major in English). Church, parish, ancient landed monastery in Glamorgan. First Abbot, called founder (c. 520) was Saint Illtud, called a Breton, said to have been a nephew of Saint Germanus of Auxerre, also said to have been a relative of and soldier under King Arthur. Saint Illtud is said to have invented a new plough for those vast domains. His monastery is said to have had seven halls, four hundred houses, and to have supported one hundred ecclesiastics (students), one hundred paupers, one hundred widows,[18] plus many strangers and guests, at no cost to any of the above, and churches without number.

• • •

[17] Recent spelling has been simplified in Wales; that is, Llandav or Llandaff is now Llandaf, but Landavensis in Latin, as The Book of Llandaf (Liber Landavensis).

[18] The starvation of veterans' families in such times of general devastation must have been extreme when one considers that French widows destituted under the Code Napoléon in France of the nineteenth century also starved en masse.

3. Caerleon reputedly founded by Saint Dubricius for two hundred philosophers, astronomers, and scientists. [19]

When we turn to an American scholar and clergyman, Dr. William Cathcart, editor in 1894 of the Baptist Encyclopedia and author of *The Ancient British and Irish Churches* (Philadelphia, 1894), we hear confirmation of the Rev. Rice Rees as to the importance of Saint Dubricius:

> One of the powerful agencies for extending the Gospel among the ancient Britons was the establishment of great monastic schools, where the Bible was studied and literary instruction imparted. These institutions are said to have been founded, soon after A.D. 429, by Dubricius and Iltutus, supposed disciples of Germanus (p. 54).

He goes on to say that the fame of Dubricius was increased because of his knowledge of the Old and New Testaments so that scholars from every part of Britain sought him out, not only the uneducated, but also the masters of philosophy and other disciplines, to study under him. At his hall in Hentland on the Wye River he had with him as students one thousand clergymen working in literature and divinity. The students supported themselves (on the patrimonial estates of Dubricius, it would appear) by agriculture and fishing.

Cathcart concludes his study of fifth-century Britain with these words: "The Britons for centuries held the chief doctrines and practices of the Baptist denomination" (p. 58).

One last voice should be heard before we leave the subject of schools to which both Merlin and Saint Dubricius are so closely connected. The Rev. David Davies, writing from Penarth, Wales, in 1924, clears up the issue of authority in the Celtic Church

•   •   •

[19] Here again, due to lack of confirmation and to reason, one suggests that Carlisle was the place of this monastery and school.

by showing "that the Church of (Saint) David (of Wales) drew its authority from Jerusalem, the home of the first Church of Christ, and was, therefore, wholly independent of the church that derived its authority from Saint Peter" (p. 45). In this church, he adds, the "special title of 'Archbishop,' " as it was bestowed upon Saint Dubricius, was not "expressive of any metropolitan dignity," but rather designated him as " 'first among equals' by reason of exceptional piety, gifts, prominence, or extended service" (p. 47). Rev. Davies asserts categorically that the term "Saint" as applied to such early clergymen as Dubricius merely meant that he was born into a Welsch, ecclesiastical tribe.[20]

The churches dedicated to Saint Dubricius stand just west of the bend of the Wye River, in eastern Wales. They are given by William Rees in his *Historical Atlas of Wales*, from northwest to south, as Moccas, Madley, Ballingham, Wormbridge, Llanwarthyn, and Henllan (Hentland).[21]

. . .

[20] See note in *The Ancient Celtic Church and the See of Rome* (Cardiff, 1924), pp. 68–69.

[21] *Historical Atlas of Wales*, Plate 25a.

10

THE
MURDER
OF
MERLIN

. . . .

MERLIN

I

Merlin's blows are strokes of fate,   v. 16
Chiming with the forest tone,
When boughs buffet boughs in the wood;
Chiming with the gasp and moan
Of ice-imprisoned flood;
With the pulse of manly hearts;
With the voice of orators;
With the din of city arts;
With the cannonade of wars;
With the marches of the brave;
And prayers of might from martyrs' cave.

Ralph Waldo Emerson.
Poems. Vol. III.

* * * * * * *

When he edited the Prose Lancelot in 1872, Paulin Paris noted a peculiar phenomenon often occurring whenever Merlin's relationship to the Lady of the Lake is concerned: as it approaches the end, their story no longer develops progressively from one episode into another. Thus, concerning Merlin's murder, one finds only scattered accounts, as if from witnesses separated from each other by sealed doors behind which, unable to follow the testimony of the others, each can relate only his own shocked recollection of what he thought he saw, or heard, or read, or concluded all by himself.

The *Prose Lancelot* copy stored in the archives of France and which has recently been proposed as the original or primitive source, exemplifies this scattering or divergent practice. Quite independent of corroborative testimony, the narrator spins off his own disparate findings: first, that Merlin was not born in Carmarthen, Wales but in a port of Scotland near Ireland, that is, "en la maresche de la terre d'Escoce et d'Irelande." If he was born on the March of Scotland as one goes to embark for Ireland, then he was born on the Rhinns of Galloway, at or near his own "Fountain of Bredigan."[1] Merlin was twelve years old,

* * *

[1] It is critical to compare Paulin Paris's text and commentary to the recent critical edition of the same manuscript called A (original) Manuscript B.N. (Bibliothèque Nationale in Paris = National Library of France) fr. (written in Old French) and 768: *Lancelot du lac,* edited by Elspeth Kennedy, 2 vols. (Oxford and New York, 1980), Vol. I, p. 21, l. 24ff.

one is now asked to believe, when he counseled Uther Pendragon, and at that time Merlin possessed from his father the Devil (or from his father who was a devil) "all the secrets of human knowledge." The Lady of the Lake was commonly seen accompanying him. Merlin was nonetheless in his lifetime, continues the "original" copy of the *Prose Lancelot*, venerated as a "holy prophet," and also as almost "a sort of god." Since the Lady of the Lake directly acquired her own knowledge from him, this "set her above all the women of her time."

The author does not need to explain his own premise or point of view toward all this. He steers a straight course, maintaining his inviolability and keeping a wide distance: *knowledge is evil*, and especially of the past. "The more one knows, the more evil one becomes," he writes expressing his corollary. Sniffing disdainfully, the author of Manuscript A concludes the two must have made an unholy compact: he will teach her *everything*, which obviously includes sex. There lurks here, implies the author, a real danger of guilt by association.

The original connection between Merlin and Niniane/Vivian from this point in the development of their history becomes suspect. What else did Merlin teach her besides sex? He taught her magical words enabling her to enclose a person forever! He taught her how to exhaust a man so totally that she could thereafter keep him asleep as long as she wished! Like one of the Three Sisters, she could weave a spider's web of enchantment around all men!

Every now and then, the author fishes up other sources (which Paulin Paris theorized must have been short poems or stanzas put together into a prose narrative that is suspiciously choppy) that say it differently:

1. Niniane/Vivian would not yield to Merlin's desire for sexual relations. Why not? Because she said her father had threatened to kill her if she lost her virginity. If she made love to Merlin, the news would get back to her father.

246

2. Whenever Merlin got too near her, she put two words of conjuration on his knees(?), and he dropped off. As soon as he awoke, he believed that he had had her. Therefore, by Merlin's own mouth she is called his "paramour."

3. How was Merlin able to sleep? He could fall asleep, you see, because he was half mortal and only half demon. She must have killed him while he slept!

4. "Finally the Lady learned so much from Merlin that she ended up enclosing him in a grotto in the Perilous Forest of Darnantes, which hems in the Sea of Cornwall (the Rhinns of Galloway lie north of the Solway Firth) and the kingdom of Sorelois, the Isles. From that time on, Merlin was never *seen* again, and nobody would say what place had confined him."

5. When Merlin was twelve years old, he was taken to Uther Pendragon. Afterward he went off to haunt the deep ancient forests of Scotland.

6. Merlin found Niniane/Vivian on the March of "Lesser Britain" (that is, smaller Britain = Scotland). "He loved her, but she defended herself. She swore to be his if he would teach her particularly how to enclose somebody permanently, by words, so he could never get out, and how to make him sleep permanently so he would never awaken [Manuscript 768, edited by Kennedy, Vol. I, p. 23, 1. 7ff].

" 'Por quoi,' dist Merlins, volez vos ce savior?'

(For what [reason], said Merlin, do you want to know this?)

" 'Because if my father knew you lay with me or anybody else lay with me, I would kill myself. Be careful not to teach me any false knowledge; if you do, I shall leave you forever.' Because she knew writing on parchment, she managed to put Merlin to sleep whenever he came to her. Her means were two words of conjuration so he never could take her virginity

247

nor know her carnally. She had trouble with his devil half, which never fell asleep; but finally she wound him around so well she put him inside a cave . . . she was Lancelot's same damsel, the one who bore him into the Lake" (pp. 23, 1. 24–24, 1. 2).[2]

"Vivien" by Alfred Lord Tennyson follows suit (last 8 vv.):

> *Then, in one moment, she put forth the charm*
> *Of woven paces and of waving hands,*
> *And in the hollow oak he lay so dead,*
> *And lost to life and use and name and fame.*

> *Then crying "I have made his glory mine,"*
> *And shrieking out "O foul!" the harlot leapt*
> *Adown the forest, and the thicket closed*
> *Behind her, and the forest echo'd "foul."*

While the charge against Merlin is beneath contempt, those against the Lady of the Lake merit close consideration for several reasons. She has stood, as charged, for several centuries:

1. She murdered Merlin, by
   a. enclosing him, within a forest, in
      (1) a tower of air, or words,
      (2) an oak trunk, or
      (3) a grotto (cave, cavern);

• • •

[2] In this version Lancelot's mother Elaine rode up the peak to aid her embattled husband, but her friend and relative the Lady of the Lake rode after her, bearing the baby Lancelot before her on her saddle. They found the king dying, and the Lady spurred her horse downhill and bore Lancelot into the "Lake." Often in Arthurian manuscripts the action is telescoped, as here, where the king seems to have died on the east coast (of what is now England) while the Lady's Lake is the Irish Sea. She therefore would have embarked on the west coast.

248

2. She was a harlot.

The authors of the Middle Ages did not leave it at that. Much more hangs upon this issue than murder alone, and the trial, for if she murdered Merlin, then she suffered the penalty. It is useless for the *Prose Lancelot* to continue blithely along to the touching scene that follows: the white-clad Lady of the Lake introducing her ward Lancelot to King Arthur; Lancelot standing there weeping to see her go. Or another: the Lady rescuing Arthur when the recreant Accolon wielded Excalibur against him and Morgan le Fay awaited her lover Accolon with open arms. Many questions must still be answered centuries after the events occurred.

How did Niniane/Vivian actually kill Merlin and under what circumstances? Does knowledge turn women to evil? What was her motive? Had she gone mad? Does learning injure women's brains?[3] Are we to assume the extenuating circumstance of mental incompetence on the part of the Lady and accept it as her defense? Or did she kill, if in fact she did kill Merlin, in self-defense?

The accusation of murder by the Lady of the Lake, who was considered *the most eminent woman of her time*, brought many repercussions. Judging from their understanding of physiology, medieval authors like Jean de Meung who wrote the *Roman de la rose* Continuation, a woman who refused to make love with her suitor could cause his death. In other words, any man refused sex by any female risked death. If he died, the theory went, she murdered him and therefore deserved death. Jean de Meung continued the *Prose Lancelot's* allegations, which were elevated into a literary quarrel, a *cause célèbre* that lasted at least six hundred

• • •

[3] This may seem hard to believe, but that learning might physically damage a woman's brain was widely held as late as World War I when the first American women were admitted into the Graduate Faculties at Columbia University in the city of New York.

years. The argument centered on the nature of women, which was considered to be evil.[4]

The quarrel aroused in western Europe by the *Prose Lancelot* and continued by *Le Roman de la rose* was called the "Quarrel of the Rose." It flared up all over again in the early fifteenth century with Alain Chartier's famous poem "La Belle Dame sans merci.[5] It flared up again in the case of the cardinal of France's sister, the novelist Claudine de Tencin accused in the eighteenth century of her heroine's crime. These represent only two instances of minor authors repeating or re-living cruel beliefs centuries old by their times. The original "Belle Dame sans merci" is the Lady of the Lake, called merciless because she was said to have refused Merlin as her lover. The murder charge against the former nun Claudine de Tencin also stemmed from the death of a suitor to whom she had refused sexual favors. The quarrel involved even Rousseau, whose opinion was that men, and not women, are more likely to be carried away by passion.

The *Prose Lancelot* elicited before the end of the thirteenth century a long continuation that addressed itself to the murder of Merlin. Its author claims to be a "Maistre Richart of Irlande," but the editor Lucy Allen Paton in 1966 thought differently. *Les Prophecies de Merlin* (The Prophecies of Merlin) proves actually to

•   •   •

[4] According to the expert Agatha Christie, if women murder, they do so in defense of girls, and they generally murder by poisoning their victim or themselves. The Lady did neither.

[5] That Chartier's poem of 1424 swept France by storm, although it is a trifling work, seems due to the climate of depravity at the court of King Charles VI. Other medieval poets hated women because Helen of Troy had caused the Trojan War, as Paris's mother charged her in drama. Queen Guinevere has always been hated because she supposedly caused the collapse of King Arthur's realm, but see Goodrich, *King Arthur*, Part II.

be a text in Old French, written for the most part by a Franciscan monk, probably a Venetian.[6]

Les Prophecies de Merlin [sic] contains his so-called "Merlin prophecies" or dire predictions, but in general terms only: floods, mountains that collapse, fires seen in the sky, comets, rivers that change course, coastlines that become altered, seas that dry up, torrential rains, droughts, marvelous stones, cyclones, the moon out of orbit, the stars awry or off the ecliptic; the sun displaced, and huge storms at sea. The authors became more specific in four separate areas Merlin could not have known: (1) Venice, (2) the Crusades to free Jerusalem, (3) Rome and the enemies of the papacy in the twelfth and thirteenth centuries, and (4) corruption in the Vatican. Every page reveals a certain commonality of attitude toward the world:

1. Men are seen as loving and victimized,

2. Women are seen as unloving and oversexed,

3. Old women are seen as greedy, lustful hags,

4. Young women are seen as hateful and filthy,

5. Adolescent girls are seen as evil and conniving,

6. Fear on the part of men is justified because of:
   a. unnatural birth,

. . .

[6] 2 vols. (New York, 1966). Paton also used Manuscript 593 from the Municipal Library of Rennes, France, collated with B.N. Manuscript fr. 350 and British Museum Additional 25434, neither one of which is the original text. Other manuscripts are found in Berne, Paris, and Vienna, but no original as yet. The text is of composite authorship. It shows particularly close acquaintance with Venice, port of "The Good Mariners," and also a specific knowledge of the Crusades. Because of this last area, for many Crusaders took ship at Venice, one suspects it to be an expansion of a lost Arthurian manuscript. In other words, one should take it somewhat seriously.

b. human and animal monsters,
 c. witches and evil spells,
 d. female vipers *(vipera)*:
   (1) dragons, and other
   (2) snakes.

Nobody can expect any defense of Niniane/Vivian here, of course, but it is still necessary to consider as much evidence as possible on the theory that a new mass of evidence is better than nothing at all and that murder will out—if murder occurred.

· · · · · · ·

The Prophecies of Merlin [7]

(Translation)

LXXII. Merlin: " '. . . that I truly believe that this Morgein was born from the fires of lust, and concerning the beautiful Lady of the Lake I truly believe that she was born then near Paradise. This Morgein pursues and does evil deeds, but the latter does good works. The former has good warriors killed and the latter has them rescued and assisted. The former yet will have orphans destroyed in spite of their fathers and of their mothers.

CXX. Merlin: " 'Oh, how I wish you could set down in writing,' and Merlin says this to Master Antonine, 'that the Lady of the Lake will be a friend to all people more than any lady who may be in the world nor any you know of to be alive, and shall also have this high reputation among everyone in the world, and shall be spoken of also as long ago it was spoken of a lady who

· · ·

[7] What follows is a partial translation of episodes that pertain to the question of who Merlin was and who the murderer was. They are also in Paton's Vol. I; her manuscript section numbers given, and the speakers identified. To my knowledge this material has never been translated before. (*Prophecies* is correct, and not *Prophécies*, the acute accent not often employed in Old French.)

253

lived in Vergil's time, and who was called "Luscente" because of it. [8]

CXXII. Narrator: (Merlin has met the Lady in the forest) "and so Merlin loved the Lady of the Lake with all his heart; the Lady hated him fully as much or more.

CXXIII. Narrator: "They wandered within the forest of Aurences until they came to the entrance where the grotto ("la croute") was where Merlin had had built ("estoree") the chamber and the tomb for which the Lady had begged him so long." (It was in the Forest of Darnantes—"la forest de Darnantes").

CXXIV. Narrator: "Know that as soon as darkness had fallen and the Lady of the Lake thought that she would have only a certain darkness for the night, she was disappointed because Merlin had stuck so many blocks of stone of such size in the walls that no matter how brilliant was the brightness of the night, as if the sun had thrown itself upon all the stars, (she was in darkness).
" 'Tell me, Merlin,' says the Lady of the Lake, 'will these stones ever be lifted out of here?'
" 'Lady,' says Merlin, 'negative . . .' "

CXXV: (They spent fifteen months in the forest and each month Merlin sent out messages to his Master Antonine. "Morgein" came all the time searching and searching for Merlin, and the Lady could hear her beaters and her hunting horns . . . even close to the grotto. She (the Lady) had her valets and her elderly serving women

• • •

[8] Merlin is right. She is mentioned by Vergil ("Lucinam pati") as the woman who brings babies into the light (of day): Lucina. The name was often given as a title to a goddess or to a midwife. Thus, we have learned something new about the medicine practiced by Niniane/Vivian: she was Lucina, "expert in labor."

with her—no young person, for fear Merlin would sleep with them, for which reason she wanted to kill him and also).

" . . . because she knew for certain that Merlin was in league with King Claudas of the Waste Land, (for) never Lancelot nor his two cousins (Bors and Lionel) could survive until their majority, without his having them slain, either by poison or by some other means, and neither from his schemes nor from his enchantments would she be able to guarantee them.

CXXVII. Merlin: " 'Lady,' says Merlin, 'this know thou truly, that before thou hast passed away from this century shall I be put into the earth. . . . It shall be just as I tell thee,' says Merlin.

" 'Since thou art to be put in the ground before me,' says the Lady of the Lake, 'I beg thee to lie down in the tomb where we shall both repose, for I wish to see if I shall have a wide (enough) portion of this tomb, and if my bones will lie there at ease. And if they were not to be at their ease, I should beg thee to make me a wider one.'

(They went hand in hand to see the tomb, which was splendid and which pleased her, but she wanted it made larger.)

" 'In God's name,' says Merlin, 'it is large enough and well enough made so that thou wilt take thine ease, and I shall show that to thee plainly.'

CXXVIII. Narrator: "Merlin went inside the tomb and lay down, and then speaks and says, 'Lady,' this says Merlin, 'now look and see if thou wilt have a large enough place, and long enough and wide.'

"And when the Lady of the Lake who had brought him to this experiment (found it) so well sealed both within and without, just as he had told her it would be (to the degree) that no man in the world no matter how learned would ever be able to unlock him, neither so much nor so little. When Merlin saw himself in such a

255

place where he had every good reason to know that never again would he ever be able to issue forth from it in any way whatsoever . . .

"'Merlin,' says the Lady of the Lake, 'is it thine opinion that I am the White Serpent that you prophesied about on innumerable occasions, the one who had come from Little Britain and who cohabited with the half-man in the Forest of Aurences, and the White Serpent left the forest in high spirits. Come true has this prophecy, I see clearly, just as thou hadst told me other times.'

CXXIX. Lady of the Lake: "'Merlin,' says the Lady, 'certainly thy prophecies are not contravened by me, but I wish thee to spend the remainder of thy life inside here. And I shall tell thee why.[9] Know truly that I have put thee inside here because thou used to go around to all places where thou went saying thou hadst played around with me, because of which I was acclaimed a whore by the very mouth of Morgein herself. For which I now wish to take my revenge of the White Serpent upon thy very body, for thou has robbed me of my whiteness, as thou goest around saying, and because thy prophecies have been distorted . . . of which I am willing for thee to know that I am still a virgin.'

Merlin: "'And for this do I wish that he (Master Antonine) have it written down that the intelligence of a man ("sens d'ome") is worthless when compared to the wiles of a woman ("engien de fame") and tell him that any man who shall subject himself to a woman shall be as humiliated as I am . . .'

(Narrator: "The horse desires the spur and the woman, the club.")

"'Merlin,' says The Lady of the Lake, 'since thou hast wished it, I will go to him, but meanwhile I wish thee

• • •

[9] Here she gives her third and last reason for her approaching murder of Merlin.

256

to tell me, if thou knowest the answer, how long a time thou wilt be able to hold thy wits within thy body.'

CXXX. Merlin: " 'Lady,' says Merlin, 'the flesh above me will be rotted away before a month has passed, but my spirit will not fail to talk to all those who shall come here.'

" 'Tell me, Merlin,' says the Lady of the Lake, 'how many noblemen will come here?'

" 'Lady,' says Merlin, . . . 'one nobleman alone shall come here before the Lady of the Lake shall have passed out of this century, and (he shall be King Segurans of Babylon and Abirons).' [10]

" 'Tell me, Merlin,' says the Lady of the Lake, 'shall there come nobody after my death?'

" 'Lady,' says Merlin, 'from that time on . . . shall be commenced a quest in which there shall be joined inside this forest more than a thousand warriors. . . .'

CXXI. Narrator: "What should I tell you? Know it as true that the Lady of the Lake was in that place more than a month, and then asked Merlin if his flesh had rotted, and he said yes, it had. And at that departed from there the Lady of the Lake, and went away into Wales where she found Bishop Antonine, who the many, many prophecies of Merlin had had written, all those Merlin had sent him by messengers, as we have already clearly stated. And the Lady of the Lake also narrated all that had occurred from that day backwards. . . . (The Bishop was sorely bereaved, . . . for much loved he Merlin with all his heart). Then she crossed over to the Isle of Man or Wales ("Gaulle"), which was a sea voyage of

· · ·

[10] King Segurans appears in the lineage of Galeholt le Brun. Babylon is the birthplace of the feared Antichrist. The reference is to Merlin's demon ancestry, specified elsewhere as another reason why the Lady murdered him.

three days. She went home where she was raising King
Ban's son (Lancelot) and his two cousins (Bors and Lio-
nel). She also raised Tristan's brother Meliadus, who later
became her lover, and who then visited Merlin's tomb,
received his farewells, and delivered more of his proph-
ecies to 'Master Antonine. . . . Subsequently, the Lady
generally put it thus: 'Too bad that Merlin was lost.' "

(Quests for Merlin summarized: the news of Merlin's death
reached Queen Guinevere, who sent her damsel Mabiles whom
she had raised in her tower, and whom she trusted greatly, for
she had business with Merlin. When "Morgain" heard the news,
she was glad to be able to supplant him because, ugly as she
was, "Morgue" would be because of her learning more feared
than Merlin. Of all the questers only Meliadus several times
found the hidden tomb because the Lady had directed him. She
also taught Mabiles the route to follow. Mabiles also met Master
Antonine, who advised her that Merlin would nevermore be seen
until on Judgment Day he issued forth from the Forest of Dar-
nantes. Queen Guinevere was so accomplished in all queenly
pursuits, being the most beloved personage of her age, and all
the questers loving her so much, that she made them all wish
to join the search parties. The Queen was called "fontaine de
hauteur"—spring of loftiness. The questers came to naught, for
none could discover the grotto.)

CXXXVII. Narrator: "In this section, says the book, Me-
liadus, who was the lover of the Lady of the Lake, had
come to the place where Merlin had been inserted, who
already had his flesh rotted away. And then heard Me-
liadus the voice of the spirit of Merlin."

Summary follows: (She had decided never to go there with him,
but he had sworn on his father's soul to force her or break re-
lations. She loved him so desperately that she could not con-
ceive living a single day without him. She arranged matters so
nobody in her household could tell where she was. She left the
Lake one morning with her lover and only four valets whom she
loved, had raised, and promised to ennoble. They considered
her their mother, so frequently did she call them "Fitzroy.")

(What should I say to you? she took ship to "Huiscestre" [Winchester, or Edinburgh] where the cemetery was, where the stones from Ireland had been brought, where the Saxons had attacked, where the tournament was held. They traveled under full canvas until they landed there and were warned "Morgain" was about. The Lady knew what was believed to be such an impossible route [that nobody took it], but which she could use safely. Only Merlin otherwise used it for traveling; it then passed through the Forest of "Arvencez.")

(She left her valets. She dismounted. She climbed up to the "head of the mountain" ["au chief de la montaigne"], and Meliadus would gladly have surrendered all his worldly goods never to have set fearful foot near that horrible entrance, much less inside the grotto. Inside the rock all was charming, however, "delitablez," in short, all was delightful.)

("I've gone out of my head to do this," she said ("sui issue de mon droit creant"). But he took her hand and made her look at all the beauty Merlin had created there.) "Don't praise the tomb," said Merlin's spirit.)[11]

> CCXXXVII continued. Narrator: "Within lie the bones of the most learned mortal man who ever was in the world, and the flesh of him has rotted, but his spirit is there enfolded without issuing forth, all days ever more."
>
> "I must tell you he is dead, and so is Master Tholomez, and the Roman Emperor, and all those he led into the Jerusalem lands."[12]

．　　．　　．

[11] This passage is summarized for two reasons: (1) so that the reader can watch a different narrator who has a flair for amusing fictions and (2) to show his thoughtless, muddled geography (Huiscestre, Vincestre, Vinciste, We[n]cestre; Arvencez, Arvances, Avrenches).

[12] This is included to demonstrate for the reader how Paulin Paris arrived at his theory of lost Arthurian material from separate stanzas (laisses in French), or separate epics long since lost. What follows is also not related to Merlin in any way.

CXLII. (New) Narrator: "And then speaks The Lady of the Lake and says, 'Tell me, Merlin,' says the Lady of the Lake, 'have I sinned because of having enclosed thee?' "

" 'The sin is absolutely not so great,' says Merlin, 'as the fact that thou hast turned to some rather evil deeds which will be spread about the world, like the countless maidens who will have lost their honor, like other bad carnal sins ("Karoudes"), like evil charms, which through (the world) have run, of which countless men will also be as if blinded, as I was also, accused of concupiscence, in which sin many damsels disappointed me, just as they misled other men.'

" 'Concerning which I wish that Master Antoinne [sic] take note in writing that all the filth in the world resides in the body of women for entrapping men, nor can a mortal man's heart hold up against their wiles. And moreover say I this for aged women as for little ones, and knowing that whenever they will pit their wits to the deception of men, they shall resemble eels which, when a man thinks he is holding them by the middle of the head, he has only got hold of one, and her by the tail!'

" 'Therefore I wish Master Antoinne [sic] to put it in writing that when men shall think that women really belong to them and that they desire for them all the good in the world, they shall be deceived of it, for if women were to find some things to their taste, that it would please them more, they would feel none too great a shame, even were he to grasp them by the tail, just as one can an eel.'[13]

" 'Ha!' says the Lady of the Lake to Merlin, 'thou goest

•   •   •

[13] Latinists find this sentence very amusing in the French, the author having found himself unable to construct a contrary-to-fact French condition in secondary sequence (seussent? eussent?), and undecided about a pleonastic "n."

on saying all this evil about all the other ladies because of thy love of me! Thou thoughtest once that I should have loved thee, but thou wert deceived, and thou knowest it's the truth.'

" 'For what reason, for which one hast thou gone along cheating me?' says Merlin.

" 'I (cheated) thee,' says the Lady, 'so that thou wouldst teach me all that which made thee learned.'

" 'Lady,' says Merlin, 'you have by your very own words, cornered yourself, and all other women are going to cheat other men in order to get their wealth and in order to roll drunk in their own over-sexuality.[14]

When the Lady of the Lake hears this, she bows her head and draws herself back, nor ever again, so long as she remained in the cave, did she address another word to him."

CLXXXVIII. Narrator: When the wise clergyman (Raymon de Galles) "saw the cliff where Merlin was, he recognized it at once from the fact that Meliadus had so frequently described the rock's appearance, and he saw the headland (mountain), which was struck repeatedly as does the sea when it is roused . . . saw clearly before him the whole crag and the grotto and the tomb into which Merlin had been inserted. And then he realized that of everything he had seen, all of it was nothing compared to this grotto, so delightful did it appear to be to him. But then when he saw the marvel of this headland (mountain) beaten (by the waves), and how it had been made (sculpted), he told himself that in his view no earthly (man) would dare set his feet there to pass across the face of the cliff, and were he to put his feet there he would soon thereafter be treacherously swallowed up. He beheld about him so many marvels of fine art that

•   •   •

[14] The abrupt change from "thou" to "you" comes in the French like a slap in the Lady's face.

he knew this adventuresome approach (to the cave) had been effected by means of great skill. [15]

Folio 148ᵃ (pp. 487–88): ". . . Here lies the wise clergyman (Raymon de Galles), he who left his great treasure to Merlin after his death, and placed excellent safeguards for its disbursement. Then as soon as this wise clergyman had been laid in earth, as you have just heard, the chaplain who remained at that site began to read the prophecies of Merlin where he discovered in writing that Merlin had said to the Lady at the very hour when he was buried in the tomb:

'I wish you to know that on Judgment Day Our Lord will have you come before Him, and when you shall have come, He will inquire of me, and you shall tell Him the whole truth, and He shall order that I come to Judgment, and in such manner as I am here, to this tomb I shall be led, but I know for sure that never shall the enemies in hell have any part of my soul, of which I request all those who have been baptized that they be joyous, if they are truly repentant and have confessed their sins, for the pity of the Saviour of the world is so vast that sky and earth are bowed down beneath it.' "

.   .   .

[15] Paton explains the plots of Queen Morgue and King Claudas against the Lady of the Lake, and Merlin's involvement, which ultimately gives the Lady another reason for murdering him, p. 372, #2ff. Raymon de Galles bequeathed his estate to Merlin.

11

THE VOICE
FROM BEYOND
THE GRAVE

· · · · · · ·

· · · · · ·

(THE CAVE IN ITHACA)
. . . and at the head of the harbor is a slender-leaved   v. 102
olive and near by it a lovely and murky cave
sacred to the nymphs . . .

The water flows unceasingly. The cave has two gates,   v. 109
the one from the north, a path for men to descend,
while the other, toward the south, is divine. Men do not
enter by this one, but it is rather a path for immortals.

The Odyssey.
Homer.
(In *Porphyry: On the Cave of the Nymphs,*
translated and introduced
by Robert Lamberton,
1983) p. 21.

．　．　．　．　．　．　．

Following the murder, the hunt was on for Merlin's grave. His wisdom and his magic were still required from that grave. Other men soon would be so affected by his legend that they roamed the forests of Scotland, King Arthur's same "Caledonian Forest," calling themselves "Myrddin," Merlin's name in British, as in modern Welsh.

At the time of Merlin's death, Scotland and Wales still presented to invaders from Ireland on the west, the Scots or Gaels, and the Anglo-Saxons on all coasts, a united Celtic realm in which to quest for Merlin. The names "Scotland" and "Wales" came into history after Merlin's death, long after the Angles had driven their wedge across Britain to sever them, as now, into these two Celtic lands.

From the day of Merlin's death, King Arthur finds himself deprived of his chief adviser and battle-leader. The king will not long survive the interment of Merlin's body into the tomb, the "enserrement" of Merlin. After another six years Arthur will have reached his final day at the horrible battle of Camlan, a word so fatal, a calamity so distressing that the Welsh people today call a great defeat, or a rout, "camlan." Their records of *Triads*, which they kept secret for another fifteen hundred years, list for all who wish to read them, as do the Welsh people in mute suffering, the seven survivors of the Battle of Camlan. It was fought at the *Camboglanna Fort on Hadrian's Wall. Merlin's name* is not among the survivors, as expected. Nothing had been heard from him since 536. The *Triads* also give the date of Arthur's last battle: 542.

The Welsh *Triads,* their sacred lists of threes by which they committed to memory their ancient history, mention Merlin only as one of their three holy "bards," or prophets. The second of the three bards is one of Merlin's successors, the poet and mad monk Myrddin, who went insane during another later battle about 573. The third is Taliesin, a wondrous poet.

Concerning the demise of Merlin, we have *Les Prophecies,* considered in translation and partial summary in Chapter 10, and one of their sources, the *Prose Lancelot.* At first reading, they seem a great disappointment. But standing back from them and letting their general thrust sink in, one may be able to see through to the heart of the matter. If one examines Homer's *Odyssey,* one is not flying off on a tangent for both Odysseus and Merlin are great heroes of the ancient world. Merlin's death and Arthur's bring that world to a close.

In Book XIII of the *Odyssey,* the prestigious Odysseus is returning home to the island of Ithaca after the long and terrible Trojan War, where he was largely responsible for victory. His prime characteristics have been courage, strength, high intelligence, craft, charisma, optimism, and love of his native land. Like Merlin, he is a strategist and a traveler who after long hardships has won his way home to his native land. In these last years, during a period of peace, he returns to the woman he has cherished all his life, his wife Penelope. She sits and weaves, like one of the Fates. As Odysseus steps ashore at a bay belonging to the Old Man of the Sea, he stands beside a lone olive tree. In medieval literature the epic hero also dies beneath a lone pine tree.[1]

On this bay Odysseus finds a cave with two entrances, one from the south and one from the north. It lies well hidden by greenery just above the crashing waves. Odysseus enters it to

• • •

[1] See Ernst Robert Curtius: "Epic Landscape," in *European Literature and the Late Middle Ages,* translated by Willard R. Trask (New York, 1953) p. 200ff.

hide his treasures. Although the authors of *Les Prophecies* never knew it, Merlin's cave also was full of magical treasures, which were much admired by the Lady of the Lake and later recorded by the *Triads* of Wales. Within the cave, or near its mouth, boiled up the sweet waters of knowledge, which Augusta Gregory borrowed, or which her Irish ancestors borrowed, from Pindar or from Homer's *Odyssey*. This "fountain" of Merlin and the sweet spring, like the Holy Wells that one can now visit throughout Wales and Scotland, are held to be "one of the world's great secrets." Every probe comes up against the veils of charm and mystery. Both Merlin and the Lady concealed their secret well, but it is probable that they performed the sacrament of baptism there.

Additional evidence of that age's baptisms is an ancient altar found near the Roman walled city of Deva (Chester, in England), which bore the dedication:

TO THE NYMPHS

AND

FOUNTAINS

THE TWENTIETH LEGION [2]

THE VALIANT AND VICTORIOUS

Another altar to the Nymphs was found in Scotland:

TO THE FIELD DEITIES

AND THE DEITIES

OF BRITAIN

ON THE ANTONINE WALL [3]

• • •

[2] Permanently stationed in Chester for some five hundred years, guarding against invasion from Ireland.

[3] Between Glasgow–Dumbarton and the Firth of Forth, near Edinburgh.

Altars dedicated in Cumberland and Scotland to the pagan field god of Rome, Silvanus, have also been found; and it is interesting to realize that Merlin's successor Myrddin is often called "Silvester." Under no circumstances, however, should Merlin be thought to have wandered about in the pagan woods, wreathed in flowers, and half-crazed, encountered by Saints Kentigern and Waldhave, or that he was goat-legged like the great god Pan.

Merlin should rather be thought of as a man securely attached to royalty, to landed estates, like Saint Dubricius himself, not only administering his inherited lands in Wales but also cognizant of what was happening in the world around him. How else could he have organized the defense of Britain prior to and alongside King Arthur? That campaign was waged successfully during Merlin's lifetime. He may be said in that sense to have died in peace.

On the other hand, Merlin failed to die in a period of safety for intellectuals, if one looks at an important event when Merlin was already some eighty years of age. Ten years before Merlin's departure for his cave, which was to be his first place of interment, the world was shaken to its heart by the execution of one of Rome's greatest noblemen, the theologian Boethius. At the age of fifty, Anicius Manlius Severinus Boethius of the consular Praenestine family at Rome was summarily disgraced, tortured, and beheaded for his writings and teachings. A consul under the Visigoth Emperor Theodoric, Boethius had been forced from his lavish home and lodged in a hideous prison between Milan and Pavia.

The voice of Boethius is one of the few voices from beyond the grave in the sixth century, whether from his theological writings or from his theistic masterpiece, *The Consolation of Philosophy*.

King Arthur has no voice from before or beyond the grave. Neither Morgan nor Niniane/Vivian has a voice, except, like Arthur, through their living descendants among the Celts. Even the great Saint Germanus has no voice, except as his teacher remembered him. Saint David of Wales has no voice. Like Boethius and like Merlin, Saint Patrick still has a resounding voice that thrills with its ardor. Merlin has the voice of his *Prophecy*.

The voice of Boethius that haunted men after his tragic death must have alarmed Merlin as it alarmed all contemporaries, who could not help fearing a future under the new rulers in Europe. Especially fearful were those who, like King Arthur and Queen Guinevere, called themselves "Romano-Britons," more especially those other great landowners from the ecclesiastical tribes such as the children of Brychan, who were, like Saint Dubricius, born and educated to be eminent scholars, churchmen, and educators on the largest scale.

Repeatedly, one is struck by the similarity between Boethius and Merlin, each with his undaunted voice from beyond the grave. During the period of his imprisonment, Boethius knew what end awaited him. Like Merlin, he foresaw the day of his rapidly approaching death. Then into his cell stole a beautiful woman, who diagnosed for Boethius his mortal wound, which she then offered to heal. In *Les Prophecies* the dying Merlin also has a beautiful woman minister to him. It is his physician, the Lady of the Lake, parallel to her whom Boethius calls Philosophy, the Love of Learning.

Philosophy not only heals Boethius but prepares him patiently for his hours of agony. She promises him a release. Paraphrasing her early conversations with the abject Boethius, she asks essentially who he thinks he is. I am a mortal, a man, he replies. Then that is your problem, your fear, and your disease, she replies. "Thou hast fogotten what thou art." Are you only bones, flesh, and blood? If you think so, then that has caused your illness. Do you think that evil men are truly powerful and happy? You are wrong. Do you think that the world is governed by fate and chance? You are wrong. True thinking, which is our nature, will console you. Divine reason will comfort you. Fear, hope, and sorrow have clouded your mind. Much later, after several long consulations, she concludes:

There is, if you will not dissemble, a great necessity of doing well imposed upon you, since you live in the sight of your Judge, who beholdeth all things.[4]

The more one reads the words of the Lady Philosophy, the more one accepts the premise that Merlin educated a real young woman like her in the person of his student and then his beloved and loving Lady of the Lake. Rome had perhaps set a style which its lost province followed. Boethius and Merlin are, in fact, not alone in their death scenes but are accompanied by similarly educated women. Saint Patrick likewise is often believed to have been ministered to, at the hour of his death, by a Saint Bridget,[5] who wrapped him in his winding sheet. King Arthur was accompanied to Avalon, or to the Isle of Avallach, says the Welsh *Triad*, by Queen Morgan, and he was, adds a *Triad*, interred in a hall of the (Grail) Castle. This castle cannot now be taken as Catholic Christian, for the Catholic Church has never accepted all of Celtic Christianity, nor the Holy Grail either, as orthodox Christian.

Saint Germanus of Auxerre, France, who twice visited Britain to stamp out the Pelagian heresy, as Saint Augustine was stamping it out in Rome during the lifetimes of Boethius and Merlin, also has his part to play. Saint Germanus, too, died in Ravenna while on an embassy from the pope.

The biographer of Saint Germanus, for the saint, being primarily a man of action, left no writing of his own, was his teacher

• • •

[4] *Boethius*, and so on, Loeb Library classics (see Bibliography), pp. 143, p. 167ff., and p. 411.

[5] This cannot perhaps be taken as yet for historical truth because of the difficulties of chronology. There were possibly twenty-five different women called Bridget, or those who took her name to honor her. In Wales she is called Saint Ffraid.

Constance de Lyon.[6] Saint Germanus fell ill in Ravenna, says Constance, and there he died seven days later, on July 31, 448. His enemy Pelagius from Britain had finally in 431 been condemned in Rome by the Council of Ephesus, says Constance. He adds that Germanus ordained Saint Patrick as bishop in Auxerre in 432, a fact that many people doubt. Saint Germanus announced his approaching death to his throngs of followers. In his last illness, his whole life having been one of utter self-deprivation, he was attended by the Roman Empress Placidia in person. With her own hands she dressed his body for its first funeral services in Ravenna before it was transported back to Auxerre in France.

In his *Celtic Folklore*, Vol. I, (p. 397ff.) the highly esteemed John Rhŷs tells about Saint Teilo of South Wales and the center of pilgrimage that became Saint Teilo's Well. This saint employed a favorite maid from Pembrokeshire. She was a remarkably beautiful woman like the Lady of the Lake. The serving maid was granted the privilege of attending the saint while he lay upon his deathbed. He ordered her, a year hence on the anniversary of his death, to carry his skull to a certain well and to leave it there for the sick to drink from. She would, he said, be blessed as a vehicle for their cure. The saint predicted that drinking from this skull would cure children of whooping cough, which as late as the 1920s in the United States was a major cause of infant and child mortality.

John Rhŷs concluded (p. 400):

But consider for a moment what has happened: the well paganism has annexed the saint, and established a belief ascribing to him the skull used in the well ritual.

•   •   •

[6] This *Life* is one of the more trusted eyewitness accounts of the Dark Ages since it was written only thirty years after the death of Saint Germanus.

In other words, the faith in the well continues in a measure intact, while the walls of the church have long fallen into utter decay. Such is the great persistence of some primitive beliefs; and in this particular instance we have a succession which seems to point unmistakably to an ancient priesthood of a sacred spring.

Noteworthy is the Lady of the Lake questioning Merlin about how soon his flesh would have decayed. Like poor, starved Saint Germanus, Merlin presumably had in his old age little or no flesh about his bones.

Reading these accounts of ancient deaths and funerals, one wonders whether it was only Merlin's death that occurred in the cave under the seaside crag on the Rhinn of Galloway at Whithorn, his remains being later transported elsewhere. The *Prose Lancelot* tells how one of Lancelot's principal duties was the reinterment of his ancestors, other Lancelot kings, who were removed to safer burial plots on Man or in the western isles.

Merlin's case also calls to mind another immortal, the wonderful Pythagoras who was also a priest, but of Apollo at the Delphic Oracle, before he founded his school at Crotona in Italy. Two points of similarity lead to Merlin a thousand years later: (1) both possessed loud voices from beyond the grave and (2) both sought, examined, and accepted as a beloved student a gifted preadolescent girl. Theoclea continued the work of Pythagoras at Delphi much as the Lady of the Lake continued Merlin's.

Edouard Schuré found several other points in common. Theoclea, like the Lady, also maintained her virginity, for "physical love, dimly seen, seems to them a rape of the soul, a pollution of their undefiled, virginal being."[7] Theoclea, like Merlin and probably Niniane/Vivian, also belonged to a priestly family, where the priestly dignity was hereditary. Both Theoclea and

• • •

[7] *The Ancient Mysteries of Delphi: Pythagoras* (New York, 1971), pp. 38ff.

Niniane/Vivian presided at a sacred fountain, spring, or well. Pythagoras and Theoclea presumably continued a secret chain of initiates, a "chain of wills" that restricted their special secrets within the minds of the initiates. Saint John Chrysostom is reported to have declared: "The initiates will understand." The practices of Christianity were still novel and perhaps feared.

Schuré (see his note 12, p. 130) brings us back to Merlin, for in temple language, he says, "Son-of-the-Woman," which we also have agreed may be the etymology in Celtic of the Latin name *Merlinus*, "designated the lower stage of initiation" into the priesthood, where "woman" meant "nature," or progenitor. The second-stage initiates were called "Sons-of-Men," and the final-stage initiates were called "Sons-of-God" because they had studied astronomy, or the "cosmogonic science."

The last section of Merlin's *Prophecy*, as well as his first place of interment and his prophecy of his approaching death, discussed in Chapter 12, point to him as having reached an equally advanced degree of education in astronomy. The "Great Initiates" have often been listed: Sophocles, Solon, Plato, Cicero, Heraclitus, Pindar, Pythagoras, Moses, and Saint Paul.[8] The initiate is said to have been laid in a great stone coffin, where he remained enclosed for three days. It is a long, impressive line, indeed, to Merlin.

The Welsh *Triads* explain that King Arthur was confined thrice "under the stone," and his third "prison" seems to have been the same small Bardsey Island where the bones of tens of thousands of Celtic holy persons were later used for the making of fences.[9]

Before a final consideration of *Les Prophecies*, it should prove useful to examine briefly Book XIII of Homer's *Odyssey*.

• • •

[8] See, among many such works, *Secrets of the Great Pyramid* by Peter Tompkins (New York, 1971) and *The Great Pyramid* by D. Davidson and H. Aldersmith (London, 1941) (Vol. I).

[9] See *Triads*, edited by Rachel Bromwich, pp. 133, 140, and 143.

Very mysteriously Homer speaks there of the cave where Odysseus hid his treasures. A brilliant interpretation of Homer's text was written by the scholar Porphyry: *On the Cave of the Nymphs* (ante A.D. 300). Before one entered this cave, Homer intended, said Porphyry, that a person must lay aside all material possessions, that he must strip naked and advance like a poor supplicant before a holy shrine. The body must beforehand have been starved of its flesh. All that is purely physical must already have been discarded. Then, and only then, could Odysseus *communicate with Athena*, the Greek *goddess of wisdom*, who would advise him how next to cast off every smothering lust of body and soul so that the candidate could begin to take the path toward pure perfection. After all purification, after the loss of all its enveloping flesh, the soul might aspire to the waters of wisdom.

Following this marvelous exercise in hermeneutics, where apparent contradictions of Homer's text have been reconciled, where the true meaning of his words has been elicited, and the unsaid, truly wonderful message from beyond the grave has been read, Porphyry revealed his major discovery: *the cave symbolizes the cosmos.*

Similarly, one might see that as he approached his death, Merlin had arrived at the last or cosmic section of his *Prophecy*. From the inside, as he looked in darkness up to the roof of the cave, Merlin saw the inverted bowl of the heavens, his northern nighttime sky.

Returning then to *Les Prophecies*, one can recall Niniane/Vivian charged with having enclosed Merlin, with being a harlot, with employing magic, and with possessing knowledge (which in a woman always led to evil). Refuting this, the evidence shows that Merlin went willingly into his tomb, that he actually approached it calmly, hand in hand with the lovely Lady. It was their mutual tomb, such being the custom, with honeycomb slots for each separate body. Far from murdering Merlin, the fond Lady was much more likely to be assisting him in her capacity of the loving Lucina, who ministered to mothers bearing their pains of childbirth. She planned to sleep beside her beloved teacher Merlin and already knew from him the date of her own death. It was to be soon, he had revealed. In all this, then, there occurred no murder at all. There exists none of the usual motives for murder. Nor was Niniane/Vivian accused at the time. She survived Merlin and took his place ministering to King Arthur and to Queen Guinevere, whom she did not survive. (Had she lived longer, the Lady might even have saved the gallant queen from the snake pit where she died.) The Lady left descendants in Wales.

The truth seems patent: Merlin had prepared the cave, which was lavishly sculpted, as their tomb. He commenced his last hours or days willingly. *Les Prophecies* was obviously prepared by amateurs unable to read or remember what had gone before, equally unable to anticipate what was to follow. As a joint effort, it fails to present a convincing text. Frequent changes in narrative focus jolt the reader, for example:

Sections	*Changes*
LXXII, CXX, CXXVII	Merlin praises the Lady; they love each other.
CXXII	Abruptly the Lady hates Merlin.
CXXV	Morgan is called a huntress, a concocted charge, for it is Arthur who is remembered as a hellish hunter across the dark sky.
CXXVIII	Inappropriate folklore regarding the "White Serpent" from France, where she is called the *Vouivre* ($<$ *vipera*). [10]

. . .

[10] See Marcel Aymé's novel of 1943, *La Vouivre.*

	Theory: All women hate women; ergo, Morgan hates Niniane.
CXXIX	Theory: All women wish to be battered or beaten. Error: One thousand warriors quested for Merlin? *Prose Lancelot:* Thirty questers. [11]
CXXI	Error: Queen Guinevere was very beloved? Not so.. Error: The Lady called everybody "Fitzroy"? No, only Lancelot.
CXLII	Very peculiar about-face by granting dignity to the Lady after Merlin has excoriated her and called her formally "vous."

Much of *Les Prophecies* is therefore psychologically untrue and false from the viewpoint of Arthurian records. In fact, the Lady remained for a month (CXXI), tending Merlin until he had expired.

And the place where he expired was an ancient hospital, a healing shrine replacing or continuing temple areas such as those that functioned in Greece until about A.D. 200 and were by then eight hundred years old. The Greek god of medicine Asklepios was reputed to be the son of Apollo, the god of prophecy, and

• • •

[11] Ten went "left" with Sagremor, ten went straight ahead with Yvain, and ten took the right fork, with Gawain.

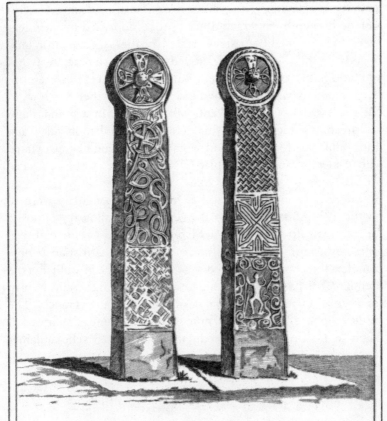

MAEN Y CHYFAN

STONES OF LAMENTATION, or
WEEPING CROSSES: Wales

of an earthly mother. The ruins of his shrine at Epidaurus, Greece, include his tomb, to which a mass processional led his devotees every four years. His patients rested in the sanctuary for long periods of time while they enjoyed the mild climate, rest, hot and cold baths, and draughts of pure spring water. His prescriptions have survived: cover the head in rainy weather, wash without the assistance of a servant, take exercise in a gymnasium; eat bread, cheese, celery, and lettuce; drink lemon juice and drink milk; go for walks, and worship. The goddess associated with Asklepios is Athena.[12] Her Christian descendants are Queen Morgan herself, and the sad Lady of the Lake.

Merlin's healing shrine, cave, spring, and sanctuary were all on the Whithorn peninsula, the Rhinns of Galloway, opposite the northern tip of the Isle of Man, a distance of some eighteen miles. By Merlin's time, the place had been a Christian temple complex for about a hundred years and had been built by the premier Christian saint and missionary to Scotland, Saint Ninian (or Nynia) in memory of Saint Martin of Tours, France. The medieval poet of Scotland, Thomas of Erceldoune, confirmed as much in his prophecies, as edited by the noted scholar James A. Murray in 1875:

> And mervelus merlyne is wastede away   v. 567 (p. xxxii)
> Wyth A wykede womane—woo mycht sho bee!—
> Scho has closede him in a cragge of cornwales coste.

The old accusation of murder still continues, but True Thomas identifies the place of Merlin's burial as on the Horn of "Wales," now called promontories (rhinns) of Galloway: "Galles" is the French spelling of "Wales." Murray quotes the many prophecies of Merlin that were still current in medieval Scotland.

· · ·

[12] See A. Charitonidou's "Epidaurus: the Sanctuary of Asclepius," in *Temples and Sanctuaries of Ancient Greece*, edited by Evi Melas (London, 1970), p. 89ff.

WHITHORN
Rhinns of Galloway, Scotland

A cross found at Whithorn Priory at Whithorn (now being excavated): site of the first Christian church in Scotland, founded as Candida Casa by the premier saint of Scotland, Saint Ninian, early fifth century.

Saint Ninian's Chapel is on the Isle of Whithorn. Restored ruins are on the old Pilgrim's Way. Saint Ninian's Cave (Merlin's Cave) is at Physgill, four miles southwest of Whithorn, on the coast. Crosses carved on the cave have been defaced. The cave faces south-southwest; its floor is 4 meters above normal high water; there is a stream quite close to the cave.

The current view, writes my correspondent G. Langshaw (Historic Buildings and Monuments, Edinburgh), is that "Candida Casa was at Whithorn, about 4½ miles away; alternately, it might have been at Isle of Whithorn, the same distance away."

The Isle of Whithorn is what the Arthurian texts call "Merlin's Isle."

**SAINT NINIAN'S CAVE
EARLY CHRISTIAN CROSSES**
Priory Museum, Whithorn, Scotland

Two small slabs of stone found near Saint Ninian's Cave (Merlin' Cave), at the sea edge on the "fossilised upper beach," 5 km. south-southwest of Whithorn, Galloway, Scotland. Slabs are now lodged in the Priory Museum, Whithorn.

Both slabs show typical cup-and-ring depressions carved in the stone, like the dot-and-circle decorations characteristic of early Christian carving.

See Ronald W. B. Morris, pp. 159–160.

According to public knowledge (see guidebooks) Arthur's Cave is located near where he defeated the giant, on the southwestern coast of Anglesey. Its mouth is closed at high tide, but this cave would doubtless have hidden his army, for it is a mile long. Above it rises a hilltop where King Arthur is said to have buried his treasure. His cairn is not far away:

> Near Arthur's Cairn on the shoulder of Snowdonia
> Lie the remains of the famous giant Ricca

whom Arthur slew in single combat. The giant, too, slumbers under a stone mound "on a ridge cold and vast."

Merlin's second cave yawns at the ocean's edge below the fallen bluffs of Tintagel Castle in Cornwall, southern England. One can scramble down the cliff and enter it easily. Its floor is paved with flat black stones of slate and round or egg-shaped stones of white quartz. The reason this headland and ruins are called Arthur's birthplace stems from two factors: (1) that Cornwall was also named "Dumnonia," like Brittany, France, and the Rhinns of Galloway and (2) that soon after Arthur's death and Merlin's that area adjacent to the much-later medieval castle called "Tintagel" was settled and Christianized by the descendants of the same Brychan and his grandson, the Saint Dubricius who had crowned King Arthur in Carlisle.

The cave that was Merlin's actual place of death and first insertion into the tomb is today called Saint Ninian's Cave, "5 km. SSW of Whithorn, at sea edge, on fossilised upper beach," says the archaeologist Ronald W. B. Morris in *The Prehistoric Rock Art of Galloway & the Isle of Man* (United Kingdom, 1979), p. 159. The cave was "first reported by the royal Commission on Ancient Monuments of Scotland (1914), at which time" only "small slabs" were found near the cave. "Fragments of two Christian Crosses" now lodged in the Priory Museum in the village of Whithorn, display carvings called cup-and-ring. The late keeper of the national Museum of Antiquities of Scotland, R. B. K. Stevenson, a leading authority on Scottish Early Christian carvings, has observed that "while the Cross itself in early Christian days represented the *physical* crucifixion, the symbols at the four points of the Cross and at its centre, with perhaps no actual Cross outlined, represented the spiritual side of the resurrection" Thus, one of these broken crosses may have been carved by Merlin's instructions and intended for him and his student, the great lady Niniane/Vivian.

An ancient gravestone from Whithorn also shows a carved emblem, the Chi-Rho sacred monogram, or first two letters in the name of Christ.[13] Merlin's Whithorn is known to be the oldest Christian site in Scotland.

The earliest British monks are thought to have been Pelagius (who disturbed the Christian world when he overwhelmed Rome with his learning and eloquent Latin), Puplicius (Saint Peblig, who founded the monastery of Llan Beblig), Saint Ninian (who founded *Candida Casa*, his monastery at Whithorn), and King Arthur's uncle Constans, (the grandson of the Constantine who was killed c. 411), and the Bishop Patrick (who was born in Ireland, or Wales, or near Dumbarton, Scotland, about 373).

Fodor's *Guide to Scotland* locates Saint Ninian's chapel in the far west of Galloway, above the shores of Wigtown Bay. The route to Merlin's Cave is the A 746, once a pilgrim's way and also the "royal route" traveled by King Arthur, says a Perceval text, when he went there to worship. The early Scottish kings and peers always planned to make a pilgrimage to this Isle of Whithorn, which is actually a promontory, once in their lifetimes: the fourth-century cell, school, and chapel of Saint Ninian, Whithorn village, and the sandspit "isle." Saint Ninian's Cave, which is located "near Glasserton," and which is in the care of the Secretary of State for Scotland (as of June 24, 1986), is the one where the evidence from the French manuscripts places the death and first burial of Merlin. However, it should be noted that not all scholars agree.

•   •   •

[13] See also M. D. Anderson's *Looking for History in British Churches* (New York, 1951).

In the notes (p. 383ff.) to her translation of the *Mabinogion*, Charlotte Guest gave the older contrary evidence for the location of Merlin's Well at Broceliande/Bredigan, said to lie near Concoret in Brittany, the modern name "Concoret" having replaced "Broc'hallean," thought Villemarqué, who was the earliest of the Arthurian scholars from Brittany and a contemporary of Tennyson. Villemarqué reported his emotional visit to that site in *La Revue de Paris* (May, 1837). Geoffrey of Monmouth's translator and adaptor, Wace, had changed its name from "Barenton" to "Brecheliant" in the twelfth century, and had visited a site in Brittany, which he claimed was Merlin's Fountain. He was disappointed to have seen no fairies thereabouts and disgruntled at having put himself to such pains for nothing. Prior to 1978, a visit was made by Ronald Millar who reported having seen the place-name "Brekilien" on a *"circa* sixteenth-century map of Brittany," replacing the modern place-name Paimpont. He thought he had found Merlin's "Spring" and Merlin's "Rock." He knew he had found the ruins of Henry II's twelfth-century monastery. The Abbé of Trehorenteuc informed him *in situ* that the Arthur legends had been brought to Brittany by veterans of Hastings after 1066.[14]

The best of these observers was Villemarqué, who reported near Concoret a fountain flowing near two rocks and nearby a wooden cross in an "immense amphitheater crowned with somber woods."

While the various observers failed to discover all the features of the scene, such as the cave, the sea, and the crag, the medieval French writers added a metaphorical name that has always puzzled Arthurian scholars. The best recent textual and critical scholar has been William A. Nitze, who tackled this problem in 1943: What is an *esplumoir*? When Merlin said he was going to retire into his "esplumoir" and never be seen again,

. . .

[14] *Will the Real King Arthur Please Stand Up?*, "To the Valley of No Return," (London, 1978), pp. 45–59.

what did he mean?[15] Nitze turned to another French text by Raoul de Houdenc where the hero Meraugis searched for and found the "esplumoir." One morning Meraugis came to the seashore beside a road, where he saw a very "hideous" cliff running back some distance inside the mountain. The rock was not only very high but all of one piece. Perhaps ivy encircled its entrance. Upon the domed summit the hero saw twelve damsels sitting on the grass. Rain or shine, they always sat there prophesying, but only about the future. Therefore, when Merlin said *esplumoir*, he meant his cave at Bredigan after all, where he would remain like the merlin/hawk molting and mewed, or henceforth forever in mew from the world.

While the translators were fortunate to be dealing in the noun *esplumoir* with common roots (*plume* = feather, and *mutare* = mutate, change), they were less fortunate when they fell upon the British *cruc* = a barrow. Acton Griscom and Robert Ellis Jones discovered an old, commonly repeated error while editing Geoffrey of Monmouth (VIII, 8). When Eldol cut off Hengist's head, he "raised a great cry over his head," as was the custom in burying a "Saxon chieftain" (*Jesus College, Oxford* manuscript LXI). In their note 80 the editors remark: "The Ms. has *cri*, therefore *cry* has been retained in the (English) translation; but the original word was undoubtedly *cruc* = a barrow, which a number of other texts have here, while others have *bryn* = a mound, and still others have *karnedd* = a cairn.

Therefore, when the French texts claimed erroneously that Merlin "cried" out for help as he lay in his stone coffin, they erred and aroused an unjustified anger in all hearts against that "wily" Lady of the Lake, who had supposedly murdered him so cruelly.

• • •

[15] Merlin's remark comes at the end of a text called *Didot-Perceval*, translated by Dell Skeels (Seattle and London, 1966), p. 94 and note 20. See also Nitze's "The Esplumoir Merlin," *Speculum*, Vol. XVIII (1943): 69–79.

While Queen Guinevere sent only a damsel to learn the whereabouts of Merlin from the Lady, King Arthur ordered a quest, which was undertaken by thirty heroes. Many others, such as Bademagus, sub-king of Urian, went to hear Merlin's "cries" from within his tomb; the questers followed the usual routes:

1. starting point: Merlin's *perron* or rock past the plains called "walescog" = Val Escoce = Vale of Scotland, at the intersection of seven roads (that is, Carlisle),

2. the Valley of the Dead, where the two best heroes fought,

3. the intersection at a spring, where a terrible massacre took place,

4. the lone pine tree of heroes, beside a meadow and a spring,

5. a convent beside a great meadow, a river, and the shore of the Queen's Lake (that is the Irish Sea), a chapel on a rock and a "barrow," or Saint Ninian's Whithorn.[16]

King Arthur's questers spent many months rescuing each other from their several series of mishaps. Merlin was, as he had predicted, never again seen.

Everybody knew the reason he was never seen, for as Ralf Higden has explained in his *Polychronicon*, his remains were removed to Bardsey Island, the Welsh Enlli off the south shore of the Carnarvon peninsula, and there added to the twenty thousand Druids there interred. The later "Druids" were so well mourned by the great Thomas Gray that everyone has been searching Britain for them ever since, with a great lack of success. Gray wrote his beloved, and celebrated poem "The Bard" after hearing a blind harper perform on a Welsh harp:

· · ·

[16] Directions in the introduction of the *Grand-Saint-Graal*.

On dreary Arvon's shore they lie,
Smear'd with gore and ghostly pale,
Far, far aloof th'affrighted ravens sail;
The famish'd Eagle screams, and passes by.
Dear lost companions of my tearful art,
Dear, as the light that visits these sad eyes,
Ye died amidst your dying country's cries.
No more I weep. They do not sleep.

Nobody seems to have proved the existence of Druids in Britain during Merlin's lifetime, although the Arthurian corpus does speak of pagan priests such as Bademagus (Baldwin) at the Grail Castle. Those writers who depicted him as receiving words from Merlin beyond the grave were tarring both men with the same brush. The supposition that Merlin was a pagan bard, even that he was a pagan sun god, continued in learned circles from Thomas Gray to John Rhŷs in 1886.[17] He thought that Britain's first name was "Merlin's Enclosure": *Clas Myrddin*. This sun god Myrddin would have married Elen of the Hosts, daughter of Old King Coel, the god of sky and war. Myrddin, said Rhŷs, was the British Zeus worshiped at Stonehenge, which was, he said, a temple of Apollo. Thus, the god would have been "imprisoned" on the Salisbury plain in a "tour withouten walles, or withoute any closure." Thence he would have been removed westward to Bardsey Island at the westernmost point of Carnavonshire, Wales. Edward Davies, in 1809, had already related Myrddin to Stonehenge, its seven score stones making a mystical 140. Many medieval writers fancied such numerology and gematria almost as much as they doted on astrology.

While no text proves a connection between Merlin and Myrddin, much less between Merlin and Stonehenge, authori-

· · ·

[17] "The Hibbert Lectures," published as *Celtic Heathendom* (London and Edinburgh, 1888).

ties for hundreds of years have put Merlin's second interment on Bardsey Island:

Merlinus ipse natus est in Cambria

(Merlin himself was born in Wales)

or

Ad Nevyn in North Wallia
Est insula permodica
Quae Bardisia dicitur, . . .

(Toward Nevyn in North Wales
There is a very small island
Which is called Bardsey.)

Merlin will be torn away from Stonehenge only when good reasons are offered.[18]

Gerald of Wales, prelate and sometime champion of his mid–twelfth-century contemporary, Geoffrey of Monmouth found a copy of Merlin's *Prophecy*. His translation, if he ever finished it, has not survived. Elsewhere he declares that there must have been two Merlins:

1. Merlin I was born at Carmarthen in Wales, and it was named after him. He was a contemporary of Vortigern.

2. Merlin II was born in Scotland. He was King Arthur's Merlin.[19]

But John Rhŷs said Elen, who was the god Myrddin's wife, had built Carmarthen and its fortress, the highest in Wales. Any

• • •

[18] See Goodrich, *King Arthur*, Part I, Chapter 2, p. 55ff. for my best argument thus far.

[19] *The Journey through Wales*, p. 192; *The Description of Wales*, p. 226.

number of scholarly editions of the Merlin manuscripts will give the accounts of all the minor authors who listed two or more separate Merlins, or two separate Merlins, Merlin as a Druid, a bard, a conjuror, a sorcerer, the tendency being to belittle him as time passed and he dwindled further and further back in time toward a vanishing point.[20]

The Welsh archives, *Annals*, and *Triads* have the oldest, categorical distinction and may clear up as much as possible—the controversy over the two Merlins. The earliest translators of the *Mabinogion*—Joseph Lot in France, Charlotte Guest in Wales, and the French scholar Edmond Faral in 1929—all drew attention to the Welsh historical records;

Triad 25: The three greatest (or primitive) bards of the Isle of Britain are:

Myrddin Emrys (that is, Merlinus Ambrosius),

Myrddin ab Morvryn (the Merlin of the *Vita Merlini*),

and Taliesin.

In his book on Taliesin, D. W. Nash pointed out a further complication: in a poem Taliesin said he had once been called "Merddin" (Myrddin).[21] Charlotte Guest wanted all to know that both Myrddins mentioned in *Triad* 25 were born in Wales, the second in Caerleon-of-Usk where Geoffrey of Monmouth erroneously kept putting King Arthur. In other words, everybody is guilty of the confusion of the Merlins since the middle of the twelfth century.[22]

• • •

[20] See, for instance, "Two Merlins or One" by Henry B. Wheatley, editor for the EETS of *Merlin*, Original Series 10 and 112, Vol. I.

[21] *Taliesin, or, the Bards and Druids of Britain* (London, 1858).

[22] See Paul Zumthor's *Merlin*, p. 65 passim, but he does not take a stand for one or another Merlin.

H. L. D. Ward, who studied the question of the later Merlins who lived after Merlinus Ambrosius, and particularly in Scotland, determined that neither "Merlin Silvester" nor the twin of a Merlin called "Lailoken" was the real, original Merlinus Ambrosius.[23] After long examination Ward also dismissed a body of Welsh poetry attributed to Merlin. He considered the poems composites, so largely rewritten in the twelfth century as to be virtually worthless as documents and very poor poetry at that.[24]

However, two or three Merlins and three or four graves does not exhaust the claims. Andrew and John Lang researched the grave of Myrddin, who is probably the second Merlin listed in *Triad* 25: Myrddin son of Morvryn. His genealogy is still preserved in Wales. As the Langs reported, the poet or bard Myrddin ab Morvryn was buried in a grave in the border area of Scotland, at the town of Drummelzier near where the Powsayl Burn flows into the Tweed River. This Merlin, who went insane during the Battle of Arthuret about 573, wandered in the Tweed Uplands for as long as fifty years. His grave, when the Langs saw it, was under a thorn tree in the churchyard. This grave is the second Merlin's resting place, or grave 2. The first and third graves belong to the prophet Merlinus Ambrosius, who counseled four British kings: the cave at Whithorn near the temple complex, where Merlin died; and the next burial site on Bardsey Island.

Chris Barber writes in *Mysterious Wales* (pp. 114–15) that today Bardsey still has the bodies of twenty thousand saints and one cross to commemorate them all. In the middle of the island may be found the ruins of an abbey dedicated to Saint Mary, built during the thirteenth century upon the site of the Celtic monastery. It had been founded by Saint Cadfan, who was Mer-

• • •

[23] "Lailoken (or Merlin Silvester)," *Romania* XXII (1893): 504–26.

[24] See *The Black Book of Carmarthen* (1, 16, 17, 18), *The Red Book of Hergest* (1, 2), and the bibliography for editions and translations.

lin's contemporary and probably one of his pupils. The island of Bardsey is only three miles in circumference.

The evidence that Merlin and not Myrddin was buried on Bardsey is found in what surrounds the deceased: the Treasures of Britain. Only a statesman, educator, benefactor, and immensely wealthy and prestigious warrior, and a grandson of someone royal like Brychan, *of royal and priestly blood*, would have been buried along with the sacred Treasures of Britain and in one of the safest and holiest places in all Britain—Bardsey Island.

Charlotte Guest lists from *The Red Book of Hergest* the Treasures in the various editions of the *Mabinogion*, which she published the first time between 1838 and 1849. In her second edition (London, 1877), the list is more or less as follows:

1. a flaming sword,

2. a platter, or basket providing food,

3. a horn providing drink,

4. a chariot providing a ride wherever one desired,

5. a halter that captured horses all by itself,

6. a knife that could carve for twenty-five at one slice,

7. a cauldron that boiled food only for the brave,

8. a whetstone that guaranteed death by the hand holding the sharpened knife,

9. a garment that fitted only those of noble birth,

10. a pan that cooked whatever one desired,

11. the gold ring of Lunette,

12. a chessboard with gold and silver pieces that played by themselves,

13. the mantle of King Arthur ("whoever was beneath it could see everything, while no one could see him.")[25]

The fourth grave, Merlin's final resting place, was not prepared for him until about 1120. His remains lie there in state today.

. . .

[25] Since the thirteen treasures are sometimes listed in books of magic, I have compiled a list of "magical instruments" and/or "accessories," or "objects of magical powers" from Lewis Spence's *An Encyclopaedia of Occultism* of 1960 (new edition of New Hyde Park, 1968) collated with the same from Glenys Goetinck's *Peredur* (see Bibliography): altars, animals, cauldrons, censers, chalices, chessboards, lamps, lances, mantles, platters, golden rings, rods, spears, and swords (which both name). My thanks to a doctoral candidate in psychology, Molly Ann Squire, for having directed me to the Spence book.

12

ECLIPSE
OF THE
SUN

EPILOGUE
Spoken by PROSPERO

Now my charms are all o'erthrown,
And what strength I have's mine own;
Which is most faint: now, 'tis true,
I must be here confin'd by you,
Or sent to Naples. Let me not,
Since I have my dukedom got
And pardon'd the deceiver, dwell
In this bare island by your spell;
But release me from my bonds
With the help of your good hands.
Gentle breath of yours my sails
Must fill, or else my project fails,
Which was to please. Now I want
Spirits to enforce, art to enchant;
And my ending is despair,
Unless I be relieved by prayer,
Which pierces so that it assaults
Mercy itself and frees all faults.
As you from crimes would pardon'd be,
Let your indulgence set me free.

The Tempest.
William Shakespeare.

・　・　・　・　・　・　・

Present memory of Merlin is uncannily accurate when one considers the pull of forgetfulness upon the generations, as well as the loss of knowledge due to mischief and to time. Most people have heard of Merlin. Many recall him with a smile as of imagined kindred, or at least, as if he had been an unlost friend. Children think the magic he did was harmless prestidigitation, all white, not malevolent, and never hate-filled. He won his battles by virtue of his stealth, dissimulation, guile, forethought, all based upon the understanding that intelligence means mastery. When he entered into open warfare, he was fortunate since he opened his own gate, rushed out on his own horse, and carried the banner he chose. Before the carnage began, he blessed the other warriors and forgave them. What about himself?

One of the five major courses Merlin had to pass before he qualified for the teaching profession was entitled "Preparation for Death." This course in philosophy was required of all advanced students in late classical times.

Merlin is always remembered standing beside or close behind King Arthur, whom he certified before the assembled dignitaries, rulers, and concerned persons, as their rightful king who would with honor and success defend the realm. Merlin engineered the alliances and educations of Arthur and of Arthur's finest warriors: Lancelot, Tristan, Gawain, and Perceval. He also chose two other pupils who have themselves virtually dropped into mystery despite their many notable descendants: Morgan "le Fay," and Niniane/Vivian, the Lady of the Lake. It has been forgotten that Merlin was also a healer or that he prob-

ANCIENT GRAVESTONES

1. Whithorn

2. Wales

3. Catacombs at Rome

4. Wales

The sacred Christian monogram = Chi-Rho, from the first two Greek letters of Christ:

X P I C T O C = Greek alphabet
CH R I S T O S = Latin alphabet

ably officiated at rites of baptism or that he died in a cave on the south shore of Scotland.

This forgetfulness is no doubt related to the multiple meanings of the name Merlin. What was Merlin's other name? His real name? By what name is he recorded in official history, rather than in the pseudo-historical narratives in Old French?

He was certainly called "Merlin" when disguised he passed borders, fjords, rivers, seas, and forests on the business of the kingdom. Associated with the phenomena of weather, he was able to "bring" down whirlwinds, storms at sea, thunder and lightning precisely beamed so as to set enemy camps afire. One may assume that he was not only a scientist, physicist, and astronomer but also a weatherman. Perhaps like his predecessors at Rome, he could predict conditions by observing the flights of birds in the four quadrants of the sky, the Augurs' *regiones*. He was apparently a falconer, his own merlin having brought down a string of game birds for Arthur's field larder. Thomas Malory remembered the picture: Merlin carrying them hung about his belt.

But the best and fondest picture of Merlin is as genial Father Time: flowing white curls, long white garments, right hand holding the scroll of annals, looking with kingly eyes on Perceval, whose back is turned. Or one hears Merlin's laughter as he tells his followers that he is about to climb up into his *esplumoir*, to be mewed up forever, like and unlike the merlin in annual moult. Or he is the merlin-fish of vernacular Scottish, an ocean-goer who took the tiller himself when with the Lady he crossed the sea one night—probably traversing the stormy Firth of Forth, Stirling Castle Rock to Edinburgh Castle Rock, and Holyrood. On nearby Calton Hill he had constructed his everlasting monument for Uther and the Celtic dead.

Most remarkable of all his marvelous achievements, Merlin prophesied, not in the manner of the Roman Cicero, but in that of the ancient Hebrews, specifically in John the Baptist's style. Merlin's was the Hebrew prophet's broken voice shining its light upon an ever-darkening world, another voice in the wilderness.

Did Merlin understand, or did he only repeat what was to his mind a divine communication, where he functioned solely as spokesman?

The Hebrew word *nâbi* means to bubble, like a fountain. The prophet, whose words bubble up like water from the depths of earth, interprets only. He cannot explain. He dare not explain, for what he says comes to him by sudden, broken illumination. He is only the instrument through whom man may, if he so desires, be comforted. The effort is not Merlin's, but man's. The teacher practices but does not preach.

The ancient Hebrews chose their prophets with the same care Merlin used to select Arthur and test him publicly. The Hebrew prophets studied at special colleges designed only for them. They were also ancient annalists (historians) by profession, as was Merlin, prepared secondly for oral teaching, which is their definition of prophecy.

Why is Merlin's *Prophecy* darkly worded? First, so that no listener or reader is coerced into any belief, one way or another. Second, so that no disappointment can occur. Third, so that effort brings benefit. No effort, no benefit. Fourth, because a prophet speaks under no obligation to teach any one specific point: he is not merely an ordinary teacher, whose results should always be measured. Fifth, his speech is veiled by necessity and therefore fragmentary, metaphysical, allusive, and abstracted from fixed relations of time, persons, causes, and places. Last of all, his prophecy may be double in its application or may unfold only at the end of a listener's lifetime.

From a technical, literary point of view, Merlin's *Prophecy* is memorized, direct address, a late, classical example of the art of extemporaneous speaking, *ars dicendi*. As such, it follows the rules laid down by Cicero, Quintilian, and especially by the later commentaries of Macrobius (c. 400). Formal studies in oratory and memory development, which Merlin would have done, included not only vocabulary, figures of speech and style, grammar, rhetoric, and subject matter but also the works of the

Roman dramatists, narratives dealing with history, and genealogies. The treatises used as a basis for the curriculum of future orators recognized three kinds: judicial, deliberative (that is, prophetic because political, historical, and persuasive), and panegyrical (praise of rulers). In his *Prophecy*, Merlin discards the formula for a written piece such as a lawyer's brief to be presented to legislators. Instead of an *exordium*, he uses a dedication. By way of narrative procedures, he employs allegory, symbolism (especially of animals), metaphors, a fable (or Roman *exemplum* = moral tale), digression, and scattered utterances such as a prophet would utter under direct inspiration from outside himself.

His *Prophecy* returns in its last mnemotechnical section to the standard classical rules of composition with its *peroratio*, or cosmic conclusion, which resembles that of John on Patmos.

At all times Merlin employs the recommended discourse of the great orators, specifically Cicero's manner. Cicero had used this manner in retirement as he tirelessly rewrote his prosecution of the Roman governor Verres (Governor Boar), whom he made notorious for the pillaging of Sicily, from which Verres had stolen and removed countless major treasures of Greek and Roman art. Quintilian, who was teacher of Silver Latin at Rome and a prolific author, defined that style and manner as "stylus ornatus," "le style orné," or formal and ornamented discourse. French critics have further defined it in the modern Romance (Roman) languages as the oratorical style, the very heart of French prose as practiced by Rousseau.

The underlying thesis, which is Merlin's characteristic stance and artistic doctrine, resembles that of symbolists: "the words mean what you think they mean." Therefore, Merlin's *Prophecy*, on a literary scale as just defined on a philosophical/theological level, means what each reader can construe as a meaning. Otherwise, we may conclude that a literary piece, composed according to the tenets of symbolism, requires more active collaboration on the reader's part than a piece written according to the doctrine of realism. Realism satisfies a more passive reader, in others words. Merlin's symbolic *Prophecies* demand therefore a dialogue between author and reader.

Merlin has avoided many of the standard subject matters of most orators. He uses no dedication, no identifications of speaker, place, and qualifications, no apology for himself (such as Cicero employed to disarm the defense counsels of Governor Boar). What Merlin employs most effectively are two of the ancient commonplace subjects that gave much material to prophets: the world has deteriorated utterly, and the world now is upside down. That the world had declined into catastrophe must have been a commonly held opinion of the educated Romano-Britons of Arthur's day as they gazed out from their tranquil estates and palatial villas upon the invaders that drew nearer every day.[1]

One of Merlin's reactions was to write the *Prophecy*, which assuredly was not addressed by a seven-year-old to King Vortigern (Chapter 3). By the *topos* of an upside-down world, Merlin makes clever use of the similitude of impossibilities, which may be termed an early contrast of thesis and antithesis. As Merlin attempts to see clearly into the muddled events of his own day, always the hardest of tasks for any intellectual, his images proliferate: heron's eggs hatch into beasts, wolves swim in the sea,

• • •

[1] Ecclesiastical histories have recorded another such observer, the noted British scholar Pelagius, who was personally so unfortunate as to have seen the sack of Rome in 410, when the imperial city fell to Alaric and the Goths. Pelagius is writing a letter here to a woman named Demetrias:

> This dismal calamity is but just over, and you yourself are a witness how Rome, that commanded the world, was astonished at the alarm of the Gothic trumpet, when that barbarous and victorious nation stormed her walls and made their way through the breach. Where were then the privileges of birth and the distinctions of quality? Were not all ranks and degrees leveled at that time and promiscuously huddled together? Every house

women are snakes, a maiden's truce cup is poisoned (the deaths of Uther and Ambrosius?), the lioness's cubs turn into foxes, and especially, the houses of the zodiac are awry, out of their usual tracks across the sky. Merlin shows his classical education under Quintilian as he gives a virtuoso display of metaphors, their copiousness being Aristotle's measure of identifying a genius in literature. Merlin skillfully draws upon Quintilian's figures, doling out pyrotechnical displays of exclamation, hyperbole, apostrophe, metonymy, in addition to allegory and the constant animal metaphors that urge the philosopher's angry charge: man is a beast. As a philosopher he had taken a course called "The Ascent of Man" and probably hoped he could by his chastisement halt man's beastly metamorphoses.

Since historical fiction had not yet been devised, Merlin selected the best medium at hand, which was oratory in the style called "ornate-difficult" (*ornatus difficilis*). A critical cause set him in motion, which was the cataclysmic overthrow of his known world. In the face of this catastrophe, he was almost a helpless observer until he had decided upon courses of action.

What could a learned philosopher do when faced with chaos? Merlin's first recourse was to defend the Celtic realm by counseling the good rulers (Uther, Ambrosius, and Arthur) and by

. . .

was then a scene of misery and equally filled with grief and confusion. The slave and the man of condition were in the same circumstances, and everywhere the terror of death and slaughter was the same; unless we may say that the fright made the greater impression upon those who obtained the most by living. Now if flesh and blood have such power over fears, and mortal men can frighten us to this degree, what will become of us when the trumpet sounds from the sky, and the archangel summons us to judgment; when we are not attacked by sword or lance, or by anything so feeble as a human enemy, but when the artillery of heaven, all the terrors of nature, the militia, as I may so speak, of God Almighty, are let loose upon us?

301

effecting the ouster of the ill-advised Vortigern. Merlin could then come to actual blows, wage war himself, map campaigns, and actually secure a realm (Ireland, Scotland, Cornwall, Wales) for those Celts who managed to survive and then rear children. Merlin then could supervise the education of the best boys and girls among that generation. He could then face death gracefully after having ministered to all comers at his healing shrine and fountain. Last of all, he could leave his schools, his newly Christianized Castle of the Holy Grail and his temple complex at Bredigan, Galloway. Most important, he could bequeath two other imperishable monuments:

1. *The Annals of Scotland*, reported lost since the Middle Ages but at least partially recoverable in the pages of Geoffrey of Monmouth and succeeding Arthurian literature, and

2. The *Prophecy*.

The Greek genius Thucydides wrote his history of the Peloponnesian War under the threat of its overwhelming catastrophes. Saint Augustine wrote major works of history and he corresponded with Pelagius after the fall of Rome to Alaric in 410. Merlin was born in its aftermath. His idol, the great Homer, had written the *Iliad* in memory of the Trojan War, and the *Odyssey* also. Julius Caesar had written *Concerning the Civil War* after the defeat of Pompey at the fall of the Roman Republic. Victor Hugo wrote *Les Misérables* after the bloody humiliation at Waterloo. Tolstoy wrote *War and Peace* after the terrible French invasion of Russia. Oswald Spengler expressed his views in *The Decline of the West* after the disastrous World War I. In those times throughout western civilization when annihilation threatened, great thinkers have considered the questions that Arnold J. Toynbee (writing in the shadow of World War II) put: "How does a culture behave in times of crisis? How do people react? Who survives?" It is this line of thought, this line of *littérateurs* into which Merlin and his *Prophecy* fit.

The writers of these cultural landmarks all approached the problem from a philosopher's stance and from literary training. One can describe war, no matter one's training. The creative imagination goes to work to interpret, as Merlin did, the horrors and the savagery of conflict. For such reportings the "fabulatory function," upon which Henri Bergson lectured, takes over and recreates images like Merlin's "fable." But how will a writer achieve peace in his time? Will Merlin kill all the animals? Or will he lament simply, "Ve!" "Woe is me!" He overcomes the problem of how to describe war with his flashes, his visions that soar and subside, his brief bolts of light, his nonpersonal stance without editorializing, without asides, without explanations, without argument.

Many a novelist has struggled to find a narrative voice with which to relate the commotion of battle. None has managed to define peace satisfactorily. If any of them found peace, it probably came through the process of writing, when beside his narrator each writer paused to lift up his eyes and ponder Merlin's cosmic conclusion. The stars he saw were topsy-turvy. By what means then did Merlin, who was by profession and long years of rigorous training a "philosopher," find peace?

To answer that question, it is necessary briefly to look backward at what major discoveries have been made concerning Merlin's life. For his time he was unique. His *Prophecy* differs from similar writings of his contemporaries, Saint Gildas for example. Merlin has even been identified as and compared to Gildas. The works of Gildas, who was probably Merlin's student, are harsh, dry, and academic to the point of pedantry. Merlin spoke and wrote differently. He stands out as more Celtic, more imaginative, more distinct than Gildas. Their voices are different, separate, and each one distinctly recognizable. So are their lives.

"Merlin" means son-of-the woman, member of the priestly tribe of the Celts. He was perhaps born of a daughter from that tribe, not from a priestly father. His father remains unknown. The place of his birth is not yet known, but Merlin had one foot in Wales and the other in Scotland. Everyone who saw him as a child knew at once that he was a prodigy. He acted like one, performing brilliantly in school and prophesying readily. Many of his prophecies were recorded over the centuries in Scotland, and they correspond generally and specifically to the written *Prophecy*. His sayings were so memorable that they influenced nations and peoples for centuries, and this is a matter of actual, known historical fact. Merlin was a noteworthy statesman, a renowned warrior, an ardent annalist, and a feared examiner—which means that he was one of the world's greatest teachers, like the teacher of Achilles and Alexander the Great and Plato. Merlin's pupils also performed memorably. His death scene is remembered to this day.

Who was Merlin, and why is his name not in the history books? Why has he been pushed aside, shrugged off as a charlatan? Why has the Lady of the Lake been accused of his murder? These are still mysteries. However, a mystery is not something unintelligible. It is only something never made plain.

So, what actually transpired when Merlin and the Lady of the Lake proceeded toward Merlin's Cave, entered it, and opened the tomb in which he lay down? Did she murder him?

The event unfolded more like a ceremony in which both officiated and which many watched. Here Merlin seems to have performed the one act of public penance that he was allowed in his lifetime; because many had intervened on his behalf, he alone was allowed to buy back all his sins. Some sin requires the prayer of an outstanding person for remission, instructed the contemporary theologian Saint Ambrose of Milan in his "Concerning Penance."[2] Since the grace of public penance can be accorded only once, said Saint Ambrose, some people reserve it for the day of their death.

The exact liturgy performed here by the dying Merlin, assisted by his favorite pupil Niniane/Vivian, has long since been

• • •

[2] "De Poenitentia," *Sources chrétiennes* 179, edited by Roger Grysom (Paris, 1971), pp. 43–50.

lost. Celtic Christianity was organized at the margins of the Roman world, in Merlin's sixth century, and upon the foundation of Saint Ninian, which was essentially monastic or eremitical. The rituals of penitence performed at Bredigan lapsed and have been forgotten. Merlin could have received forgiveness by undergoing those expiatory practices called "Penitentials" that precisely codified and spelled out the rite in the minutest detail. Samples from such instructions were published in Paris in 1969. It was the French Church that late in Merlin's century convicted Irish monks who still adhered to these earlier unorthodox ceremonies. The trend then was for the confessor to acquire more latitude until after a few more centuries he could receive absolution before completing the penance. Saint Gildas wrote his Penitential in 583, almost fifty years after Merlin's death. Saint David may have written his in c. 544, and Saint Finian his in 552. Perhaps Merlin followed the practice of Saint Patrick, whose *Confession* has survived.

The following is known of the ceremonies of public penance before 461, and Merlin presumably died in 536. Until the year 461 the confession made by the penitent was public; thus, a crowd of people probably witnessed Merlin's last moments. The ceremony had already required of him a prolonged period of fasting and cleansing of the body. During the ceremony, there were prayers, prostration of the supplicant, who was dressed in sackcloth and rags and who lay on ashes. The constant use of only the plainest food and drink and the harsh treatment of the body had doubtless long characterized Merlin as it had Saint Germanus. For "as long as a person remains in sin," said Gildas, "so long is he to do penance."[3] His penance completed and his body reduced, Merlin was at last duly transported, accompanied by the thirteen treasures of Britain, to interment with the Druids and Saints on Bardsey Island.

Now that his death scene has been understood more reason-

• • •

[3] Gildas "On Penance." In *Gildas.* Edited by John Morris, p. 85.

ably, this summary completes the principal points concerning Merlin and his life. It does not answer the question of his name in history, for surely a man so exalted that he was buried with the thirteen treasures of Britain has a place of note in history. The proof for who he was will be located along the same route as the proof for when he died.

The first clue to the historical presence of Merlin as a dignitary of the highest importance comes in the same place where Arthurian literature was born, in the dense Latin pages of Geoffrey of Monmouth. Geoffrey did some fancy footwork around Merlin, stepping in close for a brisk *pas de deux* and pirouetting out on the double, all innocence and guile. First he gives us Merlin and Vortigern, Merlin and Uther, Merlin and Aurelius, Merlin and the *Prophecy*, Merlin and Arthur. Then abruptly he offers Arthur and the Archbishop Dubricius at "Caerleon," which was in reality Carlisle. Geoffrey then caught himself in a trap; requiring Dubricius at Carlisle, he had to drop Arthur as much as a thousand miles off into southern Wales. But when Dubricius in a loud voice from the hilltop exhorts Arthur's men to make Badon Hill a wonderful victory for Arthur, then Geoffrey summons the archbishop up into Scotland at Dumbarton Rock. After the French and English manuscripts describe Merlin's wars beside Arthur in North Wales, Geoffrey brings him back beside Dubricius, a most pious man, a great healer, an astronomer with two hundred student astronomers in his observatory at Caerleon in southern Wales. He then associates Dubricius with Saint David of Wales.

Gerald, prince of Wales, who was a Geoffrey endorser, here added that Merlin had prophesied that Saint David would become archbishop at Caerleon, and so he was elected there, as archbishop, unanimously. Despite their fancy footwork, neither Geoffrey nor Gerald succeeded in obtaining their coveted archbishopric in Wales. Nor could either manage to sweep Merlin under the carpet and keep him quiet there.

The various other accounts of Dubricius (Dubritius) down through the centuries are eye-opening. In fact, they are astonishing. On the one hand, like the case for Merlin, nobody knows where Dubricius was born or when and where he died. On the other hand, it is known that Merlin was interred among the Saints and Druids on Bardsey Island, and that the thirteen treasures of Britain were buried with him.

The name and fame of Dubricius has never faded from the memory of historians, who are aware of his supreme importance and of the "lost" archives concerning his life and place of birth. In his "Assertion of King Arthure" of 1544, John Leyland lists fifteen sources for British history of the fifth and sixth centuries, concluding firmly that he knew that Arthur was "the chiefest ornament of Brittayne, and the onely Myracle of his time." He also knew "Dubritius" (the change in spelling apparently occurs in the Renaissance) as "Archbishop of Caerlegion upon Usk" (Wye River in Wales). Leyland says King Aurelius died by poison, that his brother Uther "ruled a few yeares," followed by his son "Arthure," *who ruled because of the assistance given him by Dubricius.* Arthur

> who with bold courage fet [set] upon the *Saxones* in many battels, and yet could he not utterly roote them out of his kingdom. For the Saxones has subdued unto them/selves the whole compasse of the Island which stretcheth from the water of *Humber* unto the Sea *Cattenessinum* or Scottish Sea (No. 11, p. 22).

Leyland's source, he claims, was a life of Dubricius written by John Stow. He adds the King Arthur donated fragments of a wooden cross from Jerusalem to a "towne of Lodonesia" (Lohian, Scotland) near to Melrose (Abbey), and that he did not dower Glastonbury, where there was no monastery during Arthur's time; that is, the Benedictine Abbey of Glastonbury was only built centuries after Arthur's time. The old Merlin prophecy remembered by True Thomas in medieval Lothian claims both Arthur and Merlin for the north of Britain:

The first roote of this war shall rise in the north,
That the Isles and Ireland shall mourne for them bothe . . .

Recent *Dictionaries of Saints* by Donald Attwater (1958) and John J. Delaney (1980) give Dubricius as having lived about the year 545, which is probably incorrect. Merlin died before 542 when Arthur fell at Camlan. The legend that says Dubricius was born in Wales is repeated by three recent lexicographers, but if so, he was not born in Carmarthen, Wales. Both Charlotte Guest and John Rhŷs have pointed out that this place, the Roman Maridunum, was founded ages before either Merlin or Dubricius lived.

The historical Dubricius was a very wealthy landowner who founded monasteries or colleges inside Wales to which he "attracted followers." He became Bishop of Llandaf (Church-on-the-Taff River) Monastery, and was the Archbishop of Caerleon (*recte*, Carlisle) who crowned King Arthur, as well as the "metropolitan of Wales" (head of Wales as an ecclesiastical province). He was interred on Bardsey. The religious settlements he endowed with his own lands and estates were situated in what are now identifiable geographically as the "borders of Herefordshire and Monmouthshire." Dubricius consecrated Saint Samson (Galahad) as Abbot of Caldey Island in the archdiocese of Cardiff, Wales.

The long biography of Saint Dubricius, whose feast day is November 14, contradicts these recent dictionaries. In his massive *Lives of the Saints* (Edinburgh, 1914) Rev. Sabine Baring-Gould calculated that Dubricius died about 524. Gould based his book on the monk Benedict of Gloucester's *Life of Dubricius*, written about 1170.

The Welsh name of Dubricius was Dyfrig, says Gould. He must have been born in old Wales, either on the banks of the Gwain River in Pembrokeshire or on the banks of the Wye River in Herefordshire. The problem here stems from the fact that the name of the river where he was born is given in Latin only, unfortunately not in Celtic, and so *Vaga, Vaginensis* could designate either Welsh river. He was a grandson of the great patriarch Brychan, king of Brecknock, eastern Wales. Thus, Dyfrig, called Dubricius by the Latin annalists, was born a saint because he was born into the Celtic priestly tribe.

The Welsh scholar Rev. Rice Rees had already noted in 1836 that the name Dyfrig resembles that of Saint David *(Devi Sant)* and that both names in Welsh mean "waterman." By itself, this has no particular significance, for which reason later biographers ignored it; but to a reader of Arthurian literature, it divulges its hidden meaning. It solves a puzzle of the last hundred years posed by the *Prose Lancelot,* which otherwise contains a reputable, authentic telling of Lancelot's childhood, except when it insists he was "taught" by "mermen." The best Arthurian scholars of the early twentieth century threw up their hands and relegated all to fairyland, preferably Irish. *King Arthur* (1986) explains that the translation changed from "mermen" to "sailors" because Lancelot was educated on the Isle of Man. But if both Dyfrig and Devi were "watermen," then the Old French should have been translated as "Baptists."

One finds an identical puzzle in Rabelais, where the Oracle is mysteriously called "Bacbuc" or "bottle," names that give us such modern family names as "Butler" and "Boutell," meaning Protestant evangelist, one who carried with him on his journeys a bottle of holy or baptismal water. It has been argued that Rabelais was himself an "impenitent evangelist," his mysterious disappearance from the Paris hospital where he, like Merlin, was a doctor of medicine, was due to his execution for his unlawful, religious beliefs.[4]

According to Gould's encyclopedia of saints, Dyfrig founded

•   •   •

[4] *Rabelais. Oeuvres complètes,* edited by Jacques Boulenger and Luciene Scheler (Paris, 1959).

the monastery of Hentland-on-Wye in Erchenfield (Hereford-shire), where he spent seven years as a teacher. He was conse-crated Bishop of Llandaf monastery shortly after the year 470 and raised to Archbishop of Caerleon about 490. He is always reported to have attended or have persuaded Saint David to preside at the Council of Llandewi-Brefi in Wales, where the teachings of Pelagius were condemned, but Gould cannot ac-cept these details, believing quite correctly that Dubricius died before 569. In any case, it now appears that all records of that council have been lost. Gould accepts the connection between Dubricius and Samson (sometimes thought to have been his pupil, Lancelot's son Galahad), reporting that Samson called him "Dubricius papa."[5]

Samson's name sounds correct, for Gawain was also edu-cated by a saint called "papa," which has always been mistran-slated as "pope." Dubricius is believed to have fled into Wales from Lothian, where Merlin was said, by the *Alternate Prose Lan-celot,* to have been born. That Dubricius was an immensely wealthy landowner tallies with history since his holdings were coexten-sive with the Roman province of *Britannia Secunda.* The churches dedicated to Dubricius today are in Herefordshire, close to the Wye River, both referred to in Merlin's *Prophecy* in connection with water rights to the east of them, and specifically London's water as flowing from Merlin's lands in Wales.

Rees pointed out how common it was during those days for the prominent churchmen to travel back and forth, as Gildas did, from one part of the Celtic realm to another: Brittany,

• • •

[5] In 1982 Chris Barber wrote of another legend concerning Dubricius in Wales, that when he ordained Samson as deacon, a white pigeon flew in at the window and settled on the youth's shoulder. The bird remained there until the ceremony was completed and the young man ordained. Then Samson arose to receive holy communion. Saint Samson died twenty years after Dubricius, in Dol, Brittany, in 565.

modern Wales, Ireland, and to modern Scotland, especially around Edinburgh or the Lothians. Those Britons who had found a refuge in the north "when pressed by the Saxons and Picts," says Rees (p. 167), retreated to safety in southern or eastern Wales.

Such displacements in the descendants of Brychan were recorded because this was one of the three royal tribes of the Britons whose children (twelve sons and twenty-four daughters) over the generations frequently married into the royal lines of the Scots in Argyll. There the royal name "Arthur" recurred in the dynasty of Dalriada (the Irish Scots) for the second time in history. As grandson of Brychan, Dubricius was a celebrity in the Celtic realm from the day of his birth. His mother's name is given in Latin as Eurdila, and his father is assumed politely to have been the king of Herefordshire (Archenfield).

In 1934 Arthur Wade-Evans in *Welsh Christian Origins* gave a different pedigree for Saint Dubricius, which is revised as follows:

Emperor Maximus
(who died at Segontium,
North Wales, in 388*)*
m. Helena
⋮
Constantine (d. 411)   *King Erb of Archenfield* (Ercing and Gwent)
⋮
Constans (a monk)   *Ambrosius*   *Uther m. Ygerne*   *Efrddyl m. Peibio*
                                 ⋮   (Ebrdil)
                                 ⋮   (Eurdila)
                                 ⋮   ⋮
                              Arthur   *Saint Dubricius*
                            (born c. 475)   (born c. 450)

According to the above arrangement, King Arthur and Saint Dubricius were first cousins because of a fourth child of Constantine, who was a daughter. Wade-Evans believed that Saint Dubricius was the great-grandson of Constantine and the great-nephew of Ambrosius. Geoffrey of Monmouth had said that Arthur was a descendant of Constantine. Wade-Evans added that Saint Dubricius was born in Wales (or western England) at Madley, c. 450 (see Appendix). (According to this author's prior and independent calculations, Merlin was also born c. 450.)

This contribution of Wade-Evans is significant, for it explains the greater part of Merlin's behavior and most of the events of his earlier years.

1. why King Vortigern needed desperately to put the child Merlin to death,

2. why Merlin rallied to King Ambrosius and was accepted so readily as counselor and adviser,

3. why Merlin then transferred to King Uther Pendragon, and why he spoke so familiarly to him,

4. why Merlin was able to take the infant Arthur from his mother's arms,

5. why Merlin risked his life and interrupted his eccelsiastical and scholarly career so often to assist King Arthur,

6. and why he was able to vouch for Arthur's ancestry.

Obviously, the genealogy of Merlin needs more search inside Wales and through the Welsh libraries. Nevertheless, it would seem that Merlin was descended from two ancestral founders of ancient nobility, from Constantine like King Arthur, and also from Brychan and his ecclesiastical tribe.

Wade-Evans also says that there was formerly at Madley a stone commemorating the birth of the child Dubricius, just as there was on the Rhinns of Galloway Merlin's Stone, or *Perron* (dolmen), at or near Carlisle.

There is at least one direct connection between King Arthur, Merlin, Saint Dubricius, and the properties in eastern Wales and western England as we know them. This connection is the rather mysterious statement in the "Marvels of Britain" section of the *Annals of Wales,* and it was noted prominently in 1927 by Edmund K. Chambers in *Arthur of Britain* and in 1929 in France by Edmond Faral in Volume I of the Arthurian Legend (*La Légende arthurienne*). Both scholars recorded the strange statement of Nennius as follows:

> Est aliud miraculum in regione quae vocatur Ercing. Habetur ibi sepulcrum iuxta fontem, qui cognominatur Licat Anir, et viri nomen, qui sepultus est in tumulo, sic vocabatur Anir. Filius Arthuri militis erat, et ipse occidit eum ibidem et sepelivit. Et veniunt homines ad mensurandum tumulum in longitudine aliquando sex pedes, aliquando novem, aliquando duodecim, aliquando quindecim. In qua mensura metieris eum in ista vice, iterum non invenies eum in una mensura, et ego solus probavi.
> (*Records,* Chambers, p. 240.)

Casually translated, for the text offers no problems of meaning:

> There is another marvel (miracle) in the region which is called Ercing (Archenfield). They have a tomb here, next to the font, which is called the Bed of Anir, and the name of the man who is buried in this tumulus (barrow), is so called: Anir. He was a son of the soldier Arthur, and he himself slew him on this same spot and entombed him. And men come for the purpose of measuring this tumulus, sometimes six feet long, sometimes nine, sometimes twelve, sometimes fifteen. In whatever measurement you measure it on that spot, again you will not find it at any one measurement (as before), and I alone have proved it.

The opposite map made by Rev. Doble in *Saint Dubricius* shows Erging (Ercing) as the present Herefordshire, or as the border area between Wales and England. This exact area supported and supports the many religious foundations dedicated to the worship of Saint Dubricius, who was, insofar as one can see, the real Merlin and King Arthur's Merlin.

In 1929 Edmond Faral concluded that this story from the *Annals of Wales* and Nennius did not necessarily mean that King Arthur killed a son in Ercing but rather that this garbled story was a memory of the King Arthur veneration transported by somebody from the north of Britain into eastern Wales. This somebody was Merlin himself, that is, Saint Dubricius.

Both Merlin and Dubricius were born to be educated for the Church, both sons-of-the-woman, born into the priestly tribe that was that of Brychan. Even Robert de Boron's text in Old French, which may be a borrowing from the Old Testament, has the baby Merlin named for a grandfather. Both personages are born of unknown fathers and in places unknown. Both kept one foot in Wales and the other in Scotland, although they were then not two separate realms but one Celtic nation undivided even from Ireland and Cornwall. Both great men were prodigies, outstanding because of learning, intelligence, ingenuity, and wisdom. Nobody has challenged this brilliance, this British genius that has influenced peoples and nations ever since they first prophesied from that height of theirs, which dwarfed even kings.

When he stole through the battle zones in a variety of disguises, he was "Merlin." When he led Arthur's advance contingent and carried the Roman dragon banner, he must also have been hailed and adored as the prodigiously wonderful "Merlin." When he put on his grandiose manner and ecclesiastical robes of state to crown King Arthur, all bowed down and lowered their eyes before their prince, Saint Dubricius, the first among all the Christian prelates of Britain, said Geoffrey of Monmouth, who cannot be silenced.

Bishop Usher of Llandaf in May, 1120, had the remains of

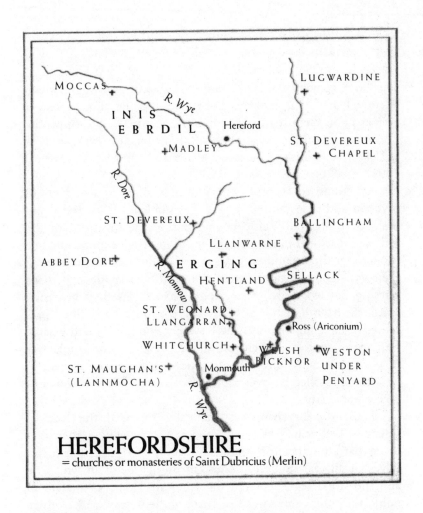

HEREFORDSHIRE
+ = churches or monasteries of Saint Dubricius (Merlin)

Notes: This is an enlargement of the map drawn by Rev. Canon Doble (Saint Dubricius, p. 33), but see his text for all the real estate holdings of Saint Dubricius, as given in the Book of Llandaf.

"Inis Ebrdil" would seem to have been the estate of the mother of Saint Dubricius: the Island of Ebrdil (Efrddyl).

"Whitchurch" might be a memory of Whithorn in Scotland.
ERGING (Ercing) derives from the Latin name ARICONIUM.

Saint Dubricius moved from Bardsey Island to his cathedral, where they remain in state today. He also commissioned *The Book of Llandaf* (Llan Dav), which includes the "Life of Saint Dubricius." This book contains the land charters of Llandaf monastery, which Wendy Davies has recently been studying. Because of recent attacks upon Geoffrey of Monmouth, included in the Appendix is a first partial translation of this "Life" from *The Text of the Book of Llandaf* as published by J. G. Evans and John Rhŷs (Oxford, 1893).

According to reports from Welsh scholars, descendants of Brychan and Constantine solved the problem of life and death that confronted all Celtic people during the invasions of the fifth and sixth centuries, which were forecasts of more to come for another three hundred years. How could they hope to retain their vast landed estates before the onrush of landless, perhaps starving but assuredly pagan Anglo-Saxons? As they fled back and forth from one corner of Britain to another, a solution presented itself compellingly. Interestingly enough, it is the same step many of today's generation are presently contemplating: how to make a significant contribution with the worldly wealth so painfully collected over a period of work? The solution? Endow a university.

Thus, the Brychans systematically followed the lead of "Merlinus Dubricius Ambrosius," and in the generation after him, as in that after the first Ambrosius, completed divesting themselves of all real property. Thus, in the garments in which he and she stood, each entered the Church. Their actions are so noble that one cannot read of them without tears. All of them practiced what they continued to preach.

Reading *The Text of the Book of Llandaf* and Geoffrey of Monmouth's *History of the Kings of Britain*, where Merlin and Dubricius are each mentioned for the first time and with great respect, one must still want to heed modern warnings.

Such a condemnation came as recently as 1958 from the theologian Christopher Brooke in "The Archbishops of Saint

David's, Llandaff and Caerleon-on-Usk."[6] These two books (*Llandaf* and Geoffrey's *History*) are "the two most considerable historical forgeries of medieval Britain," Brooke writes (p. 201). Geoffrey lied when he said Dubricius could cure disease (p. 202), he adds. Geoffrey knew that such a claim was fiction, he repeats. Saint Dubricius was "undoubtedly historical," but Geoffrey called him "primate of Britain and legate of the Holy See" (p. 209)—all lies! As for *The Book of Llandaf*, it was written either by the monk, known to Geoffrey, Caradoc of Llancarfan, or by "an assassin (hired by Bishop Usher of Llandaf) from outside the walls," or by Geoffrey of Monmouth himself (pp. 232–33).

Merlinus Ambrosius was placed on the forbidden list or *Prohibitory Index* of the Catholic Church at the Council of Trent in 1580. His prohibited prophecies, so high did they whip the courage of Europeans, were partially responsible, for the French victory under Joan of Arc in the Hundred Years War. But Joan, who was raised to sainthood in the 1920s, was burned at the stake for her efforts and probably also for the use of Merlin's prophecies as another potent weapon in another endless war over real property. But perhaps Merlinus Ambrosius was prohibited for heresy because he championed baptism as the primary, initiatory ordinance of Christianity, and a universal obligation. Dubricius would doubtless have added that it is spiritual gratification that counts. Merlin would have agreed as he made this same public confession and lay on ashes, with the Lady of the Lake to assist him, as he entered the sculpted cave.

One does not have to look very long in Church history to find Merlin as the teacher whom the Irish fairy tales called the *Grúagach*. In the early centuries when Latin was replacing Greek as the liturgical language of the Church in Rome, the earthly birth of only three persons was celebrated: Christ, Mary, and

. . .

[6] In *Studies in the Early British Church*, edited by Norah Chadwick (Cambridge, 1958), pp. 201–42.

John the Baptist. His head or icon had been assigned to Gawain to find, which he did and presented to the Grail Castle. Christ said of John the Baptist who had been born six months before Himself, ". . . among those born of woman, there is not a greater prophet." As forerunner of the Messiah, he merited celebrations for his maturity and martyrdom (August 29, A.D. 30?). John the Baptist was called "the wonderful child," for at his baptism, when he was eight days old, he praised God.

John the Baptist was set apart as a Nazarite for life obligation. He was forbidden to drink wine, to cut the hair of his head, and to approach a dead body. There were only three such Nazarites for life: Samson, Samuel, and John the Baptist. They dressed like the old prophets in garments of camel's hair attached to the body by a leather girdle. They ate only food of the desert. Merlin Dubricius seems to have been a fourth Nazarite, which would perhaps explain his hirsute appearance that struck everyone so memorably.[7]

* * * * * * *

The time of the final question is now at hand, not only for Merlin/Dubricius but also for Arthur. Despite all comparative calculations and despite the Annals of Wales, no one date is certain as yet for either personage. Arthur may have been born in 475. Merlin/Dubricius may have been born in 450. Arthur probably died at or soon after his defeat at Camlan, possibly in 542. Dubricius is erroneously said to have died as late as 612,

* * *

[7] It is uncanny that Edwin Arlington Robinson should have caught this second, major physical trait in "Merlin":

> Buried alive I told you I should be,
> By love made little and by woman shorn,
> Like Samson, of my glory; and the time
> Is now at hand . . .
>
> (Collected Poems, p. 260)

to have attended Saint David's Council in 569. We know that Saint Patrick became Bishop of the British Church in Ireland when he was about forty years old and that he died about 460. Not a single fact or reported detail of his death is known for certain. One reads that Saint Dubricius became a bishop (of Carlisle) about the year 490. If he was also then forty years of age, then he was born c. 450, as Wade-Evans had reported for Dubricius.

If Vortigern died in 459, then Merlin actually was near the reported age, seven to nine, when he prophesied Vortigern's death to the tyrant's face. Then Merlin would have been twenty-five when Ambrosius and his brother Uther Pendragon were poisoned, and when Arthur was born. Merlin must then have been forty years old when he had Arthur elected as "dux," and he had just that year, A.D. 490, become Bishop of Carlisle. Merlin was fifty when as Dubricius he orated, in 500, at Badon Hill. He then had thirty-two and one-half years to live, during which period Arthur's rule weakened and fell into the same chaos that had already swept over much of Europe. He took part in Arthur's Island Campaign, where he undoubtedly helped reconvert the Grail Castle to Christianity. Merlin there turned down both Gawain and Lancelot for final education leading to kingship of the Grail Castle. He helped Arthur maintain the peace for another twelve or so years, the golden age of Arthur and his warriors. Merlin as Dubricius crowned Arthur again in Carlisle, ascertained his rights, and championed him against the hostile warlords, after which Merlin is seventy-two years old and Arthur is forty-seven. Thirteen years later Perceval is urgently summoned for training and, if he passes the tests, for inauguration at the Grail Castle. Since Merlin approves of Perceval, he participates in this education and sponsors the youth. When Perceval presents himself at Arthur's court, there are, everybody remembers, only seven years to go until the collapse of the realm. Merlin would be eighty-five years old. He foretells his own death the following year, during an eclipse of the sun. Aged eighty-six, he is attended in death by the Lady of the Lake, who also sorrowfully receives King Arthur's wounded body five or six years later, in 542.[8]

Mathematicians and astronomers have recently written books about Stonehenge as an observatory and about Silbury Hill as another, as well as about megalithic monuments around the globe. Merlin too is reported to have been an astronomer, the same for Dubricius, both allegedly also teachers of astronomy.

Among the ancient Hebrews, says Mircéa Eliade, it was customary as a last resort in times of utter catastrophe to turn to the heavens, to the cosmic God when all lay abjectly under threat of total annihilation. An initiation-type of religious cere-

· · ·

[8] In its final section, Merlin's *Prophecy* talks about the Zodiac gone awry or reversed and the stars charting new courses off the ecliptic. The learned Cundrie also lectured on zodiacs and planets in *Parzival*. She is shrugged off even if she was Merlin's pupil. Taliesin wrote a "Song of the World" where he listed Sun, Moon, Mars, Mercury, Venus, Jupiter, and Saturn, or five known planets. And the much more ancient twelve labors of Hercules or the voyage of the Argo corresponded to zodiacal lore. The ancients could presumably have learned some astronomy from the Middle East, as the often quoted words of Diodorus Siculus suggested about 50 B.C., where he gave the Saros Cycle (about nineteen years):

> The Moon as viewed from this island (Britain) appears to be but a little distance from the Earth and to have on it prominences like those of the Earth, which are visible to the eye. The account is also given that the god visits the island every nineteen years, the period in which the return of the stars to the same place in the heavens is accomplished. . . . There is also on the island both a magnificent sacred precinct of Apollo and a notable temple . . . and the supervisors are called Boreadae, and succession to these positions is always kept in their family.

320

mony, Merlin's penance, was then performed.[9] For good reason, then, Merlin's *Prophecy* reads like the Book of Revelation, as an announcement of what stages of deterioration to expect before Judgment Day and a New Jerusalem. Thus, Merlin/Dubricius gladly underwent a public ceremony of penance.

Having found who Merlin was and when he died, one mystery more needs an explanation: Merlin predicted his own death on a day when the earth would be darkened. This darkness would cover him in the middle of the day. Night would swallow up day. At that instant Merlin would die.

Anyone who has read *Huth-Merlin* (f. 120a) must remember this passage but, apparently, nobody has mentioned it. In it, Merlin predicted his own death.

For his part Merlin could have read the *Phenomena* of Aratus from the third century B.C. in order to compose his zodiac in the *Prophecy*. No problem there. Or the Gaels may have taught astronomy, as is often alleged. *But to predict an eclipse of the sun he would probably have had to have studied Pythagoras, who some think taught the sphericity of the earth,* knew that the moon's light came from the sun, must have had or made a calendar showing the rising and setting of the largest stars, must have had the ancient Babylonian eclipse records, must have been able to track the five known planets, and furthermore, must have understood that solar eclipses occur only at the new moon.

Contemporary astronomers sometimes explain that everything known about astronomy has been learned in the last two hundred years, or even in the last forty years, from 1940–1984, as J. B. Zirker writes in *Total Eclipses of the Sun* (New York, 1984), pp. 1–3. He also tells us that the Greeks had an astronomer named Hipparchus (c. 150 B.C.), who may have developed a

• • •

[9] *The Sacred and the Profane: The Nature of Religion,* translated by Willard Trask (New York, 1959), p. 75.

theory for the motions of sun and moon. Hipparchus is also said to have discovered the mystery of *the nineteen years* Diodorus Siculus spoke of, and the phenomenon of the precession of the equinoxes.

Ptolemy's *Almagest* (c. 140 B.C.) expanded and corrected Hipparchus, adding a catalogue of stars, giving their magnitudes, calculating the distances apart of sun and moon, offering a theory of planetary motion by which the relative positions of the known planets and stars could be predicted by arithmetic and geometry. Better than those tools alone, Merlin was said to have had an observatory with two hundred watchers of the nighttime sky. The ancient Irish claimed as much.

Merlin truly resided at the very edge of his world, and of Ireland, not only geographically but also intellectually. Astronomers and astrologers were initially proscribed at Rome by Augustus Caesar in A.D. 11, however. About the year 300 Diocletian banned all divination, that is, observation of the heavens. Constantius made such studies a capital offense (c. 367, c. 373, and c. 409). "Astrologers" were publicly and legally declared enemies of the state, of Roman law, and of civic order. All practiced under pain of the death penalty.

Chaldean astronomers had already discovered that eclipses recurred after 223 months, which would be 18 years and 10 or 11 days. They also knew that the sun and moon returned to the same longitude *after nineteen years*. A short cycle of four or five eclipses may occur every nineteen years in the same part of the sky, and at the same season in the year.

In their *Eclipses of the Sun and Moon* (Oxford, 1937) Frank Dyson and R. v. d. R. Woolley say that in any one year there could be four eclipses of the sun and three of the moon, or five of the sun and two of the moon. Two eclipses of the sun per year, visible at some place on earth, appear to be the minimum. And yet there was in the nineteenth century no eclipse of the sun that was visible in Britain, and there will be none such in the twentieth century.

322

No total eclipse of the sun has been recorded as having been observed in Merlin's lifetime. Even so, this leaves us at least one ray of hope: either there was no eclipse of the sun during Merlin's lifetime or none was reported in Britain, or Merlin predicted an eclipse.

J. B. Zirker describes the period in which Merlin lived as a "void," a black hole, which stretched from A.D. 364 to A.D. 840, or from the Alexandrian astronomer Theon of the fourth century who first recorded an eclipse by date and by the time of its beginning, middle, and end, measuring the elapsed time in fifths or sixths of an hour, and whose careful records of the moon's motion are still used, to the years A.D. 840–1310, when seventeen eclipses were recorded by ten or more separate observers (p. 6ff.). Zirker then names the real astronomers:

1. Johannes Kepler (1605), who first noted the solar corona,

2. Isaac Newton (1664), who spread sunlight into a spectrum,

3. Giovanni Cassini (1706), who spread sunlight into a crown of light,

4. Edmund Halley (1715), who described the corona's shape,

5. Francis Bailey (1836, 1842), who discovered during an eclipse the beads of sunshine, hence that they were rays of sunlight streaming out between mountains on the moon: "Bailey's Beads,"

6. Francis Bailey (1890), who settled the question of the corona, that it is a part of the sun.

Zirker gave his due to Francis Bailey, who was an amateur observer and not a university professor academically trained in astronomy.

An eclipse may be partial, where the moon hides only a part of the sun's disk, or annular, where the moon is centered in the middle of the sun's disk, or on it but off center, but having a ring of light around it, or total. As Dyson and Woolley describe it, in a total eclipse there is a gradual darkening of the sun visible but with a dark section on the western edge of the solar orb. This darkening, which resembles conditions during a severe thunderstorm, increases for about an hour and a half, the time depending upon the observer's location on the earth. Gradually the temperature falls. The light on earth changes color. It is difficult for the observer to judge the hour of the day and also difficult for him to judge distance. Animals, people, but especially birds exhibit peculiar behavior, as they do immediately before and after a strong earthquake. Then, too, there follows a terrifying suspension. When total darkness comes, it comes at once from all directions, swooping over and under and about the observer. Again the silence or suspension is terrible. There is no up or down. Streams of white light faster than the human eye can follow can sometimes be seen, streaking off from the blackened sun. A white corona appears visibly around it, perhaps. Then the stars come out all over the sky. This darkness lasts, say Dyson and Woolley, at least three or four minutes, or even as long as seven and a half minutes.

The darkness on earth is caused by the moon's shadow as it falls across the earth in an elliptical path perhaps a hundred miles wide. This shadow indicates either that the moon covers the sun completely, causing a total *umbra* on earth, or that the moon covers it partially as during an annular eclipse when the shadow is also called in Lain an "almost shadow," a *penumbra*.

The moon, which moves thirteen times faster than the sun, overtakes it from the west and moves off to the east so that as the eclipse ends, the sunlight streams out again, in danger of blinding the observer permanently, from the west. Edmund Halley's chart shows the elliptical path of the *umbra* and the *penumbra*. The *umbra* sometimes passes at 5,000 mph, or at the equator at only 1,060 mph because the earth rotates in the same direction, thus decreasing the speed of the cast shadow at the earth's greatest diameter. The higher the latitude, the greater the shadow's speed. The path of the shadow in a typical eclipse is 6,000 miles long and one hundred miles wide. The average time of total darkness in a total eclipse can range from two to three minutes to four hours.

Amateur astronomers are encouraged, as R. R. Newton, quoted by Zirker (p. 45) explains:

An observation that a solar eclipse was total at a known place is an observation of rather high precision. It is not necessary for the observer to record the time accurately. In almost all cases, we need the time only within a *decade* in order to identify an eclipse; the place then determines the time with an error of only a few minutes. Thus, a person with no astronomical training can make a valuable astronomical observation.

For Merlin's eclipse to have occurred, the moon must have been new, appearing about equal in size to the sun, and their paths as projected on the sky must have intersected or met at an intersection (called a node).

Theodor von Oppolzer published in Vienna in 1887 the *Canon der Finsternisse* (*Canon of Eclipses*, New York, 1963), which lists and studies eight thousand solar eclipses that he and his colleagues were able to prove occurred or will occur between the years 1207 B.C. and A.D. 2161.

An eclipse of the sun, numbered 4143, occurred in the year A.D. 536 (pp. 160–61). It would have been visible in an elliptical path some one hundred miles wide, extending across or south of the Isle of Man, the Irish Sea, and on its extremity to south of the city of Carlisle, England. This path of the penumbra might even have been visible at Merlin's Cave, Whithorn, on the Rhinn of Galloway. Eclipse 4143 was noncentral annular; a rim of sunlight, wider on one side, shone visibly around the moon's disk, and Bailey's Beads would perhaps have been partially visible, if the sky was unclouded.

Eclipse 4143 occurred on September 1, 536, at 13 hours, 20 minutes, and 1 second. Merlin had specified it would grow dark at midday.

The midday location of Eclipse 4143 was:

longitude −12 (12° west of the Greenwich Observatory),

latitude +56 (56° north of the equator).

(See Oppolzer, Chart 83 for the year 536, IX, 1).

The new moon was at its apogee, the point of greatest distance from the earth in its orbit.

The shadow of the moon fell upon the earth from the northwest toward the southeast. It was very oblique. It was moving very fast, it seems, perhaps even at 5,000 mph.

Eclipse 4143 (noncentral, annular, or *Ringformige*) crossed the Atlantic Ocean; its commencement (Oppolzer's *Aufgangpunkt*) was in central Canada at its northernmost point. It ended (Oppolzer's *Untergangpunkt*) somewhere in the area of the Red Sea, near the northernmost promontory of eastern Africa. It lasted only about seven and a half minutes because the moon would have been in the outer portion of its orbit, the shadow falling somewhat short of the earth. The ring of light around the sun would have shone as full but lopsided. Therefore, the duration would have been brief, the shadow streaking out from the Atlantic Ocean and striking land some 250 miles northwest of the Isle of Man.

According to Edmund Halley's chart, Eclipse 4143 would have proceeded opposite to Halley's Eclipse of April 22, 1715, or would have gone from the far upper left corner of his chart to the lower right corner.

Thus, directly from Merlin: he died in his burial cave after having performed an initiatory and penitential rite in the year 536 on the occasion of an eclipse of the sun, which occurred at midday, perhaps over his second sacred Isle at Whithorn.

Marvelous to the end, Merlin typifies the imposing miracle of a magical life, for he represents in his life a cultural force that

EDMUND
HALLEY'S MAP

"A description of the Passage
of the Shadow of the Moon
over England"

people have always believed in and still believe in. His story constitutes a single, continuous, coherent master text containing all coded explanations, recommendations, symbols, and their unvoiced solutions. The man, Merlin/Saint Dubricius, a wondrous prodigy, has even now supplied history with a retrospective pattern of crisis and human response that we treasure, like his voice from so very long ago, speaking as a survivor of terrible perils and penance.

・　　・　　・　　・　　・　　・　　・

In a while they rose and went out aimlessly riding,
Leaving their drained cups on the table round.
Merlin, Merlin, their hearts cried, where are you hiding?
In all the world was no unnatural sound.

"Merlin Enthralled,"
Stanza 1.
Richard Wilbur.
In *New Poets of England and America*

TABLE OF
APPROXIMATE
DATES

Note: Please see the chronology of an American scholar who contributes to *Antiquity* magazine, Paul Karlsson Johnstone: *Antiquity* 36 (1962): 102–9. Johnstone calls his study of twenty years "A Consular Chronology of Dark Age Britain" from his collation of dates, including those of Roman Consuls. While I differ occasionally, I agree about King Arthur's invasion and conquest of North Wales (and not Gaul), which included the recovery of Anglesey from the Irish (King Urian of the Isles), c. 500.

Event	Date
Irish/Pictish invasions of Hadrian's Wall	c. 410–450
Accession of Vortigern	c. 425
Bishops Germanus of Auxerre and Lupus of Troyes to Britain regarding Pelagian Heresy	429
Saint Patrick, aged about 40, Bishop to Ireland	c. 430
Council of Ephesus: final condemnation of Pelagius	431
Saint Patrick preaching on the Isle of Man(?)	444
Papal Legates, Germanus and Lupus, to Britain	445–446
PROBABLE BIRTH DATE OF MERLIN	450
Birth of Saint Bridget	c. 454
Death of Vortigern, as prophesied by Merlin	459? 480? 490?
Death of Saint Patrick	c. 460
Death of Ambrosius	c. 475
Death of Uther Pendragon	c. 475

Event	Date
Birth of Arthur	c. 475
Last Roman Emperor deposed by Odoacer	475
Death of Saint Lupus	478
The *Life of St Germanus* written in France	478
Bishop Dubricius in Carlisle	c. 490
Arthur elected *Dux* of the British forces	c. 490
Theodoric assassinates Odoacer and takes Ravenna	493
Baptism of King Clovis and three thousand Franks, Christmas Eve	496
Arthur's victories, to that of Mount Badon	c. 500
MERLIN'S TIME OF PROPHECY COMMENCES ("1,690 weeks")	
Arthur's Island Campaign	c. 501
Arthur and Merlin hold Britain in peace	c. 500–513
Saint Kentigern (Mungo) born in Scotland	518 or 527
Saint Columba born in Ireland	c. 521
Arthur crowned king by Bishop (or Archbishop) Dubricius	c. 522
Theodoric tortures and kills the noble Roman Boethius	525
Justinian siezes power in Constantinople. By his decree the schools are closed in Greece	527
Perceval is summoned for training. (It is "seven years before the end of King Arthur's reign.")	c. 535

Event	Date
MERLIN'S DEATH. Eclipse of the sun.	536
King Arthur's Continental Campaign? Deaths of Gawain, Lancelot, and Arthur	542
The Lady of the Lake conveys Arthur to Avalon	
The Yellow Plague strikes	543
The poet Taliesin flourishes	c. 547–559
Saint Columba founds his school on Iona	563
Death of Saint Gildas	c. 570
Saint Kentigern removes to Glasgow	573
Death of Saint Kentigern	c. 603 or 612

The end of the ancient world in Britain

NOTABLE
LIVES

· · · · · · ·

Gaul/France

1. Saint Germanus of Auxerre (c. 378–448)	Papal Legate to Britain
2. Saint Lupus of Troyes (c. 383–478)	Papal Legate to Britain
3. King Clovis I (c. 466–511)	King of the Franks
4. Queen and Saint Clotilde (? –545)	Queen of the Franks

Italy/Rome/Ravenna

1. Emperor Romulus Augustulus (reigned 475–476)	Last "Roman" Emperor
2. Odoacer (c. 435–493)	Mercenary who deposed Roman Emperor
3. King Theodoric the Ostrogoth (The Great) (c. 454–526)	Superseded Odoacer
4. Boethius, Anicius Manlius Severinus (c. 475–525)	Roman statesman and great philosopher and writer

Ireland

1. Saint Patrick (c. 390–c. 460)	Bishop of Ireland, evangelist, writer
2. Saint Bridget of Kildare ("Mary of God") (c. 454–c. 523)	Greatest woman of the century

Ireland

3. Saint Columba ("Apostle of Caledonia") (c. 521–597)	Evangelist, teacher, Bible copier
4. Pelagius (fl. c. 410–431) and Celestius (? –431)	Radical British theologian finally worsted by Saint Augustine

Africa

1. Saint Augustine (Aurelius Augustinus) (354–430)	Greatest of Christian converts, authors

Eastern Rome/Constantinople

1. Emperor Constantine the Great (c. 288–337)	First Emperor to accept Christianity Reputed ancestor of Arthur
2. Emperor Justinian I (483–565)	Harsh and autocratic, anti-intellectual, pretended theologian
3. Saint Jerome (c. 347–c. 419)	Translator of the Bible

Anglo-Saxons

1. Hengist and Horsa 449–473	Invasion of Britain
2. Ella and sons 477–485	Invasion of Britain
3. King Esc 488	Kingdom of Kent
4. Cerdic and Cynric 495–530	Kingdom of the West Saxons
5. Porta and sons 501	Isle of Wight Portsmouth
6. Ida c. 547	Kingdom of Northumbria (607–685)

CERETIC OF GULETIC (Gwledig).
Christian King of Strathclyde in the
time of Saint Patrick (Fifth Century).

CINUIT

DYFNWAL THE OLD (Hen)
A later genealogy traces him through the Gwledig Maxen
(cousin of the Gwledig Cunedda) from King Coel the Old,
but it seems probable his was a female descent.

Various sons, from whom
the British Kings of
Strathclyde descended
until 908

British Princess:
Brychan Prince
in Manan (*Merlin's
tribe*).

PRINCESS LLERAN:
Gabhran, King of
Dalriada, slain 559.

AIDAN, King of Dalriada, 608.

EOCHAID THE FAIR,
King of Dalriada,
died 630, ancestor
in the female line
of the present Royal
Family

ARTHUR (This prince bore a
Cymric name; other British names
such as Rigullan and Morgan ap-
pear in the Dalriadic Royal Family
from this period).

• • •

Note: Genealogy kindly offered by Arthur MacArthur, historian of the
Clan MacArthur, U.S.A.

SUBSTANTIATION
OF THE
BOOK OF
LLANDAF

Note: Text provided courtesy of the Butler Library, Columbia University, from *The Text of the Book of Llandaf* (Llan Dâv). Edited by J. G. Evans and John Rhŷs (Oxford, 1893).

I. "The First State of the Church of Llan Dâv" . . . pp. 68–71.

1. Church founded 166 years after the Incarnation, when King Lucius accepted Christianity.

2. The Pelagian Heresy: Bishops Germanus and Lupus sent from Gaul to abolish this heresy.

"They consecrated the blessed Dubricius Archbishop of Llandaf [because he was] the highest Doctor of the Church [who had been] elected by the king and also by all the parochial clergy. When this dignity had been conferred upon him by Germanus & Lupus, they established for him an episcopal seat [that is, a bishopric]."

II. CHARTERS OF LLANDAF   pp. 71–78

Territories

Rights

Privileges

Obligations

Duties

Location: all on the "left side" of Britain, on the banks of the Taff and the Wye rivers, in the district called "Ercing."

345

III. CHURCHES IN THIS BISHOPRIC

Note: There is no evidence for the consecration of Dubricius by the emissaries from Gaul, and the dates are also wrong.

IV. "READINGS CONCERNING THE LIFE OF SAINT DUBRICIUS"   pp. 78–86

1. The story of the birth of Saint Dubricius, how his grandfather tried to drown and then burn his pregnant mother, and how he was healed by a touch of the baby's hand.

2. The grandfather of Dubricius endowed the baby with vast landed estates.

"And from that hour he grew so in estate and in time developed so in learning that he was sent away to study advanced letters gladly and with great devotion to his studies. And just as he had been in babyhood, he developed into maturity as a person of great prudence, deliberation, eloquence, and learning. And afterwards he became renowned, equal in presence and in erudition. His fame increased until his experience both in the Old and the New Law extended throughout all Britain. And so from all parts of Britain students thronged to him, not so much the untutored ones as the learned men, and even the Doctors [of Law] rushed to his side to study under him."   p. 79

3. Names of twenty of his most famous students.

4. Seven-year period with one thousand students on the Wye River banks, at Hentland.

5. Residence at Mochros.

   a. Story of how the angel directed him to this site.

"The teaching of St. Dubricius radiated from there over all Britain like the light of a great candelabrum . . . inspiring all to the faith . . ."   p. 81

6. He visits establishments to give correction and advice, and to ordain bishops [like Samson].

V. BARDSEY ISLAND

Weary of travels and the onerous duties of his ecclesiastical responsibilities, Saint Dubricius retired to Bardsey Island, where he lived in the strictest solitude as a hermit, there among the bones and bodies of martyrs and twenty thousand saints.

VI. TRANSLATION TO LLANDAF CATHEDRAL   p. 84

The body (or bones) of Saint Dubricius was translated to Llandaf Cathedral by Bishop Urban of Llandaf in the twelfth century. David was then Bishop at Bangor.
     The ceremonies at Llandaf.   pp. 85–86

Note: "The Reformation destroyed nearly all the liturgical books of Wales," says Rev. Canon Doble in his *Saint Dubricius* (p. 30), for which reason the *Book of Llandaf,* whatever its shortcomings, is of prime interest. Rev. Doble confirms that the body of Saint Dubricius was translated from the Island of Enli (Bardsey Island) on Friday, May 7, 1120, and that it arrived in Llandaf on Sunday, May 23 of that same year. Otherwise, as Rev. Doble adds, little is known about Saint Dubricius at Llandaf—exception made always for what is learned from poor, maligned Geoffrey of Monmouth, who *in 1120* labored in nearby Monmouth, probably mystified at what he had found about the parallel: Saint Dubricius/Merlin.

347

*SAINT
DUBRICIUS
BY ARTHUR
WADE-EVANS*

North of Gwent beyond the Monnow was the Romano-British kingdom of Erging or Archenfield, now in Herefordshire, but historically part of Wales. It was so called after the Roman town of Ariconium at Weston-under-Penyard.

The great saint of Erging was Dubricius, great-grandson of Constantine son of Maximus. He was born at Madley (c. 450), a mile south of the Wye and some six miles west of Hereford. A stone marked the spot, remembrance of which survives in the name Chilstone, "child's stone."

His mother was Efrddyl, who, notwithstanding the story told of her as of Nonn, mother of St. David, is to be regarded as one of the many women, who figured in the monastic movements in Britannia. Herself a saint, and the mother of a son who achieved distinction for like reason, she ranks with St. Helena, St. Non, and St. Gwladus, mother of St. Cadog.

She was also a woman of secular importance, not only as daughter of King Peibio of Erging and granddaughter of Constantine, but also as inheritor of the northern part of Erging, which took from her its name of Ynys Efrddyl. She is the patron saint of Madley, alias Llanefrddyl, as also of another Llanefrddyl in Llandenni, Monmouthshire. His name is also found near Llangynfil by Monmouth and in the boundaries of Llandeilo Fawr, Carmarthenshire.

Dubricius's first place was Hentland, "old monastery," near the Wye, where for seven years he had a thousand clerks engaged in the pursuit of divine and secular learning. Among these

were Ufelfyw, Merchwyn, Elwredd, Gwynfyw, Cynwal, Arth-
foddw, Cynnwr, Arwystl, Inabwy, Cynfran, Gwrfan, Elhaearn,
Idno, Gwrddogwy, Gwernabwy, Lleuan, Aeddan, Cynfarch, all
famous at one time, but now well-nigh forgotten.

After seven years Dubricius moved to Moccas in Ynys Efrddyl,
some four miles from Madley, where for many years he lived
according to rule, his doctrine radiating through all Britannia as
a lamp on a stand.

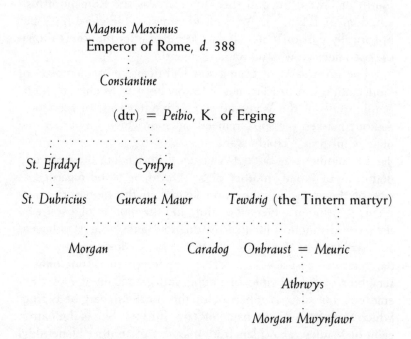

Magnus Maximus
Emperor of Rome, *d.* 388

Constantine

(dtr) = *Peibio*, K. of Erging

St. Efrddyl   *Cynfyn*

St. Dubricius   *Gurcant Mawr*   *Tewdrig* (the Tintern martyr)

Morgan   *Caradog   Onbraust* = *Meuric*

Athrwys

Morgan Mwynfawr

It was during this time that Dubricius, paying visits to Llan-
twit Major, the great monastery of Illtud, on the Glywysing
(i.e., the Glamorganshire) coast, ordained St. Samson as dea-
con, and afterwards a priest (*c.* 504).

Dubricius was also wont to spend the greater part of Lent
in a monastery on Caldey Island, near Tenby. This was under

the Abbot Pyr, whence the island in Welsh is called Ynys Byr, and the mainland opposite Maenor Byr, i.e., Manorbier. On one occasion Dubricius deposed the cellarer of the monastery, appointing Samson in his place. On the death of St. Pyr he made Samson abbot. From this it would seem that Dubricius owned the house.

At a synod held in Llantwit Major, Dubricius being present, Samson was elected Abbot of that place. Later, on the Feast of St. Peter's Chair, February 22, 521, Dubricius consecrated Samson bishop.

In harmony with all this, that St. Dubricius lived in Erging, that he moved across the South, that he was wont to consecrate bishops, we have evidence that he held properties, on which monasteries were founded, not only in Erging, but also outside as in Gower and westwards (the church of the martyrs at Caerleon was also his), and that his disciples founded monasteries, of whom several were bishops consecrated by himself, as Aeddan at Mavurn in the Dore Valley, Arwystl at Llangoed below Builth, Gwrfan at Treceiro on Lake Syfaddan, Ufelfyw at Llancillo, and Inabwy, who has left his name at Llandinabo.

We must, of course, put out of our minds the idea that these were "diocesan bishops," or that one "succeeded" the other as having jurisdiction over a defined area. Nevertheless, it is hard not to believe that in some sense Dubricius was represented in the tenth century by that "Cameleac, bishop in Archenfield," whom the Danes seized in A.D. 918, and whom King Edward ransomed with forty pounds. This was the Bishop Cimeilliauc of the Book of Llandaff, but (needless to say) there is no mention of Llandaff in the Anglo-Saxon Chronicle, which records the incident, only that he was bishop in Archenfield, i.e., Erging.

SELECTED BIBLIOGRAPHY

. . . .

Notes to the Reader: Arthurian texts are often called "romances," but this should not be taken to mean that they are fictional love stories. The theory of literary form or genre was not developed until the nineteenth century in France. The medieval French word *romans* merely meant a work, a text, written in a "modern" romance language, as distinguished from Latin. Thus, it usually meant a work written in some form of Old French. The English language derived largely from this or from these forms of Old French. Therefore Old French is rather easy and amusing for an American to read, as it is for any native speaker of English.

However, Arthurian texts are often called "Romances" in an effort to downgrade them, or to dismiss them as pure invention. Not all scholars would agree with me, or with other twentieth century critics, that fiction also is true. It has been customary since the eighteenth century to use the word "fiction" to scorn literature.

Arthurian texts may be purchased in any one of several series: Basil Blackwell at Oxford, Les Classiques Français du Moyen Age in Paris, The Arthurian Romance Series, edited by Cedric E. Pickford at Cambridge University. See Pickford's *Merlin*, for example, 3 vols., in print again as of 1986–87.

This bibliography is selected only. It is only partly annotated, not that all the books listed are not important equally, but that rare and unusual books have swept me with enthusiasm, to such a degree that I wanted to recommend them to the reader's attention.

Adams, Alison, Editor. *The Changing Face of Arthurian Romance* (Cambridge, 1986). *Festschrift* in honor of Cedric E. Pickford (1926–1983).

Adams, Frank. *The Clans, Septs, and Regiments of the Scottish Highlands* (Edinburgh, 1908, etc.).

Alanus de Insulis (Alain de Lille, France). *De prophetia Merlini Ambrosii Britanni* (Frankfurt, 1603).

Allen, J. Romilly, and J. Anderson. *The Early Christian Monuments of Scotland* (Edinburgh, 1903).

Anderson, M. D. *Looking for History in British Churches* (New York, 1951). See p. 42 for Chi–Rho sacred monograms, particularly on a gravestone at Whithorn.

Anwyl, Edward. *Celtic Religion in Pre-Christian Times* (Chicago, 1906). Taboo on eating hen, hare, and goose. Deities:

Moccos = pig,
Tarros = bull,
Epona = horse goddess,
Mullo = ass,
Artio = bear goddess,
Damona = sheep.

Argyll, Duke of. *Scotland As It Was and As It Is*, illus. See Vol. I (Edinburgh, 1887). "The View Columba saw from his Monastery of Iona"—p. 12; Woodcut from the duke's drawing *in situ*: Cambrian Sandstone.

Arnold, Matthew. *The Poetical Works of Matthew Arnold*, edited by A. T. Quiller-Couch (London, New York, and Toronto, 1909 and 1942). "Empedocles on Etna," pp. 94–126: Merlin, Perceval, Chiron, Achilles.

Bain, Robert. *The Clans and Tartans of Scotland* (Glasgow and London, 1938).

Baring-Gould, Rev. Sabine. *Curious Myths of the Middle Ages* (London, 1867).

Bell, A. R. L. "Muspilli: Apocalypse as Political Threat." *Studies in the Literary Imagination*, Vol. 8, # 1 (Spring, 1975), pp. 75–102.

—. "The Bayeux Tapestry and the Norman Conquest," Educational Video Lecture, *Medievalists-at-Work Video Series* (Spring, 1980), California State University at Long Beach.

—. *The Folklore, Background, and Artistic Interpretation of The Descent to Hell Motif in Early Western Medieval Literature* Thesis presented to the Graduate Faculties, University of Maryland, January 4, 1971.

—. "The Road to Santiago de Compostela: The French Connection" Inaugural Lecture, Long Beach Ebell Club, October 10, 1983.

Benson, L. D. *Art and Tradition in "Sir Gawain and the Green Knight"* (New Brunswick, N.J. 1965).

Boethius, A. M. S. *Boethius: The Theological Tractates and The Consolation of Philosophy*, translated by H. F. Stewart and E. K. Rand; and "I.T.," edited by H. F. Stewart (1609). (Cambridge, Mass., and London, 1962).

Borderie, Arthur Le Moyne de la. "Les Véritables prophéties de Merlin; examen des *poèmes attribués* à ce barde." In *Revue de Bretagne* III (1883): 21–49, 89–115, 211–29; and in book form of same title (eighty pages), (London and Paris, 1883). An excellent study of the poems attributed to Merlin.

Borlase, Rev. William. *Observations on the Antiquities Historical and Monumental of the County of Cornwall* (Oxford, 1754 and 1769).

Bottomley, Gordon. "Merlin's Grave." In *Scenes and Plays* (New York, 1929).

Bowen, Emrys George. *The Settlements of the Celtic Saints in Wales* (Cardiff, 1966).

Brandl, Alois. *Thomas of Erceldoune. Sammlung englischer Denkmäler in kritischen Ausgaben* (Berlin, 1880).
Important work because of this late medieval record of Merlin's prophecies, some of them verbatim.

Branston, Brian. *The Lost Gods of England*, illus. (London, 1974).
See Chapter IV, "Wyrd," and Chapter VII, "Frig."

Brewer, Elizabeth. *From Cuchulainn to Gawain* (Totowa, N.J., 1973).
Brewer also studies the beheading threat in Cuchulain(n), Carados, and Lancelot, but her main contribution is the "fantasy" of Gawain that has the power of myth; "other poems could not reconstruct the logic of the story." See the turning castle of King Curoi of Munster, Ireland, and the black, hairy churl (that is, Merlin).

Bromwich, Rachel, Editor. *Trioedd Ynys Prydein* (Cardiff, 1961).

Brooke, Christopher. "The Archbishops of St. David's, Llandaff and Caerleon-on-Usk." In *Studies in the Early British Church*, p. 201–42 (Cambridge, 1958).

Brooke, Dorothy. *Pilgrims Were They All: Studies of Religious Adventure in the Fourth Century of Our Era* (London, 1937). See "Pelagius."

Brown, Arthur C. L. "Arthur's Loss of Queen and Kingdom." *Speculum* XV, 1 (1940): 3–11.
Abduction is mythological, not real, Brown claims, and Irish. Tower of the Dead made of glass or iron, plus reeds, glass or stone tower, bogs, sword/water bridges, hedge of serpents, wall of mist, lions,

seven or three concentric walls, iron gates, iron spike with human head, ditches, stone tower.

Brugger, E. "Der dichter Bledri-Bleheri-Breri." *Z. f. franz. Spr. u. Lit.* XLVII (1925): 162–85.

—. "L'Enterrement Merlin." *Studien zur Merlinsage Z. f. rom. Philol.* XXIX (1906): 56; XXX (1906): 169; XXXI (1907): 239; XXXIII (1908): 145; XXXIV (1909): 99; XXXV (1910): 1.

Bund, Willis. *Archaelogia Cambrensis.* Vol. XI, Series V, No. 41, p. 276 ff. (Cardiff, 1924).
See for an explanation of the Welsh title "Saint," indicating birth in an ecclesiastical tribe.

Cathcart, Rev. Wm. *The Ancient British and Irish Churches including The Life and Labors of St. Patrick* (Philadelphia, 1984).
Illustrated and excellent for reproducing original texts, like the writings of Saint Patrick, in translation. Maps. See pp. 39–59 for years 400–600.

Catullus, C. *Catulli Carmina* (Brussels, 1970).
Peleus and Thetis = parents of Achilles (his feet faster than a stag's). Their famous wedding hymn or epithalamion crops up rather often in the Arthurian corpus.

Chadwick, Nora K. *The Druids* (Cardiff, 1966).

Concilium Tridentinum. (Canons of the Council of Trent). See appendix for Merlin prohibited: *Librorum prohibitorum index* (Venice, 1574).

Constance de Lyon. *Vie de Saint Germain d'Auxerre.* In *Sources Chrétiennes,* Vol. 112. edited by René Borius. (Paris, 1965)
This is the only life of Saint Germanus, written by a master scholar in about 478, or thirty years after the death of Saint Germanus. Unfortunately, he records only a very few details and no geographical precisions about the two journeys Germanus made to Britain, in 429 and again in 445–46 to expel from Britain the Pelagians, who had been declared heretical at the Council of Ephesus in 431.

Cooper, Kate. "Merlin *Romancier:* Paternity, Prophecy, and Poetics in the *Huth-Merlin.*" *Romanic Review* LXXVII, 1 (1986): 1–24.
A refreshing new type of study that attacks the textual problems from a purely interior, stylistic, and thematic point of view. This original approach brings to bear upon the text the tools of contemporary analysis.

Cosman, Madelein Pelner. *The Education of the Hero in Arthurian Romance* (Chapel Hill, 1965 and 1966).

This is a Columbia University dissertation. See the long bibliography pp. 203–27. The heroes Cosman chose are Tristan, Perceval, and Lancelot.

Coxe, A. D. H. *Haunted Britain* (London, 1973).

See pp. 141–42 for Man.

Croix, Horst de la, and Richard G. Tansey. *Gardner's Art through the Ages* (New York, etc., 1926–1970).

See p. 234 for the Equestrian Statue of Marcus Aurelius and the theory as to why the early Christians preserved it. Merlin seems to know it. See his *Prophecy*.

Curtin, Jeremiah. *Myths and Folk-Lore of Ireland* (London, 1890, 1975).

Davies, Rev. David. *The Ancient Celtic Church and the See of Rome* (Cardiff, 1924).

This is an excellent, scholarly refutation of the charges that the Celtic Church was united to Rome, even before Saint Augustine was sent to Canterbury at the end of the sixth century. Copious footnotes.

Davies, Wendy. *Wales in the Early Middle Ages* (Atlantic Highlands, N.J. and Leicester University Press, 1982).

This is interesting to us here as situating Vortigern (Gwrtheryn) in Wales. Nothing on Merlin, Myrdin, or Myrddin.

Déchelette, Joseph. *Manuel d'archéologie préhistorique, celtique et gallo-romaine* (Paris, 1924).

Didot-Perceval, according to manuscripts of Modena and Paris, edited by William Roach (Philadelphia, 1941).

Doble, Rev. Canon Gilbert. *Saint Dubricius*, Foreword by Richard Hereford, The Right Reverend The Lord Bishop of Hereford (Guildford and Esher, 1943).

This is an illustrated pamphlet of thirty-eight pages, including representations of the churches of Saint Dubricius.

Dodds, Eric Robertson. *Pagan and Christian in an Age of Anxiety* (Cambridge, 1968).

Marcus Aurelius to Constantine.

—. *The Greeks and the Irrational* (Berkeley and Los Angeles, 1951).

Dodds reminds us that there were caves in Crete and Asia Minor considered sacred to the mystery gods of divination and prophecy. Similarly, the Lady of the Lake entombed Merlin in a cave beside the seashore.

Dryden, John. *King Arthur: or, The British Worthy, A Dramatick Opera.* Vol. VI in *Dryden: The Dramatic Works* (6 Vols., edited by Montague Summers (London, 1932).

Dumézil, Georges. *Rituels indo-européens à Rome* (Paris, 1954).

Dyer, James. *The Penguin Guide to Prehistoric England and Wales* (Harmondsworth, England, 1981, 1982).

Eliade, Mircéa. *Myths, Dreams and Mysteries* (Paris, 1957), translated by Philip Mairet (New York, 1960).

Eliade, considered among the foremost historians of religion, taught until his death in 1986 at the Universities of Bucharest, Paris, and Chicago. One of his most brilliant proofs concerns the antihistorical character of the Dark Ages.

Emerson, Ralph Waldo. "Merlin," 1874. In *The Works of Ralph Waldo Emerson*, Vol. III, *Poems*, (London and New York, 1897), pp. 130–34.

Ernault, E., *Vie de Sainte Nonne, Revue Celtique* VIII (1887); 230, 405.

Saint David's mother and Merlin's mother had much in common and were contemporaries.

Evans, J. Gwenogvryn. *The Book of Taliesin* (Llanbedrog, Wales, 1910).

Evans, Sebastian. *In Quest of the Holy Grail* (London, 1898).

A creative and imaginative work by means of a dream where the following new identities are held up:

Lancelot = Simon de Montfort,
Gawain = Fulke of Marseilles,
Alain le Gros = Alanus de Insulis,
Yglais = Mother Church,
Grail = Eucharist, but with no mention of where the Grail was concealed.

Faral, Edmond. *La Légende arthurienne*, 3 vols. (Paris, 1929).

Fawtier, R. *La Vie de Saint Samson* (Paris, 1912).

Fled Bricrend. The Feast of Bricriu. Irish Text Society, II, edited and translated by George Henderson (London, 1899).

Flutre, Louis-Fernand. *Table de noms propres . . . dans les romans du moyen âge* (Paris, 1962).

Folie Lancelot, La., edited by F. Bogdanow (Tübingen, 1965).

Forbes, A. P. *Lives of S. Ninian and S. Kentigern* (Edinburgh, 1874).

Fowles, John. *The Ebony Tower* (Boston, 1974; New York, 1975).
Wonderful for his insights on Celtic, British, and Old French literature.

Frappier, J. *Etude sur la Mort le roi Artu* (Geneva, 1968).

Fraser, George S. *Scotland*, illus., photographs by Edwin Smith (New York, 1955).

Fuller, Thomas. *The Church History of Britain*, 3 vols., edited by James Nichols (London, 1868).
See Vol. I, pp. 54–56, 83–76 for Pelagius, Saint "Dubritius," and Merlin.

Gaster, Moses. *Jewish Sources of and Parallels to the Early English Metrical Legends of King Arthur and Merlin* (New York, 1887).
As we have seen, Gaster traces Merlin's birth story to the Talmud.

——. "The Legend of Merlin." *Folklore* 6 (1905): 407–27.
The Merlin legend comes from the older cycle of King Solomon by way of intermediate versions.

Geoffrey of Monmouth. *Historia regum Britanniae*, edited by Acton Griscom and Robert Ellis Jones (London, New York, and Toronto, 1929).
The publication of this diplomatic text required a breakthrough in Arthurian studies. The editors upheld Geoffrey from the attacks against him.

——. *The History of the Kings of Britain*, translated by Sebastian Evans. Introduction by Lucy Allen Paton, edited by Ernest Rhŷs (London, 1912 and 1944).

Gerald of Wales [Giraldus Cambrensis]. *The Journey through Wales. The Description of Wales*, translated by Lewis Thorpe (London, 1978).
Gerald spoke of an unknown author of Arthur's time: "Bledhericus, famosus ille fabulator," a storyteller from South Wales who lived before Gerald's lifetime in the twelfth century. See the bibliography for articles on this "Breri," who has not been found.

Goetinck, Glenys. *Peredur. A Study of Welsh Tradition in the Grail Legends* (Cardiff, 1975).

Goodenough, Erwin Ramsdell. *Jewish Symbols in the Graeco-Roman Period*, 8 vols. Bollingen Foundation. (See especially Vol. 5), 1956.

Goodrich, Norma Lorre. *King Arthur* (New York and Toronto, 1986).
See the bibliography and appendix.

——. *Le Morte d'Arthur* by Malory, abridgement (New York, 1963), but see introduction, pp. vii–xxvii.

—. *Medieval Myths* (New York, 1961 and 1977). Translations of some Arthurian material.

—. *Ways of Love* (New York and London, 1964). Translations of thirteen medieval narratives.

Griffith, Helen Stuart. *The Sign Language of Our Faith* (New York, 1939–1961).

> Symbols: Holy Spirit (descending dove), Fish (Christ), Ox (Redeemer, St. Luke), Cup (Agony), Chi-Rho (labarium), Alpha & Omega (Father), Almond (plus Carnation, Rose) = Virgin.

Griffiths, Margaret Enid. *Early Vaticination in Welsh with English Parallels*, edited by T. Gwynn Jones (Cardiff, 1937).

> This is a master's thesis of very great interest, being a history of early prophecy and a long discussion of Merlin's successors traced back to Irish literary tradition. See O'Keefe.

Grinsell, L. V. "Early Funerary Superstitions in Britain." *Folklore* LXIV (1953): 271–81.

> Antlers of red deer were thought to have afforded protection; wounded deer ate dittany to cure wounds. Medical lore transmitted, as from Merlin.

Gruffyd, W. -J. "Bledhericus, Bleddri, Breri." *Revue Celtique* XXXIII (1912): 180.

Gryson, Roger. *Sources chrétiennes* (Paris, 1971).

> See Saint Ambrose's *"De Poenitentia,"* Vol. I, 80.

Haight, Gordon. "Tennyson's Merlin." *Studies in Philology* 44 (1947): 549–66.

Halliday, William Reginald. *Greek and Roman Folklore* (New York, 1927).

> This is an excellent work by a professor from the University of Liverpool.

—. *Greek Divination* (London, 1913).

Hammer, Jacob. "A Commentary on the *Prophetia Merlini.*" *Speculum* X (1935): 3–30; XV (1940): 409–31.

Hamp. E. P. "Viviane or Niniane—A Comment from the Keltic Side." *Romance Philology* VIII (1954): 91.

Hanning, Robert W. *The Vision of History in Early Britain* (New York and London, 1966).

> This book has a brilliant chapter on Geoffrey of Monmouth's departure from a history based on Christian assumptions. Hanning calls Arthur and Merlin the leaders of a golden age. I strongly

disagree with his conclusions as they define the Arthurian romances that followed Geoffrey.

Hawkes, Jacquetta, and Christopher Hawkes. *Prehistoric Britain* (Cambridge, 1953).

Henig, Martin. *Religion in Roman Britain* (New York, 1984).
Material and data almost entirely from England.

Hervieux, L. *Les Fabulistes latins depuis le siècle d'Auguste jusqu'à fin du moyen âge*, 5 vols. (Paris, 1884 and 1893–1898).
See for possible sources of Merlin's "Fable" in his *Prophecy*.

Heywood, Thomas (d. 1641). *The Life of Merlin, sirnamed Ambrosius* (London, 1641).
Delightful first edition in the Francis Bacon Library in Claremont, California.

Hodgkin, Robert Howard. *A History of the Anglo-Saxons*, illus., 2 vols. (Oxford, 1935).
See Vol. I for an excellent and decisive handling of King Arthur, p. 179ff.

Hogg, James. *The Jacobite Relics of Scotland*, 2 vols. (Edinburgh, 1819–1821).

Holinshed's Chronicles of England, Scotland, and Ireland, 6 vols. (reprinted New York, 1965).
See Vol. 5 for translations of twelve chroniclers of Scotland.

Hooke, Della. *The Anglo-Saxon Landscape. The Kingdom of the Hwicce* (Manchester, 1985).
See page 5ff. for remarks on the Anglo-Saxon Kingdom of Mercia, the Arthurian "Northumberland." The title "Mercia," says Hooke, means "people of the March or border" and refers to the frontier between Britons and Anglo-Saxons from the late sixth through the early seventh centuries.

Hughes, Kathleen. *Early Christian Ireland* (London, 1972).
Arthurian scholars are indebted to Hughes for her many learned works.

Hunbaut, edited by J. Sturzinger and H. Breuer (Dresden, 1914).
Arthurian text.

Iselin, L. E. *Der Morganländische Ursprung der Grallegende* (Berlin, 1909).
Merlin's Cave could be studied in connection with this work on the "Cave of Treasures" from a Syrian book that explains how Melchizedec guarded Adam's tomb.

Jackson, Kenneth Hurlstone. *Language and History in Early Britain* (Edinburgh, 1953).

——. "The Wild Man of the Woods." *Report of the Yorkshire Society for Celtic Studies* (York, 1935).
Very important for the understanding of Merlin's successor Myrddin.

James, Edwin Oliver. *The Ancient Gods* (New York, 1960.)
See Chapter VI, "The Cult of the Dead."

Janson, H. W., and D. J. Janson. *History of Art* (New York, 1968).
See the Equestrian Statue of Marcus Aurelius, as mentioned in the Merlin *Prophecy*, on p. 147.

Jarman, A. O. H. "A Note on the Possible Welsh Derivation of *Viviane*." *Gallica* (Cardiff, 1969), pp. 1–12.

——. *The Legend of Merlin* (Cardiff, 1960).
This is probably the most important work ever written on Merlin, and by a Welsh scholar of great distinction. Unfortunately, it is very difficult to locate and *needs reprinting*.

Jarvis, Stinson. *The Price of Peace* (Los Angeles, 1921).
Excellent hypotheses regarding ancient astronomy in Ireland.

Johnston, R. C., and D. D. R. Owen, eds. *Two Old French Gawain Romances* (Edinburgh, 1972):
1. *Le Chevalier à l'epée*,
2. *La Mule sans frein*.

Johnstone, Paul Karlsson. "Dual Personality of Saint Gildas." *Antiquity* 22 (1948): 38–40.
This edition was edited by the great Scottish historian, editor, and geographer O. G. S. Crawford.

Jones, Ernest. *On the Nightmare* (London, 1949).
Interesting to read regarding Merlin's conception as told by Robert de Boron.

Jones, G. R. J. "Historical Geography and our Landed Heritage." *University of Leeds Review* 19 (1976): 53–78.

Jones, Owen et al. *The Myvyrian Archaiology of Wales*, (An anthology of literary antiquities assembled at Myvyr in 1801).
Second edition in one volume at Denbigh in 1870.

Joyce, Patrick Weston. *Old Celtic Romances*, translated from the Gaelic (Dublin and London, 1920).
The best collection by a first-rate scholar, Trinity College, Dublin.

Jung, C. G. *The Archetypes and the Collective Unconscious,* translated by R. f. C. Hull (Princeton, 1968).

Jung, Emma, and Marie-Louise von Franz. *The Grail Legend,* translated by Andrea Dykes (London, 1971).

Kendrick, Thomas Downing. *British Antiquity* (London, 1950).
A most interesting and impartial examination of British history as undertaken first by Geoffrey of Monmouth ("the brilliant book . . ." ". . . exclusively a study of the remote past"—p. 4). See Chapter I and also Chapter VI, "The Battle over the British History," and its eclipse.

____. *The Druids: A Study in Keltic Prehistory* (London, 1927; New York, 1966).

Kennedy, Elspeth, Editor. *Lancelot du lac* (Ms. B.N. 768) (Oxford and New York, 1980).

Kerenyi, C. *Asklepios,* translated by Ralph Manheim (Basel, 1947).
Kerenyi explains Merlin's springs to us, in that water was for the Greek oracles also a "kind of communication with the depth of earth" (p. 27).

Knox, Ronald A. *Enthusiasm: A Chapter in the History of Religion* (Oxford, 1950).

Krappe, Alexander Haggerty. "La Naissance de Merlin." *Romania* LIX (1933): 12–23.

____. "L'Enserrement de Merlin." *Romania* LX (1934): 79–85.
An aggressive attack on any claim to originality of *Merlin* or the Celtic corpus, by a well-read Orientalist.

Kushner, Eva. *Le Mythe d'Orphée dans la littérature française contemporaine* (Paris, 1961).
Published by the Society of French Professors in America and the Council of Arts of Canada.

Latham, R. E. *Medieval Latin Word-List from British and Irish Sources* (London, 1965).

Leach, H. G. "De libello Merlini." *Modern Philology* 8 (1911): 607–10.

Lewis, I. M. *Ecstatic Religion* (London, 1971).

Lewy, H. *Chaldaean Oracles and Theurgy* (London, 1956).

Leyland, John. *Assertio inclytissimi Arturii regis,* translated by Richard Robinson, (London, 1582) as an appendix to Wm. Ed. Mead's *The Famous History of Chinon of England,* EETS, Original Series 165 (London, 1925).

—. *The Itinerary of John Leland the Antiquary*, 9 vols., edited by Thomas Hearne (Oxford, 1744).

See Vol. 9 for Merlin, and Vol. 8 for Dubritius (Dubricius). There is an index at the end of Vol 9.

Libanius. *The Julianic Oratons*, 3 vols., edited and translated from the Greek by A. F. Norman (Cambridge and London, 1964).

See Vol. I, Orations 17, 18, and 24 for late Roman religious beliefs and practices.

Literature of Wales, Oxford Companion to the, edited by Meic Stephens (New York, 1986).

Lockyer, J. Norman. *The Dawn of Astronomy* (Cambridge, Mass., 1964).

Loomis, Roger Sherman. "Bleheris and the Tristam Story." *Modern Language Notes* XXXIX (1924): 319–29.

Another search for the elusive author, and see Gerald of Wales.

—. *Celtic Myth and Arthurian Romance* (New York, 1927).

Loomis was the greatest of the Arthurian mythologists until his death at Columbia University in 1966.

—. *Morgain La Fée and the Celtic Goddesses. Speculum* XX (1945): 183–203.

—. *Wales and the Arthurian Legend* (Cardiff, 1956).

Nothing new here, a summary of mythology largely of Ireland. Loomis rejects translations by Rev. Edward Davies, and by J. G. Evans, p. 134ff.

Lot, Ferdinand. "Encore Bleheri—Breri," *Romania* LI (1925): 397–408.

A study concerning the Arthurian author named Bledhericus who worked in Latin. Lot attempted to isolate him. See Gerald of Wales.

—. "Etudes sur Merlin." *Annales de Bretagne* XV (1900): 325, 505.

Study from a foremost Breton scholar.

Loth, Joseph. *Les Mabinogion*, 2 vols. (Paris, 1913).

First French translation.

Lyra Celtica, edited by E. A. Sharp and J. Matthay. Introduction to poetry by William Sharp, (Edinburgh, 1932).

Mabinogion, translated by Charlotte Guest, edited by Ernest Rhŷs (London, 1906).

This first edition is priceless because of its notes, as we saw in the case of the Fountain in Brittany, Chapter 11.

Malinowski, Bronislaw. *Myth in Primitive Psychology* (London, 1926).

This whole book applies directly to Merlin's legend or "sacred myth."

Marx, J. *Nouvelles recherches sur la littérature arthurienne* (Paris, 1965).

Merlin en prose du XVe siècle, edited by H. B. Wheatley. EETS (1899).

Merlin. *Prophecy.* Latin Commentaries on the Prophecies of Merlin.
    See editor Henry B. Wheatley's list and discussion from his intro-
    duction to *Merlin,* pp. xlviff passim, and see Zumthor.

Micha, Alexandre. "Les mss. de *Merlin* en prose de Robert de Boron,"
    Romania 19 (1958): 78–94, 147–74.

Michel, Francisque, and Thomas Wright. "Galfredi de Monumeta *Vita
    Merlini*" (Paris and London, 1837).
    But see edition by John Jay Parry (Urbana, 1925). I question
    Geoffrey of Monmouth's authorship of this *Vita Merlin,* which is to
    my mind a comical spoof written to spite Geoffrey and amuse his
    foes.

Middle English Metrical Romances, edited by Walter Hoyt French and Charles
    Brockway Hale (New York, 1930).
    See "The Avowing of King Arthur, Sir Gawain, Sir Kay and Bald-
    win of Britain," pp. 607–46.

Middleton, Christopher. *The Famous Historie of Chinon of England* and *The
    Assertion of King Arthure, Regis Britanniae, (Assertio Inclytissimi Arturii),*
    edited by Wm. Mead. EETS, Orig. Series 165 (London, 1925).

Milman, Henry Hart. *History of Latin Christianity,* 4 vols. (New York,
    1863–67; London, 1883).
    See Vol. I for Boethius.

Monipennie, John. *Certayne Matters concerning the Realme of Scotland,* ("As
    they were Anno Domini 1597") (London, 1603).
    Partial copy lent by Arthur MacArthur, courtesy of the Special
    Collection, Newberry Library, Chicago. We learn (p. 5) some-
    thing new: that Abernethie was the "Regall seate" of the Picts, and
    "Metropolitaine seate of thee Bishop";—afterward Saint Andrew.

Morris, Ronald W. B. *The Prehistoric Rock Art of Galloway and The Isle of
    Man,* illus. (Poole, England, 1979).
    For Saint Ninian's Cave, see pp. 159–60.

Myers, F. W. H. *Essays Classical* (London, 1883).
    Myers shows how Greek oracles reflected over a period of one
    thousand years (c. 700 B.C.—c. A.D. 300) the spiritual needs of
    the Greek people. See "Greek Oracles," pp. 1–105, by this most
    distinguished scholar.

Nash, D. W. *Taliesin; or, The Bards and Druids of Britain* (London, 1858).
    Excellent comparison of the lives of Merlin Ambrosius, Merlin
    Sylvester, Saints David and Dubricius.

Nashe, Thomas. *The Works of Thomas Nashe*, Vol. I, edited by Ronald B. McKerrow (London, 1910). First printed in 1594 as *"The Terrors of the Night* ("A Discourse of Apparitions" or treatise of forty-one pages).

New Poets of England and America, edited by Donald Hall, Robert Pack, and Louis Simpson (New York, 1957 and 1974).

Nilant, F. *Romuli Fabulae Aesopicae* (Leyden, 1709).

This would seem to be a possible source of Merlin's '"Fable," from this Roman collection dating from Augustus Caesar's reign.

Nilsson, Martin Persson. *The Mycenaean Origin of Greek Mythology* (Berkeley, 1932).

Historical reminiscences in mythical form, proves Nilsson, commonly survive the centuries, as is also the case with Merlin.

Nitze, William A. "An Arthurian Crux: 'Viviane or Niniane,' " *Romance Philology* VII (1953): 326–30.

——. *"The Esplumoir* Merlin." *Speculum* XVIII (1943): 69–79.

——. *The Old French Grail Romance: Perlesvaus* (Johns Hopkins University, 1902).

A major emphasis in this doctoral thesis concerns the Grail as a healing agent and the formula by which each candidate (Gawain, Lancelot, Perceval) announces his presence at the examination, which is also seen in "Testing," Chapter 9 in this book.

Of Arthur and of Merlin, 2 vols., edited by O. D. Macrae-Gibson. EETS 268 (Oxford, 1973 and 1979).

O'Keefe, J. G. *"Buile Suibhne,"* Being the Adventures of Suibne Geilt, a Middle-Irish Romance. Irish Text Society XII (London, 1913; Dublin, 1952).

This story is connected to the Wild Man of the Woods, or Merlin's successor Myrddin. See Margaret Enid Griffiths.

Olrik, Axel. *The Heroic Legends of Denmark*, translated by Lee M. Hollander (New York, 1919 and 1976).

Onians, Richard Broxton. *The Origins of European Thought about the Body, Mind, the Soul, the World, Time and Fate* (Cambridge, 1954).

O'Rahilly, C. *Ireland and Wales: their Historical and Literary Relations* (London, 1924).

Oswald, Felix. *The Secret of the East* (Boston, 1883).

Owen, A. L. *The Famous Druids* (Oxford and New York, 1962).

Only one mention of Merlin, quoting from Rev. Edward Davies's book on *The Mythology and Rites of the British Druids*, p. 13. Three references to Druids on the Isle of Man, but no association between Man and Merlin.

Paien de Maisieres. *La Mule sanz frain,* edited by B. Orlowski (Paris, 1911).

Arthurian romance.

Palgrave, Francis (1788–1861). *History of the Anglo-Saxons* (Cambridge University Press, 1921).

Palmer, John. "Rock Temples of the British Druids." *Antiquity* XXXVIII (1964): 285–87 and Plate LII.

Palmer considers Borlase's suggestion that there were ancient temples, such as Brimham Rocks, much larger and more spectacular than Stonehenge (which Geoffrey of Monmouth's translator, Wace, attributed to Merlin).

Pannekoek, Antoine. *A History of Astronomy* (New York, 1961).

Paris, Gaston, and J. Ulrich, eds. *Merlin,* (Huth manuscript), 2 vols., S.A.T.F. (Paris, 1886).

Paris, Paulin. *Romans de la Table Ronde,* (Paris, 1868–1877), 5 vols., but see Vol. I. p. 80:

". . . il sera facile de prouver . . . que l'*Ambrosius,* le *Sylvester,* et le *Caledonius* . . . ne sont qu'une seule et même personne," or Paris considered that there were three Merlins but only one man whence all three derived.

Parke, H. W. *Greek Oracles* (London, 1967).

Parke describes the site of Dodona: at the foot of a low hill, at the head of a deep valley, 1,600 feet above sea level, east of a mountain with many springs, near a well-wooded area. Only the higher altitude separates this description from Merlin's Isle or Cave. Both are sites of frequent thunder and heavy storms.

Parry, John Jay, ed. *The Vita Merlini.* University of Illinois Studies in Language and Literature (University of Illinois Press, 1925).

Parry's proof that Geoffrey wrote this work is generally accepted, but I disagree. See also Clarke, Basil, ed. and trans., *Life of Merlin, (Vita Merlini)* (Cardiff, 1973).

Excellent text, notes, and indexes.

Parry, Thomas. *A History of Welsh Literature,* translated by H. Idris Bell (Oxford, 1955).

Paton, Lucy Allen. "Notes on Merlin in the *Historia Regum Britanniae* of Geoffrey of Monmouth." *Modern Philology* 41 (August 1943): 88–95.

—. *Les Prophecies de Merlin*. MLA Monograph Series, 2 vols. (New York and London, 1926–1927).

—. *Studies in the Fairy Mythology of Arthurian Romance* (New York, 1960).

Peate, Iorwerth. "The Gorsedd of the Bards of Britain." *Antiquity* (1951) 13–15.

Pennant, Thomas. *A Tour in Wales*, illus. (London, 1773).

Excellent eyewitness accounts of North Wales history, culture, landscapes, and resources. Very good account of the massacre of monks and scholars at Bangor.

Perceval Continuations (I and II) of the Old French "Perceval," 2 vols. edited by W. Roach and R. H. Ivy (Philadelphia, 1949–1955).

Picard, Charles. *Ephèse et Claros* (Paris, 1922).

Picard, who was the director of the French School of Athens, points out that the stigma associated with women priests dates from the Oracle at Claros in Asia Minor: the Asians did not like women priests (p. 213). This dislike then comes apparently from Asia Minor directly, with Christianity at its points of origin. The feminine clergy were called Mellissas *(Melissai)*.

Piggott, Stuart. *The Druids*, illus. (London, 1968).

Masterful Chapter I, "The Problems and the Sources."

Plinval, G. de. *Pélage, ses écrits, sa vie et sa réforme* (Lausanne, 1943).

Excellent account of the British monk Pelagius, champion of the underprivileged.

Porphyry. *De Antro Nympharum* (On the Cave of the Nymphs), translated by Robert Lamberton (Barrytown, N.Y., 1983).

Porphyry lived c. 234–c. 305.

Powell, T. G. E. *The Celts* (London and New York, 1958).

Price, Glanville. *The Languages of Britain* (London, 1984). See especially Chapter 7, "British," p. 84ff.

Procopius. *The Secret History*, translated by G. A. Williamson (London, 1966).

Procopius's voice (c. 500–c. 562) from beyond the grave reveals the hideous secrets of the horrible Justinian and his ex-prostitute Empress Theodora in Constantinople.

Prophecies de Merlin, edited by Lucy Allen Paton, from manuscript 593 in Bibliothèque Municipale of Rennes, France. MLA (New York, 1966).

Prose Lancelot. See *The Vulgate Version of the Arthurian Romances*, 7 vols., edited by H. O. Sommer (Washington, 1908–1916).

Pseudo-Shakespearian Plays (Introduction and Notes), edited by Karl Warnke and Ludwig Proescholdt (Halle, 1883).
The Birth of Merlin; or, the Childe hath found his Father. Written by William Shakespear with William Rowley. London. 1662. The five-act play is on pp. 1–77. Neither scholar finds any trace of Shakespeare in this play.

Quinet, Edgar. *Merlin l'enchanteur,* 2 vols. (Paris, 1860).

Rahner, Hugo, S. J. *Griechische Mythen in christlicher Deutung* (Zurich, 1957). Rahner points out a common culture and common practices of paganism and Christianity, such as kissing the altar, crossing the threshold of the sanctuary with the right foot. He notes the borrowing of baptism from Dionysus, and the wisdom of Pythagoras borrowed, which refuses to communicate with impious persons, to deliver up mysteries to any passerby, to reveal mysteries to the scoffers.

Rees, Rev. Rice. *An Essay on the Welsh Saints; or, the Primitive Christians usually considered to have been the Founders of Churches in Wales* (London, 1836).
See Section IX (the Welsh Saints from the Accession of Vortimer A.D. 464 to the Death of Ambrosius A.D. 500) and Section X (The Welsh Saints from the Accession of Uther Pendragon A.D. 500 to the Death of Arthur A.D. 542), pp. 161–240. Rice was a Fellow of Oxford and a professor of Welsh.

Rees, W. *Historical Atlas of Wales* (Cardiff, 1951; London, 1959).
See Plate 25(a) for the six churches of Dubricius on the upper Wye River.

Reid, Margaret Jane Cornfute. *The Arthurian Legend. Comparison of Treatment in Modern and Medieval Literature: A Study in the Literary Value of Myth and Legend* (Edinburgh and London, 1938).
See Appendix A (pp. 264–66) for a chronological list of poems, plays, and prose between 1485 and 1933 on Arthurian subjects (Malory excluded).

Rhŷs, John. *Celtic Folklore, Welsh and Manx,* 2 vols. (Oxford and Edinburgh, 1901; New York, 1971).

___. *Lectures on the Origin and Growth of Religion.* The Hibbert Lectures (London, Edinburgh, and Oxford, 1898).
Merlin is studied here at considerable length.

___. *Studies in the Arthurian Legend* (Oxford, 1891).

Robert, Louis. *Les Fouilles de Claros* (Paris, 1954).

Robert, who wrote this book at the University of Ankara in 1953, points out that Romans and western Europeans commonly and in large numbers worshiped at the oracle of Claros. *Robert notes particularly worshipers from Celtic Brittany* (pp. 25–29).

Robinson, Edwin Arlington. "Merlin," 1917. In *Collected Poems* (New York, 1925), pp. 235–314.

Rolls of Parliament. Bibliothèque Nationale, Manuscript Room, Paris, France:

Chronicles and Memorials of Great Britain and Ireland during the Middle Ages:

Annales Cambriae, edited by John Williams ab Ithel.

Brut y Tywysogion, edited by John Williams ab Ithel.

Chronicles of the Reigns of Stephen, Henry II, Richard II, edited by Richard Howlett, Vols. I, II. See Vol. II for *Draco Normannicus* by Etienne de Rouen; Vol. IV for Robert de Torigny's *Chronique.*

Giraut de Cambrie (Gerald of Wales). *Opera,* 7 vols., edited by J. S. Brewer (1861).

Pierre de Langtoft. *Chronicle,* 2 vols., edited by Thomas Wright (1866).

Ralf Higden. *Polychronicon,* 9 vols., edited by J. R. Lumby (1865–1886).

Robert Manning de Brunne. *The Story of England,* 2 vols. (1887).

Ross, Anne. *Pagan Celtic Britain* (London and New York, 1967).

Many contributions to our knowledge of Merlin come from this distinguished anthropologist.

Rowland, Henry. *Mona Antiqua Restaurata* (Dublin, 1723).

Sanesi, Ireno. *La Storia di Merlino* (Bergame, 1898).

Schuré, Edouard. *The Ancient Mysteries of Delphi* (Paris, 1889), edited by Paul M. Allen. Introduction of 1961 (Blauvelt, N.Y., 1971).

Scott, Walter. *Border Antiquities of England and Scotland* (Edinburgh, 1914).

See Vol. I (p. 85) for Roman stones in the garden wall of the Howard Castle at Naworth, and (p. 45) for land charters of nearby Lanercost Priory, where the Howards and other border families are interred. Scott quotes "Horsley's *Britannia Romana,* which I can not find. I presume its author was Samuel Horsley, Bishop of Saint Asaph's (1733–1806), Flintshire, Wales. Saint Asaph's was Geoffrey of Monmouth's See.

—. *Minstrelsy of the Scottish Border* (Edinburgh, 1833).

See Vol. IV, pp. 141–43.

___. *The Lady of the Lake*, illus. (Boston, 1883).
> See the ancient-style church (Saint Bride's Chapel, p. 119), presumably unroofed, except perhaps for the priest's cell.

Skene, William Forbes. *Celtic Scotland. A History of Ancient Alban* (Edinburgh, 1887).

Snider, Clifton. "The Archetypal Self in Swinburne's *Tristram of Lyonesse.*" *Psychocultural Review* I (1977): 371–90.

Snyder, Edward Douglas. "The Wild Irish: A Study of Some English Satires against the Irish, Scots, and Welsh." *Modern Philology* XVII 12 (April 1920): 147–85.

___. *The Celtic Revival in English Literature 1760–1800* (Cambridge, Mass., 1923).
> Snyder studies literature from 1750–1800. Kendrick is much indebted for his first chapter in *The Druids* to this work, I believe.

Spenser, Edmund. *The Faerie Queene*, 6 vols., edited by Edwin Greenlaw, Charles Osgood, and Frederick Padelford (Baltimore, 1932–1938).

Stephens, Thomas. *Literature of the Kymry* (Llandovery, Wales, 1849, 1876).
> Stephens argues that ancient poems ascribed to Merlin and Taliesin are fakes written in the twelfth century. See p. 208ff. for an excellent analysis of Merlin and his successors.

Stow, John (1525?–1605). *Annals of England*
> See Vols. I, II, III of Raphael Holinshed's *Chronicles* (Vol. III = Scotland).

___. *The Annales or generall chronicle of England, etc.*, 8 vols. (Cambridge, etc. 1615).

Styan, Kate E. *A Short History of Sepulchral Crosses* (London, 1902).
> Illustrations of examples found.

Taylor, T. *The Life of St. Samson of Dol* (Brittany) (London, 1925).
> This book was not found, but T. Taylor was probably the Tom Taylor (1817–1880), who translated Villemarqué's Breton ballads and songs.

The Text of the Book of Llan Dav, edited by J. Gwenogvryn Evans and John Rhŷs (Oxford, 1893).
> This is the Latin manuscript called *Liber Landavensis*, often scorned as a forgery, written c. 1130. See Appendix for a very partial translation.

Thierry, Amédée. *Histories des Gaulois*, Vol. I, p. 246.

Priests of Delphi manipulated storms, lightning, and air electricity, which they called "cosmic fire"; and they stopped the Gauls from ravaging and sacking Delphi. They saved the Temple of Apollo. Merlin seems able to do the same, and better.

Thomas, Charles. *Christianity in Roman Britain to* A.D. 500 (London, 1981). See Chart 51 (p. 273) for the ecclesiastical and perhaps also civil administration of Saint Dubricius in southeastern Wales.

—. "The Interpretation of the Pictish Symbols." *Archaeological Journal* 129 (1963): 31–97.
I am not sure that we have learned here as much as we could learn if we really put our minds to deciphering these symbols. Arthurian texts say their stories are already "carved on stone."

Thomas of Erceldoune ("True Thomas"). *The Romance and Prophecies of Erceldoune*, ed. James A. Murray. EETS, Orig. Series 61 (London, 1875).

Tolstoy, Nikolai. *In Search of Merlin* (New York, 1985).
This excellent book on Merlin's successor Myrddin treats him as historical and associates him with a magician or shaman. Both associations seem valid, and the book deserves an important place in Arthurian studies of the century following Merlin.

Turner, Jr., John P. *A Critical Edition of James Shirley's Saint Patrick for Ireland* (New York and London, 1979).

Turner, Sharon. *The History of the Anglo-Saxons*, Vol. I (Paris, 1840).
Book I, Chapter V ". . . The Druids," pp. 39–45
Book III, Chapter III, ". . . authentic History of Arthur," pp. 167–76.
Turner suggests directions more than he offers solutions.

—. *Vindications of the Ancient British Poems of Aneurin, Taliesin, Llywarch Hen, and Merdhin, with Specimens of the Poems* (London, 1803).
This is a reply to adverse criticism Turner received for his chapters on British bards (*The History of the Anglo-Saxons*, Vol. I, 1799). Critics found his praise of Welsh bards too enthusiastic, too profuse, and too easy to demolish. Gaston Paris added that Turner had proved nothing, in any case.

Veitch, John (1820–1894). *Merlin and Other Poems* (Edinburgh, 1889).
A rather disappointing and uncritical work.

—. *The History and Poetry of the Scottish Border: Their Main Features and Relations*, 2 vols. (Glasgow, 1878; Edinburgh and London, 1903).

374

Villemarqué, Théodore Hersart de la. "Visite an tombeau de Merlin." *Revue de Paris* 41 (May 7, 1837): 47–58.

Vita Merlini, edited and translated by John Jay Parry. University of Illinois Studies in Language and Literature No. 10 (1925).

Vogel, C. "Le Pécheur et la pénitence an Moyen Age." In *Chrétiens de tous les temps* 30 (Paris, 1969).

Anthology of texts regarding penitential rules and practices.

Vroom, F. W. *The First Six Centuries: Sketches from Early Church History* (London, New York, Toronto, 1932).

Vroom, professor of divinity in Nova Scotia, writes very thoroughly on the growth of monasticism in the fifth and sixth centuries.

Wade-Evans, Arthur W. *Welsh Christian Origins* (Oxford, 1934).

Also a Life of Saint David said to have been published in 1923, but not findable. His edition of *Nennius* (Oxford, 1938) is excellent.

Waite, Arthur Edward. *The Holy Grail: Its Legends and Symbolism* (London, 1909).

See the extensive bibliography (pp. 594–618).

Ward, H. L. D. "Lailoken (or Merlin Sylvester)." *Romania* XXII (1893): 504–26.

Ward established here that neither Lailoken nor Sylvester (Myrddin) was our Merlinus Ambrosius, and I have agreed.

Warnke, Karl, and Ludwig Proescholdt. *Pseudo-Shakespearian Plays*. See "The Birth of, Merlin; or The Childe Hath found His Father," pp. 1–86, (Play attributed to Shakespear with Rowley) (Halle, 1883–1887).

Weiss, Adelaide Marie. *Merlin in German Literature* (Washington, 1933).

This is a study of the "Merlin legend" in German literature from the twelfth through the nineteenth centuries. Catholic University, Studies in German, II, III.

West, G. D. *French Arthurian Verse Romances* (1150–1300). *An Index of Proper Names* (Toronto, 1969 and 1978).

Weston, Jessie L. *From Ritual to Romance* (Cambridge, 1920).

Williams, Gwyn. *An Introduction to Welsh Poetry* (London, undated but c. 1953).

Williams, Ifor. "Wales and North." An essay in *The Beginnings of Welsh Poetry*, edited by Rachel Bromwich (Cardiff, 1972).

Wright, Thomas. *The Celt, the Roman, and the Saxon*, illus. (London, 1875).

Excellent chapter on the massacre of Druids and dark-clad women on Anglesey by Roman commander Suetonius Paulinus whose excuse was that the Druid groves had also to be cut down because the Druids had offered human sacrifices there. Thus, the Britons were defenseless again before "the avarice and luxury of Rome." Edward Gibbon eloquently defended the Druids.

Zimmer, Heinrich. *Nennius vindicatus: "uber Entstehung, Geschichte und Quellen der Historia Brittonum"* (Berlin, 1893).

A world-famous scholar defends Celtic literature. See also his *Keltische Studien* (Berlin, 1884).

—. *The King and the Corpse: Tales of the Souls's Conquest of Evil* (translation), edited by Joseph Campbell (Princeton, 1956).

Zumthor, Paul. *Merlin le prophète* (Lausanne, 1943; Geneva, 1973).

This has been the standard work on Merlin, but it has of late become very difficult to find.

See a more extensive bibliography in *King Arthur* by Norma Lorre Goodrich (New York, 1986).

INDEX

. . . .

Oxford, 68, 121

Palladini, David, 165
Paris, 47
Paris, Gaston, 49, 73
Paris, Paulin, 50, 73, 245–46, 259 n.
Parzival, 95 ff., 320 n.
Paton, Lucy Allen, 185, 220, 250–62
Patrick, Saint, 21, 45, 67, 236, 269, 282, 305, 318
Paul, Saint, 213 n., 273
Peel, 9
Peirce, C. S., 117
Pelagius, 21, 37, 66, 236, 270, 282, 300 ff., 310
Pelles (Pelles I, Pelles II, Pelles of Listenois, Perceval, Pellinor), 215, 217, 227–28
Perceval, 21, 32 ff., 47, 88, 195, 224 ff., 282, 295, 297, 319
Peredur, 52, 193, 227 n., 291
Persia, 81
Peter, Saint, 69
Peter de Langtoft, 160
Petrie, W. M. Flinders, 217
Picts, 6, 62, 63, 67, 73, 112 ff., 196 ff., 218, 311
Piggott, Stuart, 128
Pindar, 267, 273
Placidia, Empress Galla, 271
Plato, 45, 56, 273, 304
Plutarch, 193 n.
Pomponius Mela, 193 n.
Porphyry (Porphyrius, Malchus), 264, 274 ff.
Preseli Mountains, 180
Prophecies de Merlin, Les, 250–62

Prophecy, 10 ff., 19, 37, 75 n., 87, 123–57, 161, 219 n., 224, 269, 287, 298, 299, 300, 303, 320 n., and ff.
Prose Lancelot, 59, 95 ff., 162, 198, 214, 224, 245, 249 ff., 266, 309
Proserpina, 45, 190
Prospero, 20
Provence, 26
Pyrenees Mountains, 20
Pythagoras, 272, 273, 321

Queen of Sheba, 53
Quintilian, 298, 299, 300

Rabelais, François, 309
Ravenna, 69
Red Book of Hergest, 219, 289 n.
Rees, Rev. Rice, 237 n., 237–41, 309
Rees, William, 242
Reid, Margaret J. C., 20, 50
Revelation or Apocalypse, 111, 116, 321
Rhinns of Galloway, 59, 173, 193, 201 n., 217, 223, 225, 245, 278–87, 313
Rhys, John, 199 n., 210, 220, 227 n., 271–72, 286 and n., 308, 316
Richard of Ireland, 250–62
Ritho (Rhitta), 177 ff., 180
Robert de Boron, 41 ff., 50 ff., 314
Robert of Brunne, 160
Robinson, Edwin Arlington, 318
Romano-Britons, 5
Rome, 5, 23, 27, 36, 37, 49, 55,

384

Tolkien, J. R. R., 187 n.
Tolstoy, Leo, 302
Tolstoy, Nikolai, 18
Tompkins, Peter, 273 n.
Toynbee, Arnold J., 302
Trappe, J. B., 187 n.
Trask, Willard R., 266 n.
Triads, 75, 178, 265–66, 273 and
   n., 288
Tristan, 101, 217, 228, 295
Troyes, France, 52
Turner, Sharon, 51
Turpin, Archbishop, 20
Tynwald Hill, 231

Ulrich, Jacob, 72–73
Urban, Bishop of Llandaf, 240
Urian Rheged, King, 238
Urien (Urian, Rion), King, 94 ff.,
   103, 166, 170 ff., 185 ff., 192,
   195, 223 ff., 228, 285
Usher, Bishop of Llandaf, 314
Uther Pendragon, King, 5, 8, 13,
   26, 36, 53, 60, 85, 89, 91 ff.,
   93 ff., 223, 297, 301, 311, 312,
   319

Vatican, 56, 251
Veitch, John, 50
Vergil (Publius Vergilius Maro),
   6, 55, 254
Vermont, 24, 79 n.
Vestal Virgin, 207
Villemarqué, Hersart de la, 51,
   209–10, 283
Virgin, The, 11
Vita Merlini, 77–78, 96 ff., 115–
   16, 185 n.
Vortigern (Gwrtheyrn), King, 8,
   13, 36, 48, 53, 57, 63 ff., 66,

Vortigern (continued)
   85, 126 ff., 181, 223, 287, 300,
   302, 312, 319
Vroom, F. W., 49

Wade-Evans, Arthur, 311 ff., 319
Waldhave, Saint, 9, 48, 267
Wales, 6, 13, 18 ff., 22, 24, 29,
   34, 38, 43, 50, 54, 63, 68, 74,
   86 ff., 115 ff., 118, 128,
   133 ff., 161, 174, 175 ff., 180,
   200–01, 214 n., 218, 224, 233,
   235 ff., 238 ff., 265, 267, 271,
   287, 302, 306, 308 ff.
Ward, H. D. L., 289
Webster, 23
Weston, Jessie L., 51 ff.
Whithorn (Witerna), 173 ff., 217,
   224, 229, 272, 279–84, 289
Widow Lady of Camelot, 95 ff.
Wilbur, Richard, 329
William of Newburgh, 113
Winchester (Edinburgh), 73
Winefred, Saint, 27, 200, 231
Winterbottom, Michael, 63–64
Woolley, R. v. d. R., 322 ff.
Wye River, 114, 161, 241, 307,
   308

Ygerne, Duchess, 93 ff., 98, 311
York, 85, 128
Yvain (Owein), 192, 196, 217,
   229–30; Yvain, 50, 229 n.,
   230 n.

Zimmer, Heinrich, 231–33
Zirker, J. B., 321 ff.
Zodiac, 156–56, 320 n.
Zumthor, Paul, 38, 57 n., 117 n.,
   288 n.